# CliffsTestPrep®

## Nursing School Entrance Exams

# CliffsTestPrep®
# Nursing School Entrance Exams

*by*

*Fred N. Grayson*

*Contributing Authors*

Tracy Halward, PhD

Sharon Shirley, MA

Mark Weinfeld, MA

**WILEY**

Wiley Publishing, Inc.

## About the Author

As an independent book developer and publisher, Fred N. Grayson has published hundreds of books in conjunction with many major publishers. In addition, he has written and/or coauthored dozens of books in the test preparation field.

## Publisher's Acknowledgments

### Editorial

**Project Editor:** Kelly Dobbs Henthorne

**Acquisitions Editor:** Greg Tubach

**Copy Editor:** Kelly Dobbs Henthorne

**Technical Editor:** Philip R. McKinley

### Composition

**Proofreader:** Arielle Mennelle

Wiley Indianapolis Composition Services

**CliffsTestPrep® Nursing School Entrance Exams**

Published by:
**Wiley Publishing, Inc.**
111 River Street
Hoboken, NJ 07030-5774
www.wiley.com

Copyright © 2004 Wiley, Hoboken, NJ

Published by Wiley, Hoboken, NJ
Published simultaneously in Canada

Library of Congress Cataloging-in-Publication Data:

Grayson, Fred N.
  Nursing school entrance exams / by Fred N. Grayson.
    p. cm. -- (CliffsTestPrep)
  ISBN 0-7645-5986-9 (pbk.)
  1. Nursing schools--United States--Entrance examinations--Study guides.
I. Title. II. Series.
  RT79.G73 2004
  610.73'076--dc22
2004010286

**ISBN:** 0-7645-5986-9

Printed in the United States of America

10 9 8 7 6 5

1B/TR/RQ/QW/IN

For general information on our other products and services or to obtain technical support, please contact our Customer Care Department within the U.S. at 800-762-2974, outside the U.S. at 317-572-3993, or fax 317-572-4002.

Wiley also published its books in a variety of electronic formats. Some content that appears in print may not be available in electronic books.

WILEY

# Table of Contents

## PART I: INTRODUCTION

## PART II: SUBJECT AREA REVIEWS

## Physical Science Review

# PART III: PRACTICE TESTS

# PART IV: APPENDICES

# INTRODUCTION

# Introduction

Congratulations! Because you bought this book, you obviously are interested in pursuing a career in nursing. We offer our congratulations because it is a smart choice—a field in which the opportunities are increasing annually, unlike many other career fields.

You have the choice of many different areas of nursing, which we will discuss shortly. More than two million registered nurses practice in this country, and according to the U.S. Department of Labor, "more new jobs are expected to be created for registered nurses than for any other occupation." Thus, by the time you have received your degree, you probably will have a pretty good chance to get a job right away.

## How to Use This Book

A quick glance at the contents page will show you that this book is divided into several sections. The first section is this introduction, wherein you learn about the different types of questions and how to answer them. In addition, you also garner information about the career of nursing and the different areas that you can follow. The second section contains the subject review material. Each of the major areas is presented in an easy-to-understand chapter with plenty of review questions. The single, most important approach to doing well on any test is to answer as many questions as possible that are similar in approach to those you will encounter on the actual test. We have provided these questions at the end of each review section, along with answers and explanations. Many of the answers you will know on your own from information you have already learned. Some of the information will be in the review chapters, and some of it will be new to you, but you can learn the information from the explanations of the answers.

The third section contains the Practice Tests, two full-length simulated exams. You should take each section as you would an actual exam. Each section is timed, and it would be helpful to take the tests in a quiet room, with no distractions. The purpose of taking these tests is to help you become familiar with the types of questions you encounter on any nursing school entrance exam, and the more you practice with the types of questions, the better you will do on the final test.

One word of advice: read, understand, and memorize the directions. Some of the directions are straightforward—answer the questions to the best of your ability. Others may be more complex, and it is the more complex directions that tend to confuse people, and unfortunately, take time away from the actual exam. Therefore, if you have memorized the directions, you won't have to spend additional time reading them and trying to figure out what is being asked of you.

The last section is the appendices, and we have provided lists of dozens of different Nursing Associations as well as State Boards of Nursing. Both are excellent references to keep. The associations cover many diverse areas of specialization, and a quick glance at the names probably will surprise you at the many different areas of nursing. The State Boards of Nursing are responsible for licensing, and it's worth contacting your local state board for any available information.

## Nursing as a Career

The purchase of this book means that you've seriously considered becoming a nurse. You can follow a variety of degree paths in school. The most popular, and considered minimal preparation for a professional nurse, is the Bachelor of Science degree in Nursing (BSN). You also can consider an Associate Degree in Nursing (ADN), although many nurses with ADNs often enter the BSN program. In addition, you eventually can set a course for a Master of Science in Nursing (MSN). This is an 18–24 month program and gives nurses the opportunity to specialize in a particular area of study. Normally, you should have the BSN in order to work toward an MSN, but you may take other paths.

For example, if you are already a registered nurse (RN) with an associate degree in nursing, you can take a straight path from the RN to the BSN to an MSN. If you already have a bachelor's degree in some other, non-nursing field, you can apply for an MSN program, although you probably would have to take some of the basic undergraduate nursing courses before entering the graduate program.

To receive a BSN degree, courses at the undergraduate level run the gamut from the required science courses to philosophy, history, and English compositions. For example, a typical four-year program might include the following:

| Year 1 | Year 2 | Year 3 | Year 4 |
|--------|--------|--------|--------|
| Intro to Health | Clinical Science | Clinical Science Subacute/ Chronic | Ethics |
| Intro to Chemistry | Human Genetics | Nursing Research | Psychological/Mental Health Nursing |
| Philosophy | Family Development | Literature option | Clinical Science Acute Care |
| Psychology | Anatomy & Physiology | Childbearing Clinical & Practicum | Acute Care Nursing Science and Practicum |
| History | Mathematics | Public Health | Esthetics |
| Principles of Biology | Health Care Delivery Systems | Childrearing Clinical & Practicum | Nursing Science: Leadership |
| Intro to Sociology | Health Assessment | | |
| English Composition | | | |

These are, of course, just sample courses, an amalgam from several major universities across the United States. Each school will be different, but this should give you some idea of the types of courses you might encounter. However, you must also pass a national licensing examination in order to obtain a nursing license. You may be licensed in different states, and often another state will recognize the license from your state, but if not, you will have to take another state exam. In addition, all states require you to renew your license on a periodic basis, which may involve additional educational coursework.

Where does this all lead? To a career in any one of dozens of different areas of nursing. For example, this is a list of some of the specialties that you might consider:

- Acute Care Nurse Practitioner
- Adult Nurse Practitioner (Generalist)
- Adult Nurse Practitioner—Psychiatric/Mental Health
- Adult Nurse Practitioner—Occupational/Environmental Health
- Adult Nurse Practitioner—Integrated Complementary Healing
- Adult Nurse Practitioner—HIV/AIDS
- Cardiovascular Nursing (Clinical Nurse Specialist)
- Cardiovascular Nursing/Genomics
- Cardiovascular Nursing/Clinical Research Associate
- Community-Based Care Systems
- Community and Cross-Cultural Health Clinical Nurse Specialist
- Nursing Administration
- Critical Care/Trauma (Clinical Nurse Specialist)
- Education
- Family Nurse Practitioner
- Gerontological Nursing
- Gerontological Clinical Nurse Specialist

- Gerontological Nurse Practitioner
- Gerontological Nurse Practitioner—Oncology
- Health Policy
- Midwifery
- Occupational & Environmental Health
- Clinical Nurse Specialist
- Adult Nurse Practitioner
- Oncology Nursing
- Oncology Clinical Nurse Specialist
- Oncology Nursing/Genomics
- Oncology-Gerontology Nurse Practitioner
- Pediatric Nursing, Advanced Practice
- Nurse Practitioner *and* Clinical Nurse Specialist
- Neonatal Nurse Practitioner *and* Clinical Nurse Specialist
- Perinatal Nursing Clinical Nurse Specialist
- Psychiatric/Mental Health Nursing
- Adult or Child Clinical Nurse Specialist

Many of these areas require more advanced degrees.

The Registered Nurse is the first step, however, in your career as a nurse. As mentioned, more than two million RNs are practicing in the United States today, and more new jobs are opening daily. As a Hospital Nurse (the largest group of nurses), you would work on the staff, providing bedside nursing care to patients and carrying out the proscribed medical care for the patients. You may also supervise nursing aides and licensed practical nurses. In the beginning of your career, you would likely rotate between departments, but eventually, you would be assigned to a specific department: surgery, maternity, pediatrics, and so on.

Office nurses work in physicians' offices and emergency medical centers. They work with the physician to prepare patients for examinations, give injections and medications, and even assist in minor surgery.

Nursing care facility nurses manage care for patients who are suffering from a variety of ailments from Alzheimer's disease to stroke patients and who are confined to these facilities—many of them for the long-term. A good part of their time is spent on administrative and supervisory tasks, developing treatment plans, and supervising other nurses.

Home Health Nurses provide nursing care to home-bound patients, such as those suffering from cancer or debilitating accidents, or recuperating from childbirth. The Public Health Nurse works in government and private agencies, including schools and retirement communities. The Occupational Health Nurse works in company offices and factories, providing care to employees, often administering inoculations, providing annual employee exams, and offering counseling when necessary.

# The Tests

Now that we've presented the many types of nursing careers that are available, let's take a look at what this book is all about—tests! Regardless of the type of nursing you plan to do, there will always be tests that you'll have to take in order to (1) be admitted to a nursing program and (2) to become licensed. The purpose of this book is to help you understand the types of questions that you may encounter on any of the exams that you will have to take. These are not the licensing exams (NCLEX), which are far more complex than any test you will take up to then, but instead, these are general exams that will test your knowledge of several basic areas of understanding and help determine your readiness for a nursing career.

# Types of Questions

Most of the questions you will encounter on these various exams will be multiple-choice questions. These require both knowledge of the subject matter as well as skill in answering the questions. The topics that we cover here are basic topics—the types of questions that you will find on most any test you will take. We cover five basic areas, which contain subtopics:

| Subject | Subtopics |
|---|---|
| Verbal Review | Synonyms |
| | Antonyms |
| | Analogies |
| | Spelling |
| Reading Comprehension | Paragraph Understanding |
| Mathematics | Arithmetic |
| | Problem Solving |
| | Algebra |
| | Quantitative Comparisons |
| Life Science | General Science |
| | Biology |
| | Human Anatomy & Physiology |
| Physical Science | Chemistry |
| | Physics |

The subjects are the basis for most standardized tests and usually comprise most of the types of questions you would find in any college admission test.

# How to Answer Multiple-Choice Questions

In many cases, it's a decided advantage to take a test with multiple-choice questions, and the better your skill at answering them, the better your chances are at doing well. There are three basic steps to follow.

1. The first approach is to read the question. If you read the question and immediately know the answer, look at the choices given, select the correct one, and mark it on your answer page. This is the easiest way to answer the question—you know the answer.

2. The second method is to read the question and if the answer doesn't immediately come to mind, read the answer choices. If you know the material fairly well, the correct answer will be clear to you at once. Or, if it is not immediately clear, a little thought will root out the right answer.

3. The third step is to use the process of elimination. Very simply, this process involves eliminating the wrong answers so that you're left with the correct one, or at least you've narrowed down the answer choices. When test developers create questions for multiple-choice tests, a process is often followed. In questions with four choices like those you'll find in the exams in this book, there is always one answer choice that will be undeniably correct. The other choices are called "distracters." There is usually one choice that is completely incorrect and can be quickly eliminated. The other two choices may be similar to the correct answer, but there may be clues in the answers that make them incorrect. The question set up may be something like this:

1. Question

   A. Totally Incorrect Choice
   B. Totally Incorrect Choice
   C. Correct Choice
   D. Almost Correct, but not quite correct.

In mathematics, there may be things like decimals in different places in the answer choices. For instance, there's a big difference between .106, 1.06, 10.6, and 106. Keep these things in mind as you solve math problems. They should also all be labeled correctly and consistently.

Look for "give-away words" like *always*, *never*, or *not*. Most things in the world are not *always* or *never*, and you should be careful if a question asks, "Which of the following is NOT. . . !"

By using the process of elimination, you increase your chances of getting the right answer. Remember that you are not penalized for incorrect answers on either exam, so it's worth taking a chance. What this means is that if you just guess, you have a one in four chance to guess correctly—25 percent.

But, what if you are able to eliminate one of the choices because it just seems wrong to you? You now have a one in three chance of selecting the correct answer. That's 33%, which is surely better than 25 percent.

If you're able to narrow it down to only two choices, you then will improve your chances to one out of two, or 50 percent. You just want to improve your odds of increasing your score, and you can see that it doesn't take much.

We can give you no secrets to successful test-taking. There are, however, time-proven techniques, and this book will provide them for you. Try to pace yourself as you go through the book. Review the material, answer all of the questions we've provided, and go back and review anything you didn't understand the first time around.

# SUBJECT AREA REVIEWS

# Verbal Review

## Word Knowledge

The ability tested in the verbal review portion of any of the nursing tests is your command of the language—in other words, your vocabulary. Of course, by this point in your life you might think that you have learned all of the words that you will ever learn or that it will be impossible to improve your vocabulary. On the contrary! If you are diligent and put your mind to it, you can improve your vocabulary in several ways. Here are three that will definitely help:

- Read, read, read. Pick up a newspaper, a magazine, or a novel and make note of words you do not understand. Make a list or put them on note cards. First, try to figure out the meaning of the words by looking at the context in which they are used. Make an educated guess. If you are still not sure, look up the meaning of the words and write the words and their meanings in a notebook or on note cards. Then try to make up your own sentences using the words.

- Learn a new word every day or every other day. You can get into the habit of looking up a new word in the dictionary every day. Write the word and its definition on a piece of paper. Then write a sentence using the word. This will help you visualize it. Don't pick words that are too technical or specialized (such as medical/scientific terms or proper names). Try using this new word in conversation.

- Words are made up, generally, of prefixes, roots, and suffixes. Many prefixes and roots have a Latin or Greek origin. If you can familiarize yourself with some of these, you will find that you can arrive at the meaning of some words by breaking them down. The following section will offer you some common prefixes, roots, and suffixes to help you tackle words you are unfamiliar with in the Word Knowledge section.

## Prefixes

In order to break down words you do not understand or to help you recognize why a word means what it means, you should become familiar with prefixes. Prefixes are parts of words that come at the beginning of a word and that can affect its meaning.

As an example, look at the word *synonym*. This word is made up of the prefix *syn* plus the root *nym*. If you knew that the prefix syn means *with/together* or *same* and the root *nym* means *name* or *word*, then you could conclude that the word *synonym* means *same word*. And that's what it means!

Look at another example. The word *circumvent* is made up of the prefix *circum* plus the root *vent*. If you knew that the prefix circum means *around* and the root *vent* means *go* or *come*, then you could conclude the word *circumvent* means *go around*.

What follows is a list of common prefixes that you often will find at the beginning of certain words. Following the prefix, you will find the meaning of the prefix and a word using the prefix (with a rough definition in parentheses following the word). Try including a word of your own in the space provided for each prefix. If you cannot come up with your own word, refer to a dictionary for help.

| Prefix | Meaning | Word (Definition) | Your Example |
|--------|---------|-------------------|--------------|
| ab- | away from | abnormal (away from normal) | _____ |
| ad- | to, toward | adjoin (join to) | _____ |
| a-, an- | not, without | apathy (without feeling) | _____ |
| anti- | against | antiviolence (against violence) | _____ |

*(continued)*

*(continued)*

| Prefix | Meaning | Word (Definition) | Your Example |
|--------|---------|-------------------|--------------|
| ambi- | both | ambidextrous (both hands) | _____ |
| bene- | good | benign (good or harmless) | _____ |
| circum- | around | circumvent (go around) | _____ |
| com- | with, together | communion (coming together) | _____ |
| con- | with, together | connect (come together) | _____ |
| contra- | against | contradict (speak against) | _____ |
| de- | down, away | descend (move down) | _____ |
| dis- | apart, not | discontent (not content) | _____ |
| e- | out of, from | eject (throw out) | _____ |
| ex- | out of, from | exclude (leave out) | _____ |
| hyper- | over | hyperactive (overactive) | _____ |
| hypo- | under | hypodermic (below the skin) | _____ |
| il- | not | illegal (not legal) | _____ |
| im- | not | impossible (not possible) | _____ |
| im- | into | imbibe (drink in) | _____ |
| in- | not | indiscreet (not discreet) | _____ |
| in- | into | ingest (take into the body by mouth) | _____ |
| inter- | between | interconnected (connected between) | _____ |
| ir- | not | irrational (not rational) | _____ |
| mal- | bad, evil | malign (speak badly of) | _____ |
| ob- | against | obstruct (build against) | _____ |
| omni- | all | omniscient (knows all) | _____ |
| peri- | around | periscope (view around) | _____ |
| post- | after | postgraduate (after graduation) | _____ |
| pre- | before | precede (go before) | _____ |
| pro- | for, forward | proceed (move forward) | _____ |
| re- | again, back | reconvene (get together again) | _____ |
| retro- | back | retrogression (step back) | _____ |
| se- | away from | seduce (lead away) | _____ |
| sub- | under | subhuman (below human) | _____ |
| sur-, super- | over, above | supersonic (above sound) | _____ |
| sym-, syn- | together, with | sympathy (feeling with or for) | _____ |
| trans- | across | Transatlantic (across the Atlantic) | _____ |

# Roots

Along with prefixes, roots are central to the meanings of words. If you familiarize yourself with some common roots, then you may be able to better recognize certain words or at least get a general feel for several words. By studying the following list of roots, you will be better equipped to breakdown many words and make sense of them!

Following you will find a root, its meaning, a word using the root, and a space in which you can write another word that uses the same root.

| Root | Meaning | Word | Your Definition |
|---|---|---|---|
| ami, amic | love | amicable | _____ |
| anthrop | human, man | anthropology | _____ |
| arch | chief or leader | patriarch | _____ |
| aud | sound | audible | _____ |
| auto | self | autobiography | _____ |
| bio | life | biography | _____ |
| brev | short | brief | _____ |
| cap | take, seize | capture | _____ |
| ced | yield, go | intercede | _____ |
| chron | time | synchronize | _____ |
| corp | body | corporal | _____ |
| crac, crat | rule, ruler | democracy | _____ |
| cred | believe | credible | _____ |
| culp | guilt | culpable | _____ |
| demo | people | democracy | _____ |
| dic | speak, say | dictate | _____ |
| duc, duct | lead | deduce | _____ |
| equ | equal | equity | _____ |
| grad, gress | step | progression | _____ |
| graph | writing, printing | biography | _____ |
| ject | throw | inject | _____ |
| log | study of | geology | _____ |
| luc | light | elucidate | _____ |
| man | hand | manual | _____ |
| min | small | minority | _____ |
| mit, miss | send | emit | _____ |
| mono | one | monotone | _____ |
| mort | death | mortal | _____ |

(continued)

*(continued)*

| Root | Meaning | Word | Your Definition |
|------|---------|------|-----------------|
| mut | change | mutate | _____ |
| nov | new | renovate | _____ |
| nym | word or name | pseudonym | _____ |
| pac | peace | pacify | _____ |
| path | feeling | apathy | _____ |
| pel, puls | push | compel | _____ |
| phil | like, lover of | philosophy | _____ |
| port | carry | portable | _____ |
| pot | power | potent | _____ |
| quer, quis | ask | query | _____ |
| scrib | write | manuscript | _____ |
| sed | sit | sedentary | _____ |
| sent | feel | sensory | _____ |
| sequ | follow | sequel | _____ |
| son | sound | unison | _____ |
| spir | breathe | inspire | _____ |
| tang, tact | touch | tangible | _____ |
| vac | empty | vacant | _____ |
| ven | come, go | intervene | _____ |
| ver | truth | verify | _____ |
| vert | turn | introvert | _____ |
| vit | life | revitalize | _____ |
| voc | call | evocative | _____ |

# Suffixes

Suffixes come at the end of words and usually change the part of speech (noun, adjective, adverb, and so on) of words, which also subtly changes the meaning. Becoming familiar with suffixes may help you get a sense of the meaning the word is *conveying*, even if you are not sure of what the definition of the word is exactly.

Look at a word with different suffixes to see how the part of speech or the meaning can change. For example, the word sedate means to calm or relax. The following sentences contain words that are made up of the root word sedate but have different suffixes attached:

- The doctor prescribed a sedat*ive* [something that sedates] to calm her nerves.
- The speech was delivered sedat*ely* [in a sedate manner].
- The dog was under sedat*ion* [in a state of sedation] for the long trip.
- Many office workers live a sedent*ary* [relating to nonactive] lifestyle.

As you can see, in each of the sentences, the word *sedate* means generally the same thing, but the part of speech changes. However, you can get a sense of *how* the word changes if you know what the suffixes mean.

What follows is a list of common suffixes that you may encounter at the ends of certain words. Try applying theses suffixes at the ends of words you know (or words from the preceding lists) to see how the part of speech or the meaning of the word changes.

| Suffix | Meaning | Your Example |
|---|---|---|
| -able, ible | capable of or susceptible to | |
| -ary | of or relating to | |
| -ate | to make | |
| -ian | one relating to or belonging to | |
| -ic | relating to or characterized by | |
| -ile | relating to or capable of | |
| -ion | action or condition of | |
| -ious | having the quality of | |
| -ism | quality, process, or practice of | |
| -ist | one who performs | |
| -ity | state of being | |
| -ive | performing or tending to | |
| -ize, ise | to cause to be or become | |
| -less | without | |
| -ly | resembling or in the manner of | |
| -ment | action or process or the result | |
| -ology | study of | |
| -y, -ry | state of | |

Now, using the information that you have just learned, try to apply these concepts to the different test sections. Keep in mind that all of the following sections—Synonyms, Antonyms, Analogies, and Spelling—are all vocabulary related. Answer all of the practice questions and then check your answers at the end of this section.

# Synonyms

What is a synonym? Very simply, it's a word that has the same meaning as another word. In most of the nursing entrance exams, a test of synonyms is a test of vocabulary. How well do you understand words and what they mean? Almost any kind of standardized test will present some form of vocabulary test. Try these sample problems. Select the word that most nearly means the same as the capitalized word.

1. GRAPHIC

   A. unclear
   B. detailed
   C. large
   D. childish

**B.** Graphic (graph = written or drawn) means described in vivid detail or clearly drawn out, so detailed would most closely mean graphic.

2. INDISPENSABLE

   A. trashy
   B. ridiculous
   C. necessary
   D. uninvited

**C.** Indispensable literally means not dispensable (able to be thrown away). So if something is indispensable, it is necessary; you cannot do away with it.

Now practice with the following questions. Remember that the word may not be an exact meaning, but one that is most nearly like the other word.

# Synonym Practice Questions

1. CONCOCT

   A. make up
   B. throw away
   C. go through
   D. walk around

2. SONIC

   A. relating to the sun
   B. relating to the moon
   C. relating to sound
   D. relating to the earth

3. ASSIMILATE

   A. to take in
   B. to make fun of
   C. to rob of
   D. to ignore

4. DEGRADATION

   A. happiness
   B. anger
   C. celebration
   D. poverty

5. CONTRADICT

   A. to talk about
   B. to see the future
   C. to fall down
   D. to speak against

6. SEQUENTIALLY

   A. sensibly
   B. randomly
   C. in order
   D. out of order

7. CULPRIT

   A. a shy person
   B. a shallow waterway
   C. the guilty party
   D. the most qualified person

8. OMNIPOTENT

   A. all-knowing
   B. all-seeing
   C. all-hearing
   D. all-powerful

**9.** SUBMISSIVE

   A. meek
   B. not intelligent
   C. kind
   D. strong

**10.** DEMEANING

   A. boring
   B. humiliating
   C. colorful
   D. ignorant

**11.** FLUCTUATE

   A. remain the same
   B. follow a downward course
   C. follow an upward course
   D. change

**12.** RENOVATE

   A. destroy
   B. restore
   C. return
   D. go around

**13.** INTERCEDE

   A. to bring something to an end
   B. to act as a judge
   C. to act as mediator
   D. to laugh at something

# Antonyms

Antonym tests are vocabulary tests, but unlike a synonym, an antonym is a word of opposite meaning. Some of the more common antonym pairs would be *hot/cold*, *sit/stand*, *far/near*, and *up/down*. Look at these examples.

---

**1.** Happy is the *opposite* of

   A. joyful
   B. serious
   C. sad
   D. considerate

---

**C.** The opposite of *happy* is *sad*.

---

**2.** Passive is the *opposite* of

   A. angry
   B. calm
   C. active
   D. conservative

---

**C.** *Passive* means not reacting; the opposite is *active*.

# Antonym Practice Questions

*For each of the following practice questions, select that answer that most nearly means the opposite of the given word.*

**1.** Recall is the *opposite* of

   A. remember
   B. lose
   C. forget
   D. think

**2.** Civil is the *opposite* of

   A. illegal
   B. rude
   C. reveal
   D. gracious

3. Decay is the *opposite* of

   A. descend
   B. grow
   C. accept
   D. find

4. Devoid is the *opposite* of

   A. lacking
   B. emptying
   C. having
   D. taking

5. Prelude is the *opposite* of

   A. preclude
   B. intermission
   C. interlude
   D. conclusion

6. Ooze is the *opposite* of

   A. pour
   B. drink
   C. river
   D. zoo

7. Tradition is the *opposite* of

   A. custom
   B. transition
   C. novelty
   D. treason

8. Permit is the *opposite* of

   A. license
   B. allow
   C. forbid
   D. persuade

9. Somber is the *opposite* of

   A. straight
   B. bright
   C. cloudy
   D. miserable

10. Indispensable is the *opposite* of

   A. unnecessary
   B. ridiculous
   C. trashy
   D. cheap

# Verbal Analogies

An analogy is usually a comparison of two proportions or relations. In standard usage—and for many of the nursing exams—you will encounter several types of analogies.

Each question presents two words that have some type of relationship; you are asked to select the choice that best completes the analogy, which is similar to the relationship presented in the original pair of words. There are two formats for the questions. For example, look at the following:

1. FORK is to EAT as PEN is to

   A. INK
   B. PENCIL
   C. WRITE
   D. LETTER
   E. BOOK

You first must ask yourself what the relationship is between FORK and EAT. A fork is used to eat. Thus, the next pair demonstrates a similar relationship—a PEN is used to WRITE. The correct answer is **C**.

Here's another sample question.

---

**2.** PLUM is to FRUIT as STEAK is to

   **A.**   MEAL
   **B.**   DINNER
   **C.**   VEAL
   **D.**   COW
   **E.**   BEEF

---

Although many of these choices sound correct, let's analyze them. A plum is fruit. A steak can be a meal, but not necessarily the entire meal. A steak can be dinner, but it can also be lunch. A steak is not veal, so that's incorrect. A steak comes from a cow, but it's only part of a cow. The most obvious answer would be **E**, BEEF. It establishes the same relationship between PLUM and FRUIT as STEAK and BEEF.

The second format of analogy questions that you will encounter is as follows.

---

**3.** PREMIER is to COUNTRY as

   **A.**   TEACHER is to LEARNING
   **B.**   PRINCIPAL is to SCHOOL
   **C.**   PRESIDENT is to CABINET
   **D.**   SOLDIER is to SAILOR
   **E.**   POLICEMAN is to CRIME

---

The correct answer is **B**, PRINCIPAL is to SCHOOL. The PREMIER is the leader of the COUNTRY, and the PRINCIPAL is the leader of the SCHOOL. If you look at the other choices, you can see the differences in relationships when compared to the original pair. The teacher's job is to help the students learn, and he or she is surely in charge of students, but that is not the direct relationship. The President chooses the Cabinet, but the Cabinet is only a small part of the country. Soldier to Sailor and Policeman to Crime are different relationships entirely.

Keep in mind that the relationship between the words is the most important aspect when answering an analogy question. It is less important than the actual meanings of the words. Try to establish the relationship immediately as you read the question. How are the two words related? Are they the same? Are they part of a group? Are they antonyms? It is often helpful to paraphrase the relationship.

For example, you might encounter the following:

---

**4.** FISH is to OCEAN as HORSE is to

   **A.**   OATS
   **B.**   RACETRACK
   **C.**   STABLE
   **D.**   GALLOP
   **E.**   FIELD

---

You would paraphrase this by saying, "A FISH lives in the OCEAN; therefore, a HORSE lives in the STABLE." The correct answer is **C**. While some horses may live in the field, city horses may live only in a stable. (Questions usually require you to be fairly specific.) By paraphrasing the original pair, you help yourself in identifying the correct answer.

Here's one that requires even more specific attention:

---

**5.** BAT is to BASEBALL, as

    **A.** PASS is to FOOTBALL
    **B.** CLUB is to GOLF
    **C.** BALL is to TENNIS
    **D.** SPIKES is to SLIDE
    **E.** CARDS is to POKER

---

You would say, "A BAT is used in BASEBALL." Then again, A CLUB is used in GOLF, a BALL is used in TENNIS, and CARDS are used in POKER. You can eliminate the PASS since this is not an *object* used in the game. SPIKES is to SLIDE is an entirely different relationship—you wear SPIKES in a game, but they are not necessarily used to SLIDE. How do you narrow down your choices? You do this by becoming more specific. You would now paraphrase this by saying "A BAT is used to hit a ball in the game of BASEBALL." Choice **B** now becomes the logical selection, because a CLUB is used to hit a ball in the game of GOLF.

Make sure that you start by eliminating those choices that do not express a clear relationship to the original pair. This will make selecting the correct pair somewhat easier by narrowing down the number of choices. Also be careful of choices with similar words that might be included just to trip you up. If the choice sounds too similar to the original pair, it's probably incorrect and is being used by the test-developer as a "distracter."

## Classification of Analogies

Dozens of different types of analogies exist, defined based on their relationships. However, we'll just cover a few of the major types, because these are the most common types of questions you'll find on the test.

### Synonyms

As you should know, synonyms are words that have similar meanings and are usually from the same part of speech.

---

**6.** DOWDY is to DRAB as

    **A.** QUIET is to DEN
    **B.** SAFETY is to STELLAR
    **C.** OBJECTIVE is to DISPASSIONATE
    **D.** PETTY is to ELEPHANTINE
    **E.** RECREATION is to TOYS

---

The correct answer is **C**. A synonym for **dowdy** is **drab.** One who is **objective** is **dispassionate**.

### Antonyms

Antonyms are words that have opposite meanings.

---

**7.** HAPPY is to SAD as RIGID is to

    **A.** FAULTY
    **B.** TIGHT
    **C.** CONSERVATIVE
    **D.** ALTRUISTIC
    **E.** FLEXIBLE

---

The correct answer is **E**. **Rigid** means still and unyielding. The opposite is **flexible**.

## Function

What is the purpose, or function, of the relationship?

---

**8.** HAMMER is to NAIL as

    **A.** CAR is to WHEEL
    **B.** GLUE is to TUBE
    **C.** KNIFE is to SHARP
    **D.** SCISSORS is to PAPER
    **E.** PEN is to INK

---

The correct answer is **D**. The function of a **hammer** is to hit a **nail**, and the function of a **scissors** is to cut **paper**.

## Part to Whole

In this type of analogy, the first word in the pair is part of the second word. It can also be used in an opposite manner.

---

**9.** DANCERS is to TROUPE as

    **A.** SINGERS is to CHORUS
    **B.** WRITERS is to BOOKS
    **C.** SENATORS is to REPRESENTATIVES
    **D.** TEACHERS is to PROFESSORS
    **E.** PILOTS is to JETS

---

**Dancers** are part of a **troupe**, and **singers** are part of a **chorus**. The correct answer is **A**. If you analyze each of the answers, you'll see that although the first and second choices are related, they are not parts-to-whole relationships.

## Definition

This is similar to synonyms. The first word is the definition of the second word.

---

**10.** SANCTUARY is to REFUGE as

    **A.** CAVE is to BEAR
    **B.** VAULT is to VALUABLES
    **C.** TRIUMPH is to CONTEST
    **D.** STRIATION is to STRIPE
    **E.** CARNIVORE is OMNIVORE

---

The correct answer is **D**. A **striation** is to **stripe**. None of the other choices are definitions of each other.

## Type

One word in the pair represents a type of the second word. For example, MAPLE is a type of TREE, SEDAN is a type of CAR, and ROBIN is a type of BIRD.

---

**11.** ARGON is to GAS as

    **A.** BOOK is to LIBRARY
    **B.** GESSO is to PAINT
    **C.** HEART is to PACEMAKER
    **D.** PAUPER is to MONEY
    **E.** COMPUTER is to KEYBOARD

---

The correct answer is **B**. **Gesso** is a type of **paint**. These are sometimes known as "Member and Class" analogies.

Dozens of other types of analogies actually exist—some very sophisticated and some fairly simple. To learn how to solve analogies, you must spend the time on the practice problems, study the material presented previously, and try to identify the types of pairs in each question. Analyze them and take your time with these questions in order to be familiar with the different types of analogies and to be able to recognize them quickly when you take the test.

# Analogy Practice Questions

Try these practice questions.

**1.** TOOL is to DRILL as POEM is to

    **A.** SONG
    **B.** MACHINE
    **C.** SONNET
    **D.** BIRD
    **E.** NOVEL

**2.** TALK is to SHOUT as DISLIKE is to

    **A.** SCREAM
    **B.** DETEST
    **C.** FRIGHTEN
    **D.** CONTRIBUTE
    **E.** ADMIRE

**3.** CONDUCTOR is to ORCHESTRA as SHEPHERD is to

    **A.** FILM
    **B.** CANINE
    **C.** CONTROL
    **D.** FLOCK
    **E.** GENERAL

**4.** OBSTINATE is to COMPLIANT as OBLIVIOUS is to

    **A.** CONSCIOUS
    **B.** CAREFREE
    **C.** FORGETFUL
    **D.** INTUITIVE
    **E.** NATURAL

**5.** BOUQUET is to VASE as GARBAGE is to

    **A.** URN
    **B.** ABDOMEN
    **C.** CENTERPIECE
    **D.** SEWER
    **E.** CARTON

**6.** TENSION is to STRESS as VIRUS is to

    **A.** LIVING
    **B.** DISEASE
    **C.** BACTERIA
    **D.** IMMUNITY
    **E.** MORBIDITY

**7.** BAROMETER is to PRESSURE as CALIPERS is to

- A. CUTTING
- B. HEIGHT
- C. CONSTANCY
- D. THICKNESS
- E. PLIERS

**8.** MISER is to MONEY as GLUTTON is to

- A. FOOD
- B. ENVY
- C. LITERATURE
- D. PUNISHMENT
- E. NUTRIENTS

**9.** PRIDE is to HUMBLE as HUMOR is to

- A. INTELLECTUAL
- B. ENERGETIC
- C. SOMBER
- D. SERVILE
- E. LUDICROUS

**10.** CANDID is to TRUTHFUL as CONTENTIOUS is to

- A. HARMONIOUS
- B. QUARRELSOME
- C. COHERENT
- D. MENDACIOUS
- E. UNPLEASANT

**11.** COWARD is to COURAGE as

- A. CYNIC is to DOUBT
- B. REVELER is to CHEER
- C. MISER is to GENEROSITY
- D. THINKER is to CONTEMPLATION
- E. PARTNER is to COOPERATION

**12.** IMPECUNIOUS is to WEALTH as

- A. ALACRITY is to SPEED
- B. MYSTIQUE is to MYSTERY
- C. ACERBITY is to BITTERNESS
- D. IGNORANT is to UNDERSTANDING
- E. POMPOUS is to SHOW

**13.** BIASED is to IMPARTIALITY as

- A. APATHETIC is to EMOTION
- B. STEADFASTNESS is to SOLIDITY
- C. INCONGRUITY is to DISORGANIZATION
- D. FORTUITOUS is to LUCK
- E. HONEST is to INTEGRITY

**14.** SHOVEL is to DIG as

- A. WASP is to STING
- B. BROOM is to FLY
- C. WOUND is to HEAL
- D. DETERGENT is to CLEAN
- E. CLIMB is to MOUNTAIN

**15.** POKER is to PROD as

- A. PEN is to WRITE
- B. ATTRACT is to SMELL
- C. STILTS is to CRAWL
- D. CAUTION is to SUCCEED
- E. ACTIVATE is to LEVER

# Spelling

In this section, you are asked to identify words that are spelled incorrectly. For some people, this is the easiest section on any of the nursing tests. If you're a good speller, this should be a snap for you. If you have difficulty with spelling, you'll have to spend a little more time figuring out what's right and what's wrong.

These questions have different formats. One type of question just lists several words, and you are to select the incorrectly spelled word from the list.

**1.**

    **A.** weightless
    **B.** reddened
    **C.** obstacle
    **D.** aweful

**D.** The correct spelling is *awful*.

**2.**

    **A.** invigorate
    **B.** negitive
    **C.** massacre
    **D.** courtesy

**B.** The correct spelling is *negative*.

The second type of question asks you to find the incorrectly spelled word or to indicate that no mistakes were found.

**3.**

    **A.** I will finish this project by next Wensday.
    **B.** Saturday would be a good day to go to the park.
    **C.** Apparently, he does not work on weekends.
    **D.** No mistakes.

**A.** The correct spelling is *Wednesday*.

**4.**

    **A.** Sarah asked her teacher to recommend her for the tutoring job.
    **B.** Lee wanted to study medicine.
    **C.** Have you seen the skedule for next week's meeting?
    **D.** No mistakes.

**C.** The correct spelling is *schedule*.

*Now try the following questions. In questions 1–5 select the word that is spelled incorrectly.*

# Spelling Practice Questions

**1.**

    **A.** backround
    **B.** combustible
    **C.** accustomed
    **D.** slurred

**2.**

    **A.** sacrafice
    **B.** executive
    **C.** mortgage
    **D.** restaurant

**3.**

A. idolize
B. donor
C. fuedal
D. inflammatory

*idolize*

**4.**

A. television
B. perdicament
C. hindrance
D. officious

**5.**

A. excessive
B. appraise
C. government
D. cemetary

*Cemetary*

*In questions 6-10, select the word that is spelled incorrectly. If there is no spelling error, select **D**.*

**6.**

A. Rhythm in poetry and music is based on repetition.
B. Unfortunately, Frank can't be here today.
C. He is hoping to join us tomorrow.
D. No mistakes.

**7.**

A. Phil and Felicia had an arguement about whose turn it was to walk the dog.
B. Rex sat their whining because he wanted to go out.
C. The difference between the two shades of pink is not significant.
D. No mistakes.

**8.**

A. I don't believe that doing well in school guarantees professional success.
B. Good grammer is a requirement for clear communication.
C. The grade of ninety means outstanding work.
D. No mistakes.

**9.**

A. I mailed your birthday present to you last Thursday.
B. Have you recieved the package yet?
C. Sometimes delivery services are slow.
D. No mistakes.

**10.**

A. Taylor has been studying for the chemistry test.
B. Students usually take chemistry during their sophomore year.
C. Athletes are not excused from taking the exam.
D. No mistakes.

# Summary

Most of these topics are not difficult. These types of questions require, however, some diligence in studying. For example, don't mix up synonyms and antonyms. Take your time when answering the questions but don't linger too long on any one question because it will just slow you down. To save time, read the directions carefully to make sure that you know what is being asked of you.

At the end of the book are two practice exams. Spend the time to take these tests. You will definitely reap the benefits when it comes time to take an actual test.

# Answers and Explanations

## Synonyms

**1. A.** *Concoct* means to create or come up with, like in the sentence "The two boys concocted a plan to skip school." Concoct most closely means to make up.

**2. C.** *Sonic* means relating to sound (son = sound).

**3. A.** *Assimilate* means to absorb or take in. If a group of individuals successfully assimilates, then they have converged and incorporated into one group.

**4. D.** *Degradation* is a state of poverty or squalor. It literally means "a step down" (de = down, grad = step).

**5. D.** *Contradict* literally means to speak against (contra = against, dict = speak).

**6. C.** *Sequentially* means that items are arranged in order or in a sequence (sequ = follow).

**7. C.** The *culprit* is the person who is guilty (culp = guilt).

**8. D.** *Omnipotent* literally means all-powerful (omni = all, pot = power).

**9. A.** A *submissive* (sub = under, miss = send) person is one who is meek and passive, not aggressive.

**10. B.** *Demeaning* (de = down) means something that puts one down or is humiliating.

**11. D.** *Fluctuate* (fluc = change) means to change, go up and down, not constant.

**12. B.** *Renovate* means to restore or to make new again (re = again, nov = new).

**13. C.** *Intercede* means to go between (inter = within, ced = go) or to mediate.

## Antonyms

**1. B.** *Recall* means remember; *forget* is the opposite.

**2. B.** One meaning of *civil* is polite; do not be confused by another meaning of civil, referring to citizens and their relationships with a state. *Rude* is the correct choice.

**3. B.** To *decay* is to break down or rot; *grow* is the opposite.

**4. C.** To be *devoid* is to lack; *having* is the opposite.

**5. D.** A *prelude* is at the beginning of a work of music or literature; therefore, *conclusion* is the best choice.

**6. A.** To *ooze* is to seep out slowly; if something flows out quickly, it *pours*.

**7. C.** A *tradition* is something done now that was also done in the past; *novelty* is the opposite.

**8. C.** Although *permit* can be a noun, in this item it is used as a verb, and *forbid* is the opposite.

**9. B.** *Somber* means dark and gloomy; *bright* is the best choice.

**10. A.** Something *indispensable* is required or necessary.

## Analogies

**1. C.** An example of a kind of tool is a *drill*, and an example of a kind of *poem* is a *sonnet*.

**2. B.** An intense form of *talk* is to *shout*, and an intense form of *dislike* is to *detest*.

**3. D.** The function of a *conductor* is to lead an *orchestra*, and the function of a *shepherd* is to lead a *flock*.

**4. A.** The opposite of *obstinate* is *compliant*, and the opposite of *oblivious* is *conscious*.

**5. D.** A location for a *bouquet* is a *vase*, and a location for garbage is a *sewer*.

**6. B.** An effect of *tension* is to cause *stress*, and an effect of a *virus* is to cause *disease*.

**7. D.** The function of a *barometer* is to measure *pressure*, and the function of *calipers* is to measure *thickness*.

**8. A.** The desire of a *miser* is *money*, and the desire of a *glutton* is *food*.

**9. C.** To lack *pride* is to be *humble*, and to lack *humor* is to be *somber*.

**10. B.** A synonym of *candid* is *truthful*, and a synonym of *contentious* is *quarrelsome*.

**11. C.** A coward suffers from a lack of *courage*. A *miser* lacks *generosity*.

**12. D.** A person who is *impecunious* is poor, and, therefore, lacks *wealth*. A person who is *ignorant* lacks *understanding*.

**13. A.** A *biased* individual lacks *impartiality*. An *apathetic* person lacks *emotion*.

**14. D.** *Detergent* is characteristically used to *clean*. A *shovel* is characteristically used to *dig*.

**15. A.** A *poker* is used for *prodding*, and a *pen* is used for *writing*.

# Spelling

**1. A.** The correct spelling is *background*.

**2. A.** The correct spelling is *sacrifice*.

**3. C.** The correct spelling is *feudal*.

**4. B.** The correct spelling is *predicament*.

**5. D.** The correct spelling is *cemetery*.

**6. D.** No mistakes

**7. A.** The correct spelling is *argument*.

**8. B.** The correct spelling is *grammar*.

**9. B.** The correct spelling is *received*.

**10. D.** No mistakes

# Reading Comprehension Review

## Answering Reading Comprehension Questions

Reading comprehension questions demonstrate your ability to understand what you have read. Sometimes, you will be asked about the content of the passage, and the correct answer repeats words or phrases from the passage. Some questions have an answer that repeats the content of the passage in different words. For these questions, the correct answer is a paraphrase of material in the passage. Some questions ask you to make an inference. To *infer* is to make a conclusion based on the information in the passage, although the passage itself does not state this conclusion. There also may be questions about the meaning of words in the passage, but you are not expected to know the meaning of the word before reading the passage. You can determine the correct answer choice by seeing how the word is used.

Unless it is otherwise stated, the correct answer is based on something that is in the passage. Although you might know something additional about what appears in the passage, you should limit your answer choice to information presented in the passage. The questions do not expect you to bring in other material. Answer choices that are true statements may be provided, but if they are not in the passage, they are not the correct choice. You may even know that something in the passage is untrue. Even so, if that statement is given as an answer choice, it may be correct according to the passage.

As you read the passage to get a general idea of the subject, focus on the first and last sentence of each paragraph. These sentences often contain the most important idea in the paragraph, and one of them may state the paragraph's main idea. Look for words indicating how ideas are related. Words like *but* or *however* indicate contrasts. Often, words and phrases relating to causes and effects, such as *because*, *therefore*, and *as a result*, are material about which there will be questions.

Read each question and all four of the answer choices. Eliminate any choices that seem obviously incorrect. If one answer seems to be correct, reread the portion of the passage that it is about, and if this still seems to be the correct choice, select that answer. If none of the answers seem appropriate, reread the passage to see whether you can eliminate choices or find information to determine the correct answer.

If you still are uncertain about an answer, do not spend more time on that question. Because there is normally no deduction for wrong answers, choose the answer that seems most likely, even if you are unsure. You can return to these questions if you have time to do so.

Some people find it easier to skim over the questions before reading the passage. This gives them an idea of what to look for while they read. As you take the practice tests in this book, try this method to see whether it makes it easier for you to answer the questions.

## Reading Comprehension Practice

**Directions**: This section measures your ability to read and understand written English similar to what one may expect in a college or university setting. Read each passage and answer the questions based on what is stated or implied in the passage. Circle or mark the correct answer in the book or write it on a separate piece of paper.

### Passage One

Cholera, a highly *infectious* disease, has resulted in millions of deaths time after time over centuries. It is caused by the bacterium Vibrio cholerae, first isolated by Robert Koch in 1883.

The organism enters the body through the digestive tract when contaminated food or water is ingested. The bacteria multiply in the digestive tract and establish infection. As they die, they release a potent toxin that leads to severe diarrhea and vomiting. This results in extreme dehydration, muscle cramps, kidney failure, collapse, and sometimes death. If the disease is treated promptly, death is less likely.

In many countries, a common source of the organism is raw or poorly cooked seafood taken from contaminated waters. The disease is especially prevalent after a natural disaster or other destruction that results in a lack of fresh water. Sewer systems fail, and waste travels into rivers or streams; piped water is not available, so people must take their drinking and cooking water from rivers or streams. Because people frequently develop communities along waterways, the disease can be spread easily from one community to the next community downstream, resulting in serious epidemics.

1. The word *infectious* in the first sentence is closest in meaning to

   A. communicable.
   B. severe.
   C. isolated.
   D. common.

2. According to the passage, cholera is caused by

   A. a virus.
   B. a bacterium.
   C. kidney failure.
   D. dehydration.

3. All of the following are probable causes of infection except

   A. eating food cooked with contaminated water.
   B. eating undercooked seafood.
   C. eating overcooked pork.
   D. eating raw oysters.

4. What is the logical order of the events leading to the illness?

   A. Sanitary system fails, so fresh water is unavailable; disaster occurs; people drink the water; contaminated water flows into waterways.
   B. Disaster occurs; sanitary system fails, so fresh water is unavailable; people drink the water; contaminated water flows into waterways.
   C. Disaster occurs; contaminated water flows into waterways; sanitary system fails, so fresh water is unavailable; people drink the water.
   D. Contaminated water flows into waterways; disaster occurs; sanitary system fails, so fresh water is unavailable; people drink the water.

5. According to the passage, what is a symptom of the infection?

   A. Release of a toxin by the bacteria
   B. Regurgitation
   C. Overeating
   D. Epidemics

6. Which of the following would be an appropriate title for this passage?

   A. Dysentery and Its Effects
   B. Water Purification Systems and Their Importance
   C. Results of War and Natural Disasters
   D. The Causes and Effects of Cholera

7. The word *prevalent* in the third paragraph is closest in meaning to

   A. dangerous.
   B. commonplace.
   C. unusual.
   D. organized.

8. The word *lack* in the third paragraph is closest in meaning to

   A. contamination.
   B. multitude.
   C. shortage.
   D. well.

9. According to the passage, cholera

   A. is easily passed from one person to another.
   B. is not a real threat.
   C. is no more dangerous than the common cold.
   D. cannot be passed from one to another by casual contact.

10. What can you infer from the passage?

     A. Careful cooking and hygiene practices can reduce the chance of getting the disease.
     B. Water mixed with other substances will not pass the disease.
     C. The respiratory system is the most common area of entrance.
     D. Kidney disease is the most common cause of the illness.

**Passage Two**

The *ubiquitous* bar code, developed more than 20 years ago, is not a *stagnant* product. On the contrary, the technology has been improved so that it can be used more efficiently. Much less expensive than a computer chip, the bar code can hold more information than it has in the past by adding a second dimension to the structure.

The bar code consists of a series of parallel vertical bars or lines of two different *widths*, although sometimes four widths are used, printed in black on a white background. Bar codes are used for entering data into a computer system. The bars represent the binary digits 0 and 1, just like basic computer language, and sequences of these digits can indicate the numbers from 0 to 9, which then can be read by an optical laser scanner and processed by a digital computer. Arabic numbers appear below the code.

The *traditional* bar code has been used to monitor skiers at ski lifts and to determine price and perform inventory control on groceries, drugs, medical supplies, manufactured parts, and library books—to name a few. The bar code used on grocery products, introduced in the 1970s, is called a universal product code (or UPC) and assigns each type of food or grocery product a unique code. The five digits on the left are assigned to a particular manufacturer or maker, and the five digits on the right are used by that manufacturer to identify a specific type or make of product. Traditional single dimension bar codes are not readily customizable because there is little extra space.

The two-dimensional bar code, with an information density of 1,100 bytes, allows a *considerably* greater amount of information to be coded than does the traditional bar code, including customized information. It also has built-in

11. Mark the area in the passage where the author states that waterfront communities may be susceptible to the illness from other communities upstream.

12. The word *epidemics* at the end of the passage is closest in meaning to

     A. studies.
     B. vaccines.
     C. bacteria.
     D. plagues.

redundancy, meaning that the identical information is duplicated on the same code. Therefore, if the code is damaged, it can still be read. The technology even allows pictures or text to be contained within the code, as well as bar code encryption. The new technology dramatically reduces the errors of the single dimensional bar code and reduces the enormous costs that some companies have reported in the past.

13. The word *ubiquitous* in the first sentence is closest in meaning to

     A. outdated.
     B. ever-present.
     C. new.
     D. complicated.

14. The word *stagnant* in the first sentence is closest in meaning to

     A. ever-changing.
     B. useful.
     C. stale.
     D. useless.

15. The author implies that the bar code

     A. has only recently become popular.
     B. will never change.
     C. is not useful.
     D. has existed in one-dimensional form for years.

16. The author's main purpose is to describe

     A. the current technology and newest innovation of bar codes.
     B. problems with the bar code.
     C. the UPC used in grocery stores.
     D. why the bar code is no longer viable.

**17.** Where in the final paragraph could the following sentence be logically placed?

"Thus, the manufacturer is able to add information on the bar code that it finds useful for its own tracking purposes."

The two-dimensional bar code, with an information density of 1,100 bytes, allows a considerably greater amount of information to be coded than does the traditional bar code, including customized information. **(A)** It also has built-in redundancy, meaning that the identical information is duplicated on the same code. **(B)** Therefore, if the code is damaged, it can still be read. **(C)** The technology even allows pictures or text to be contained within the code, as well as bar code encryption. **(D)** The new technology dramatically reduces the errors of the single dimensional bar code and reduces the enormous costs that some companies have reported in the past.

**18.** Which of the following can be a UPC symbol?

- **A.** A code with five digits on the left, five on the right, two different widths, and one number under each.
- **B.** A code with six digits on the left, four on the right, two different widths, and one Roman numeral under each.
- **C.** A code with five digits on the left, five digits on the right, five or six different widths, and one number under each.
- **D.** A code with five digits on the left, five digits on the right, reverse form (white text on black background), and no numbers underneath.

**19.** A UPC is a type of

- **A.** computer program.
- **B.** bar code.
- **C.** grocery item.
- **D.** scanner.

**20.** The word *widths* in the second paragraph refers to

- **A.** its size.
- **B.** its direction.
- **C.** its location.
- **D.** its content.

**21.** The word *traditional* in the third paragraph is closest in meaning to

- **A.** conventional.
- **B.** new.
- **C.** logical.
- **D.** technological.

**22.** In the past, a common use of the bar code was

- **A.** to encrypt pictures.
- **B.** to keep track of products stocked and sold.
- **C.** to act as a computer.
- **D.** to hide text.

**23.** The word *considerably* in the final paragraph is closest in meaning to

- **A.** slightly.
- **B.** technologically.
- **C.** interestingly.
- **D.** far.

# Answers and Explanations to Practice Reading Exercise

**1. A.** Infectious means communicable, or easy to pass along to others. The passage makes it clear that one person can pass the disease on to another. Notice the word "infect," which means to transmit an illness, and the suffix indicates that this is an adjective.

**2. B.** The second sentence of the first paragraph specifically states that cholera is caused by a bacterium.

**3. C.** The second paragraph indicates that contaminated food and water carry the organism and that certain raw or poorly cooked foods cause infection. However, nothing indicates that food cooked too much (overcooked) causes cholera.

**4. C.** The order of events leading to the illness is: Disaster occurs; contaminated water flows into waterways; sanitary system fails and fresh water becomes unavailable; and people drink the water.

**5. B.** Regurgitation, which means the same as vomiting.

**6. D.** "The Causes and Effects of Cholera" is the most general description of the passage. The entire passage is about cholera. Dysentery, in the first answer choice, is another illness that causes some of the same symptoms. Contaminated water is a cause of the disease, but the second choice is not a good title for the passage. The third answer choice relates to only a portion of the topic. Although war and natural disaster may cause cholera, the passage is about the disease, not the cause.

**7. B.** The context of the sentence leads you to understand that prevalent means very common.

**8. C.** Shortage is nearest in meaning to lack. Both words mean "to be without."

**9. A.** Cholera is easily passed from one person to another.

**10. A.** Careful cooking and hygiene practices can reduce the chance of getting the disease.

**11.** **"Because people frequently develop communities along waterways, the disease can be spread easily from one community to the next community downstream, resulting in serious epidemics."** This area should be marked in the passage.

**12. D.** The sentence states that the epidemics have resulted in millions of deaths, so it's clear that epidemic is not a positive thing, which helps you eliminate the first two answer choices. Bacteria makes no sense because it means that cholera "has been responsible for" bacteria.

**13. B.** Ubiquitous means "omni-present" or "existing everywhere."

**14. C.** The word stagnant means stale, "out-of-date," or "not changing." This passage states that the bar code concept is still being changed.

**15. D.** The passage indicates that the bar code has been used in various ways since the 1970s.

**16. A.** The passage covers both a review of existing technology and the new two-dimensional code.

**17. A.** The two-dimensional bar code, with an information density of 1,100 bytes, allows a considerably greater amount of information to be coded than the traditional bar code, including customized information. Thus, the manufacturer is able to add information on the bar code that it finds useful for its own tracking purposes. It also has built-in redundancy, meaning that the identical information is duplicated on the same code. Therefore, if the code is damaged. it can still be read. The technology even allows pictures or text to be contained within the code, as well as bar code encryption. The new technology dramatically reduces the errors of the single dimensional bar code and reduces the enormous costs that some companies have reported in the past.

**18. A.** The reading states that the code consists of horizontal lines, black print on a white background, with two and sometimes four different widths, and Arabic numerals underneath.

**19. B.** The passage states: "The bar code used on grocery products, introduced in the 1970s, is called a universal product code (or UPC), and assigns each type of food or grocery product a unique code."

**20. A.** Width is the noun related to the noun wide. It describes the size from left to right.

**21. A.** Traditional refers to a long-standing tradition or convention.

**22. B.** Keeping track of products stocked and sold means the same thing as inventory control. The other uses mentioned are potential uses of the new two-dimensional bar code.

**23. D.** In this context, considerably means "far" or "much."

# Mathematics Review

This section reviews all the skills you need to do well on almost any mathematics test. The material is presented in a logical manner, from basic arithmetic, through more advanced topics. We have included plenty of examples so that you can fully understand the material. In addition, you can try the practice problems to make sure that you've got a handle on these types of questions.

## Arithmetic Reasoning and Mathematics Knowledge

Several basic arithmetic and mathematics sections appear on most nursing entrance exams. The following is a brief review of arithmetic and mathematics, covering some basic information that will come in handy on these tests.

Although you might not have to know everything that we present in this section, it would be a good idea to review most of this material. In addition, take all the arithmetic and mathematics tests in this book to get a better understanding of what you know and what might require more studying.

## The Numbers of Arithmetic

### Whole Numbers

The numbers 0, 1, 2, 3, 4, and so on are called *whole numbers*. The whole number system is a *place value* system; that is, the value of each digit in a whole number is determined by the place it occupies. For example, in the number 6,257, the 6 is in the thousands place, the 2 is in the hundreds place, the 5 is in the tens place, and the 7 is in the ones place.

The following table contains a summary of whole number place values:

| Ones | 1 |
|---|---|
| Tens | 10 |
| Hundreds | 100 |
| Thousands | 1,000 |
| Ten-thousands | 10,000 |
| Hundred-thousands | 100,000 |
| Millions | 1,000,000 |
| Ten millions | 10,000,000 |
| Hundred millions | 100,000,000 |
| Billions | 1,000,000,000 |

For example, the number 5,124,678 would be read five million, one hundred twenty-four thousand, six hundred and seventy-eight.

> Write the number thirty million, five hundred seven thousand, three hundred twelve.

30,507,312

> Write in words the number 34,521.

Thirty-four thousand, five hundred twenty-one

## Rounding Whole Numbers

When you only need an approximate value of a whole number, the following procedure can be used to round off the number to a particular place:

1. Underline the digit in the place being rounded off.
2. If the digit to the right of the underlined digit is less than five, leave the underlined digit as it is. If the digit to the right of the underlined digit is equal to five or more, add one to the underlined digit.
3. Replace all digits to the right of the underlined digit with zeros.

Rounding whole numbers often helps you determine the correct answer to a multiple choice question more quickly.

> Round off the number 34,521 to the nearest hundred.

Because we are rounding to the nearest hundred, begin by underlining the digit in the hundreds place, which is a five:

34,521

Now, look to the right of the underlined digit. Because the number to the right of the five is two, leave the five as it is and replace all digits to the right of the five with zeros.

**34,500** is rounded to the nearest hundred.

> Round off the number 236,789 to the nearest ten-thousand.

Because we are rounding to the nearest ten-thousand, begin by underlining the digit in the ten-thousands place, which is three:

236,789

Now, look to the right of the underlined digit. Because the number to the right of the three is six, increase three by one, obtaining four, and replace all digits to the right of this four with zeros.

**240,000** is rounded to the nearest ten-thousand.

## Fractions

A fraction is made up of two numbers, separated by a line that is known as a fraction bar. Typically, a fraction is used to represent a part of a whole. For example, in the following diagram, note that five out of eight pieces of the diagram are shaded:

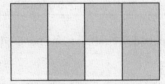

In this case, the fraction ⅝ could be used to represent the fact that five of the eight equal pieces have been shaded. In the same way, the fraction ⅜ could be used to represent the fact that three of the eight pieces have been left unshaded.

When the number on the top is *less than* the number on the bottom, fractions are said to be *proper*. Thus, the fractions ⅖, ⅝, and 3/7 are proper fractions. The value of a proper fraction is always less than one.

When the number on the top is either *equal to or greater than* the number on the bottom, fractions are called *improper.* For example, the fractions $5/2$, $7/4$, and $11/5$ are improper. If the number on the top is greater than the number on the bottom, the value of the fraction is greater than one. If the number on the top and the number on the bottom are equal, such as in $8/8$, the value of the fraction is equal to one.

A *mixed number* is a whole number together with a fraction, such as $7\frac{1}{2}$ or $3\frac{5}{8}$. The mixed number $7\frac{1}{2}$ represents the number seven plus the fraction $1/2$. As we see later, every improper fraction can be written as a mixed number and vice versa.

Classify the following numbers as proper fractions, improper fractions, or mixed numbers: $8/9$, $6/6$, $5\frac{2}{3}$, $9/4$, and $112/113$.

The numbers $8/9$ and $112/113$ are proper fractions, the numbers $6/6$ and $9/4$ are improper fractions, and $5\frac{2}{3}$ is a mixed number.

# Decimals

The numbers 10, 100, 1,000, 10,000, and so on, are called the *powers of 10.* Fractions like $7/10$, $59/100$, and $323/1000$, which have powers of 10 on the bottom, are called *decimal fractions* or *decimals.*

Decimals typically are written using a shorthand notation in which the number on the top of the fraction is written to the right of a dot, called a *decimal point.* The number on the bottom of the fraction is not written but is indicated in the following way: If the number to the right of the decimal point contains one digit, the number on the bottom of the fraction is 10, if the number to the right of the decimal point contains two digits, the number on the bottom of the fraction is 100, and so on. Therefore, $7/10 = .7$, $59/100 = .59$, and $323/1000 = .323$. The decimal .7 is read "point seven" or "seven tenths." In the same way, .59 is read "point fifty-nine" or "fifty-nine hundredths."

> Write the following fractions using decimal notation: $3/10$, $157/1000$, and $7/100$.

$3/10 = .3$, $157/1000 = .157$, and $7/100 = .07$

Note that in the last example, a 0 must be placed between the decimal point and the 7 to indicate that the number on the bottom is 100.

> Write the following decimals as fractions: .7, .143, and .079.

$.7 = 7/10$, $.143 = 143/1000$ and $79/1000$

A number that consists of a whole number and a decimal is called a *mixed decimal.* The number 354.56, for example, represents the mixed number $354\frac{56}{100}$.

> Write the following mixed numbers as mixed decimals: 76.3 and 965.053.

$76.3 = 76\frac{3}{10}$ and $965.053 = 965\frac{53}{100}$

# Percents

A *percent* is a fraction whose bottom number is 100. Percents (the word percent means *per hundred*) often are written using a special symbol: %. For example, $67/100$ can be written as 67%, and $3/100$ can be written as 3%. Note that, just as every percent can be written as a fraction, every percent can also be written as a decimal. For example, $51\% = 51/100 = .51$, and $7\% = 7/100 = .07$.

A quick way to rewrite a percent as a decimal is to move the decimal point two places to the left and drop the percent sign. Thus, $35\% = .35$. In a similar way, to write a decimal as a percent, move the decimal point two places to the right and put in a percent sign. Thus, $.23 = 23\%$.

> Write the following decimals as percents: .23, .08, and 1.23.

.23 = 23%, .08 = 8%, and 1.23 = 123%

> Write the following percents as decimals: 17%, 2%, and 224%.

17% = 17, 2% = .02, and 224% = 2.24

# Arithmetic Operations

Addition, subtraction, multiplication, and division are called the *fundamental operations of arithmetic*. To solve the word problems that you probably will encounter on most nursing entrance tests, you need to be able to add, subtract, multiply, and divide whole numbers and decimals. In this section, the techniques of doing this are reviewed.

## Addition of Whole Numbers

When numbers are added, the result is called the *sum*. The first step in adding whole numbers is to line them up, placing ones under ones, tens under tens, hundreds under hundreds, and so on. Then, add each column of numbers, beginning with the ones and moving to the tens, hundreds, thousands and so on. If the sum of the digits in any column is 10 or more, write down the last figure of the sum as a part of the answer and then "carry" the other figures into the next column.

For example, suppose that you are asked to add 37, 64, and 151. Begin by lining up the numbers in columns as shown:

$$
\begin{array}{r}
37 \\
64 \\
+151 \\
\end{array}
$$

Now, add the digits in the units column: 7 + 4 + 1 = 12. Because this number is more than 10, write the 2 below the units column in the answer and carry the one over to the tens column.

$$
\begin{array}{r}
{}^{1}\phantom{0} \\
37 \\
64 \\
+151 \\
\hline
2 \\
\end{array}
$$

Now, add the 1 (that you carried over) to the other digits in the tens column: 1 + 3 + 6 + 5 = 15. Put the 5 below the tens column and carry the remaining 1 to the hundreds column:

$$
\begin{array}{r}
{}^{11}\phantom{0} \\
37 \\
64 \\
+151 \\
\hline
52 \\
\end{array}
$$

Because 1 + 1 = 2, the final answer would be 252:

$$
\begin{array}{r}
{}^{11}\phantom{0} \\
37 \\
64 \\
+151 \\
\hline
252 \\
\end{array}
$$

Add 235, 654, and 12.

$$
\begin{array}{r}
235 \\
654 \\
+\ 12 \\
\hline
901 \\
\end{array}
$$

# Addition of Decimals

Adding decimal numbers is also very straightforward. Line up the decimal points of the numbers involved and add as you normally would. Suppose, for example, that you want to add 23.31, 19, and 3.125. Begin by writing the numbers in a column, lining up the decimal points:

$$
\begin{array}{r}
23.31 \\
19. \\
+\ 3.125 \\
\end{array}
$$

Note that the number 19 is a whole number, and, as such, the decimal point is to the right of the number; that is, 19 and 19.0 mean the same thing. If it helps you when you add these numbers, you can fill in the missing spaces to the right of the decimal points with 0s:

$$
\begin{array}{r}
23.310 \\
19.000 \\
+\ 3.125 \\
\end{array}
$$

Now, position a decimal point in the answer directly below the decimal points of the numbers in the problem:

$$
\begin{array}{r}
23.310 \\
19.000 \\
+\ 3.125 \\
\hline
. \\
\end{array}
$$

Finish by adding as described previously:

$$
\begin{array}{r}
23.310 \\
19.000 \\
+\ 3.125 \\
\hline
45.435 \\
\end{array}
$$

Some problems on the test ask you to add money. Of course, to add money, just line up the decimal points, as shown previously, and add the money. For example, expenses of $32.25, $52.35, and $97.16 would lead to a total expense of

$$
\begin{array}{r}
\$23.25 \\
\$52.35 \\
+\ 97.16 \\
\hline
172.76 \\
\end{array}
$$

Add 23.56, 876.01, 34, and .007.

$$
\begin{array}{r}
23.56 \\
876.01 \\
34 \\
+\quad .007 \\
\end{array}
$$

If you like, before doing the addition, you can put in some 0s so that all the numbers have the same number of digits:

$$
\begin{array}{r}
23.560 \\
76.010 \\
34.000 \\
+\quad .007 \\
\hline
933.577 \\
\end{array}
$$

If Brian buys three items priced at $3.45, $65.21, and $143.50, how much has he spent?

To find the answer to this problem, you need to add the three amounts spent:

$$
\begin{array}{r}
\$\ \ 3.45 \\
\$\ 65.21 \\
+\$143.50 \\
\hline
\$212.16 \\
\end{array}
$$

# Subtraction of Whole Numbers

When two numbers are subtracted, the result is called the *difference*. The first step in subtracting two whole numbers is to line them up, placing ones under ones, tens under tens, hundreds under hundreds, and so on. Then, subtract each column of numbers, beginning with the ones and moving to the tens, hundreds, thousands, and so on. If, in any step, the digit on the top is smaller than the digit on the bottom, add 10 to the digit on top by borrowing 1 from the figure directly to the left. If the sum of the digits in any column is 10 or more, write down the last figure of the sum as part of the answer and then carry the other figures into the next column.

Take the following problem as an example:

$$\begin{array}{r} 567 \\ -382 \\ \hline \end{array}$$

The first step is, of course, to subtract 2 from 7. Because 7 is bigger than 2, no borrowing is necessary, so this step is easy:

$$\begin{array}{r} 567 \\ -382 \\ \hline 5 \end{array}$$

Now, you need to subtract the numbers in the tens column. Note that 6 is smaller than 8, so we need to borrow 1 from the 5 to the left of the 6. This makes the 6 into 16, and, by borrowing the 1 from the 5, it becomes 4, as shown:

$$\begin{array}{r} ^4\cancel{5}67 \\ -382 \\ \hline 5 \end{array}$$

Next, you can subtract the 8 from the 16, which leaves 8. Finally, in the hundreds column, subtracting the 3 from the 4 leaves 1:

$$\begin{array}{r} ^4\cancel{5}67 \\ -382 \\ \hline 185 \end{array}$$

Remember that if you would like to check the answer to a subtraction problem, you can add the difference (that is, the answer) to the number you are subtracting, and see whether you get the number you subtracted from. Because $185 + 382 = 567$, you know that you have the correct answer.

Subtract 534 from 893.

$$\begin{array}{r} ^8\cancel{9}3 \\ -534 \\ \hline 359 \end{array}$$

# Subtraction of Decimals

Just as with addition of decimals, begin by lining up the decimal points of the two numbers involved. Then, place a decimal point for the answer directly below the decimal points of the two numbers. For example:

$$\begin{array}{r} 265.01 \\ -127.5 \\ \hline \end{array}$$

When performing a subtraction, it certainly helps to write in extra 0s so that both numbers have the same number of digits to the right of the decimal point.

$$\begin{array}{r} 265.01 \\ -127.50 \\ \hline 137.51 \end{array}$$

Of course, to subtract monetary amounts, line up the decimal points and subtract as usual. For example:

$$\begin{array}{r} \$324.56 \\ -\$\ 34.07 \\ \hline \$290.49 \end{array}$$

Jimmy pays a $14.51 dinner charge with a $20 bill. How much change does he receive?

Simply subtract $14.51 from $20.

$$\begin{array}{r} \$20.00 \\ -\$14.51 \\ \hline \$5.49 \end{array}$$

## Multiplication of Whole Numbers

When two numbers are multiplied, the result is called the *product*. The first step in multiplying whole numbers is to line the number up, placing ones under ones, tens under tens, hundreds under hundreds, and so on. Now, consider two possible cases:

*Case 1.* If the number on the bottom of your multiplication contains a single digit, multiply every digit in the number on top by this digit. Start on the right and move to the left. If, at any time, the result of a multiplication is a number that contains more than one digit, write down the ones digit of the number and carry the tens digits over to the next column, to be added to the result of the multiplication in that column.

For example, suppose that you need to multiply 542 by 3. Write the problem down as shown:

$$\begin{array}{r} 542 \\ \times\ \ 3 \\ \hline \end{array}$$

Begin by multiplying 3 by 2 and write the result, which is 6, below the 3:

$$\begin{array}{r} 542 \\ \times\ \ 3 \\ \hline 6 \end{array}$$

Next, multiply the 3 on the bottom by the 4 on the top. The result is 12. Write the ones digit from the 12 below the 4 in the problem, and carry the tens digit, which is 1, over to the next column:

$$\begin{array}{r} {}^{1}542 \\ \times\ \ 3 \\ \hline 26 \end{array}$$

Finally, multiply the 3 by the 5. The result of 15 should be added to the 1 that was carried from the previous column:

$$
\begin{array}{r}
{}^{1}\cancel{5}42 \\
\times \quad 3 \\
\hline
1626
\end{array}
$$

*Case 2:* If the number on the bottom contains more than one digit, begin as you did previously and multiply every digit on the top by the ones digit of the number on the bottom. Write the result in the usual spot. Then move over to the tens digit of the number on the bottom and multiply each number on the top by this number. Write the result below your previous result but position the ones digit of the result below the number by which you are multiplying. Continue on to the hundreds digit, multiplying as usual, but positioning the ones digit of the result below the hundreds digit of the number on the bottom. Continue until you have multiplied the number on top by every digit on the bottom. Finish by adding together all the "partial products" you have written.

The following example illustrates the process discussed previously. To multiply 542 by 63, set up the problem as shown:

$$
\begin{array}{r}
542 \\
\times \quad 63 \\
\hline
\end{array}
$$

Begin exactly as you did in the preceding example, multiplying the 542 by 3. After doing this, you should have written:

$$
\begin{array}{r}
542 \\
\times \quad 63 \\
\hline
1626
\end{array}
$$

Now, multiply the 542 by the 6 in the tens digit of the number on the bottom. Note that the result of this multiplication is 3,252. Also note how this number is positioned:

$$
\begin{array}{r}
542 \\
\times \quad 63 \\
\hline
1626 \\
3252 \quad
\end{array}
$$

Be very careful when multiplying to line up the numbers correctly. As the last step, add the 1,626 to the 3,252, as shown:

$$
\begin{array}{r}
542 \\
\times \quad 63 \\
\hline
1626 \\
+3252 \quad \\
\hline
34,146
\end{array}
$$

Multiply 234 by 16.

$$
\begin{array}{r}
234 \\
\times \quad 16 \\
\hline
1404 \\
+234 \quad \\
\hline
3,744
\end{array}
$$

# Multiplication of Decimals

When we discussed addition and subtraction with decimals, we saw that the very first step in finding the answer is to correctly position the decimal point of the answer. When multiplying numbers with decimals, the procedure is almost exactly the opposite. Begin by ignoring the decimal points in the numbers you are multiplying and figure out the answer as if the numbers involved were whole numbers. After you have done this, you can figure out where the decimal point in the answer goes.

To figure out where the decimal point in the answer goes, you need to do a little bit of counting. Begin by counting the total number of digits to the right of the decimal points in the two numbers you were multiplying. However many digits you count when you do this should also be the number of digits to the right of the decimal point in the answer.

A few examples make this procedure very clear. You previously solved the problem

$$\begin{array}{r} 542 \\ \times\ \ 63 \\ \hline 1626 \\ 3252\phantom{0} \\ \hline 34146 \end{array}$$

Now, suppose that instead the problem had been

$$\begin{array}{r} 5.42 \\ \times\ 6.3 \end{array}$$

Note that the number on the top contains two digits to the right of the decimal point and that the number on the bottom contains one digit to the right of the decimal point. To start, multiply as you normally would, ignoring the decimal points:

| | |
|---|---|
| 5.42 | Two digits to the right of the decimal point |
| 6.3 | One digit to the right of the decimal point |
| 1626 | |
| 3252 | |
| 34146 | Decimal point needs to be positioned |

Now, because you have a total of 2 + 1 = 3 digits to the right of the decimal point in the two numbers you are multiplying, you need to have three digits to the right of the decimal point in the product:

| | |
|---|---|
| 5.42 | Two digits to the right of the decimal point |
| 6.3 | One digit to the right of the decimal point |
| 1626 | |
| 3252 | |
| 34.146 | Three digits to the right of the decimal point |

That's all there is to it! What if the problem had been instead

$$\begin{array}{r} 5.42 \\ \times\ .63 \end{array}$$

In this case, you have a total of four digits to the right of the decimal point in the two numbers you are multiplying. Thus, the answer is not 34.146, but rather 3.4146.

Note that if you are multiplying an amount of money by a whole number, you can use the preceding process. Of course, when you do this, you have a total of two digits to the right of the decimal point in the two numbers you are multiplying, so the answer ends up looking like money, that is, it has two digits to the right of the decimal point.

Multiply 23.4 by 1.6.

$$
\begin{array}{r}
23.4 \\
\times \quad 1.6 \\
\hline
1404 \\
+ 234 \quad \\
\hline
37.44
\end{array}
$$

23.4  One digit to the right of the decimal point

× 1.6  One digit to the right of the decimal point

37.44  Two digits to the right of the decimal point in the answer

John buys four calculators, each of which costs $3.51. What is the total cost of the four calculators?

$$
\begin{array}{r}
\$ \ 3.51 \\
\times \quad 4 \\
\hline
\$14.04
\end{array}
$$

$ 3.51  Two digits to the right of the decimal point

× 4  No digit to the right of the decimal point

$14.04  Two digits to the right of the decimal point in the answer

## Division of Whole Numbers

When one number is divided into another, the result is called the *quotient*. Division is probably the most complicated of the four fundamental arithmetic operations, but it becomes easier when you realize that the procedure for division consists of a series of four steps, repeated over and over. The four steps are illustrated in the following sample problems.

Suppose, for example, that you are asked to divide 7 into 245. Begin by writing the problem in the usual way:

$$7\,)\overline{245}$$

Now, for the first step, determine the number of times that 7 goes into 24. Because 7 goes into 24 three times (with something left over), begin by writing a 3 above the 4 in the division:

$$
\begin{array}{r}
3 \phantom{00} \\
7\,)\overline{245}
\end{array}
$$

As a second step, multiply the 3 by the 7 to obtain 21 and write this product below the 24:

$$
\begin{array}{r}
3 \phantom{00} \\
7\,)\overline{245} \\
21 \phantom{0}
\end{array}
$$

The third step is to subtract the 21 from the 24. When you do this, you get 3, of course. This should be written below the 21, as shown:

$$
\begin{array}{r}
3 \phantom{00} \\
7\,)\ \overline{245} \\
-21 \phantom{0} \\
\hline
3 \phantom{0}
\end{array}
$$

The final step in the four-step process is to "bring down" the next digit from the number into which you are dividing. This next (and last) digit is 5, so bring it down next to the 3:

$$
\begin{array}{r}
3 \phantom{00} \\
7\,)\ \overline{245} \\
-21 \phantom{0} \\
\hline
35
\end{array}
$$

Now, the entire procedure starts over again. Divide 7 into 35. It goes in 5 times, so put a 5 next to the 3 in the solution.

$$
\begin{array}{r}
35 \\
7\,)\ \overline{245} \\
-21 \phantom{0} \\
\hline
35
\end{array}
$$

When you multiply and subtract, note that you end up with 0. This means that you have finished, and the quotient (answer) is 35:

$$
\begin{array}{r}
35 \\
7{\overline{\smash{\big)}\,245}} \\
-21 \phantom{0} \\
\hline
35 \\
-35 \\
\hline
0
\end{array}
$$

The procedure for dividing by two digit numbers (or even larger numbers) is essentially the same but involves a bit more computation. As an example, consider the following problem:

$$
23{\overline{\smash{\big)}\,11408}}
$$

Note that 23 does not go into 11, so we have to start with 114. To determine how many times 23 goes into 114, you are going to have to estimate. Perhaps you might think that 23 is almost 25 and that it seems as if 25 would go into 114 four times. So, let's try 4. Write a 4 on top and multiply, subtract, and bring down in the usual way:

$$
\begin{array}{r}
4 \phantom{0000} \\
23{\overline{\smash{\big)}\,11408}} \\
-\phantom{0}92 \phantom{00} \\
\hline
220 \phantom{0}
\end{array}
$$

Continue, as before, by trying to estimate the number of times 23 goes into 220. If you try 9, things continue rather nicely:

$$
\begin{array}{r}
49 \phantom{000} \\
23{\overline{\smash{\big)}\,11408}} \\
-\phantom{0}92 \phantom{00} \\
\hline
220 \phantom{0} \\
-207 \phantom{0} \\
\hline
138
\end{array}
$$

As a final step, estimate that 23 goes into 138 six times:

$$
\begin{array}{r}
496 \\
23{\overline{\smash{\big)}\,11408}} \\
-\phantom{0}92 \phantom{00} \\
\hline
220 \phantom{0} \\
-207 \phantom{0} \\
\hline
138 \\
-138 \\
\hline
0
\end{array}
$$

If at any step you make the incorrect estimate, simply modify your estimate and start over. For example, suppose that in the last step of the preceding example, you had guessed that 23 would go into 138 seven times. Look what would have happened:

$$
\begin{array}{r}
497 \\
23{\overline{\smash{\big)}\,11408}} \\
-\phantom{0}92 \phantom{00} \\
\hline
220 \phantom{0} \\
-207 \phantom{0} \\
\hline
138 \\
-161
\end{array}
$$

Because 161 is larger than 138, it means that you have over estimated. Try again, with a smaller number.

Divide 12 into 540.

$$
\begin{array}{r}
45 \\
12{\overline{\smash{\big)}\,540}} \\
-\underline{48} \\
60 \\
\underline{60} \\
0
\end{array}
$$

Remember that division problems can always be checked by multiplying. In this case, because $12 \times 45 = 540$, you know you have the right answer.

## Division with Decimals

Recall that when you added and subtracted with decimals, you began by positioning the decimal point for the answer and then added or subtracted as usual. When you are dividing a whole number into a decimal number, the idea is similar; begin by putting a decimal point for the quotient (answer) directly above the decimal point in the number into which you are dividing. Then divide as normal. So, for example, if you need to divide 4 into 142.4, begin as shown:

$$
4{\overline{\smash{\big)}\,142.4}}
$$

Note the decimal point positioned above the decimal point in 142

Now, divide in the usual way:

$$
\begin{array}{r}
35.6 \\
4{\overline{\smash{\big)}\,142.4}} \\
-\underline{12} \\
22 \\
-\underline{20} \\
24 \\
-\underline{24} \\
0
\end{array}
$$

That's all that there is to it.

A dinner bill of $92.80 is shared equally between four friends. How much does each friend pay?

To find the answer, you need to divide $92.80 by 4.

$$
\begin{array}{r}
23.20 \\
4{\overline{\smash{\big)}\,92.80}} \\
-\underline{8} \\
12 \\
-\underline{12} \\
08 \\
\underline{8} \\
00 \\
-\underline{0} \\
0
\end{array}
$$

# Arithmetic Word Problems

The arithmetic sections of most nursing entrance exams might present word problems that involve arithmetic calculations. If you have learned how to do the computations discussed previously, the hardest part of these word problems is to determine which of the arithmetic operations is needed to solve the problem.

## Basic One-Step and Two-Step Problems

Some of the word problems on the test involve only a single computation. Others are multiple-step problems in which several computations need to be performed. Examples of both types of problems are shown. Following these examples are some special types of problems that also appear on the test.

Brett earned $235.25 during his first week on a new job. During the second week, he earned $325.50, during the third week he earned $275.00, and during the fourth week he earned $285.75. How much did he earn over the course of the four weeks?

It should be obvious that, in this problem, all you need to do is add the weekly payments to find the total.

$$
\begin{array}{r}
\$\ \ 225.25 \\
\$\ \ 325.50 \\
\$\ \ 275.00 \\
+\$\ \ 285.75 \\
\hline
\$1,111.50
\end{array}
$$

An office building is 540 feet high, including a 23 foot antenna tower on the roof. How tall is the building without the antenna tower?

It should be clear that, in this problem, we need to remove the 23 foot tower from the top of the building by subtracting. This is a one-step problem:

$$
\begin{array}{r}
540 \\
-\ \ 23 \\
\hline
517\ \text{feet}
\end{array}
$$

The building is 517 feet tall without the antenna tower.

Brett has a job that pays him $8.25 an hour. If during the first week he works 21 hours, and during the second week he works 19 hours, how much money has he earned over the course of the two weeks?

This is an example of a two-step problem. One way to find the answer is to find how much he made each week by multiplying and then to add the two weekly totals:

| Week 1 | Week 2 |
|---|---|
| $\ \ 8.25 | $8.25 |
| $\times$ ___21 | $\times$ ___19 |
| $173.25 | $156.75 |

Because $173.25 + $156.75 = $330, Brett earned $330.

Perhaps you have noticed an easier way to solve the problem. If you begin by adding the number of hours he worked each week, you get $19 + 21 = 40$ as a total. Then, you only need to multiply $8.25 by 40 to get the answer.

At a restaurant, the bill for dinner is $137.50. Bill contributes $20 to the bill and then leaves. The rest of the bill is split evenly between the remaining five people. How much does each person contribute?

This is another two-step word problem. After Bill leaves, $137.50 − $20 = $117.50 remains to be paid. This has to be divided by the five people that remain.

$$
\begin{array}{r}
23.50 \\
5\overline{\smash{)}117.50} \\
-\underline{10}\phantom{0} \\
17\phantom{0} \\
-\underline{15}\phantom{0} \\
25 \\
-\underline{25} \\
00 \\
-\underline{0} \\
0
\end{array}
$$

Clearly, each person needs to pay $23.50.

## Percent and Interest Problems

These tests also contain some problems that involve working with percents and interest. Typically, these problems involve finding percents of numbers. You need to remember two things: First, the way to find a percent of a number is by multiplying, and second, before multiplying you should write the percent as a decimal.

Several examples of this type of problem follow.

A family spends 26% of its monthly income on their mortgage. If their monthly income is $2,400, how much do they spend on their mortgage each month?

This problem asks us to find 26% of $2,400. To do this, write 26% as .26 and then multiply.

$$
\begin{array}{r}
\$2,400 \\
\times \quad .26 \quad \text{Two digits to the right of the decimal} \\
\hline
14400 \\
+4800 \\
\hline
624.00 \quad \text{Two digits to the right of the decimal point in the answer}
\end{array}
$$

Thus, the monthly expenditure for the mortgage is $624.00.

Bob invests $5,500 in an account that pays 9% annual interest. How much interest does he earn in one year?

This is another one-step percent word problem. For this problem, we need to find 9% of $5,500. Begin by writing 9% as a decimal, which is .09. (Note that 9% is equal to .09, not .9.) Then multiply to finish the problem:

$$
\begin{array}{r}
\$5,500 \\
\times \quad .09 \quad \text{Two digits to the right of the decimal point} \\
\hline
495.00 \quad \text{Two digits to the right of the decimal point in the answer}
\end{array}
$$

He earns $495 in interest in one year.

Bob invests $5,500 in an account that pays 9% annual interest. How much money is in the account at the end of one year?

Note that this problem is based on the preceding one but includes an extra step. After determining how much interest is in the account at the end of the year, this amount needs to be added to the $5,500 to obtain $5,500 + $495 = $5,995.

# Ratio and Proportion Problems

Another type of word problem that might appear on these tests involves ratios and proportions.

A ratio is a comparison of two numbers. For example, a school might say that its student-teacher ratio is eight to one. This means that, for every eight students at the school, there is one teacher. Another way to look at this ratio is that, for every one teacher, there are eight students.

You might have seen a ratio written with a colon between the two numbers, like 8:1. A ratio can also be written as a fraction, like $\frac{8}{1}$. When it comes to solving word problems involving ratios, it is usually best to write the ratios as fractions so that you can perform computations with them.

In the preceding ratio, we were comparing a number of people (students) to a number of people (teachers). When a ratio is used to compare two different kinds of quantities, it is called a *rate*. As an example, suppose that a car drives 300 miles in 5 hours. Then we can write the rate of the car as $\frac{300 \text{ miles}}{5 \text{ hour}}$. If we divide the number on the bottom into the number on the top, we get the number 60 and then can say that the rate of the car is $\frac{60 \text{ miles}}{1 \text{ hour}}$ or simply 60 *miles per hour*. Sixty miles per hour is also known as the speed of the car.

When you divide the number on the bottom of a ratio or a rate into the number on the top, the result is what is known as a *unit ratio* or a *unit rate*. Often, solving ratio problems hinges on computing a unit ratio or rate. The techniques of working with ratios and rates are illustrated in the following problems.

A supermarket customer bought a 15 ounce box of oatmeal for $3.45. What was the cost per ounce of oatmeal?

The rate of cost to ounces is given in the problem as $\frac{\$3.45}{15 \text{ ounces}}$. To find the *unit cost,* you divide $3.45 by 15 ounces.

$$
\begin{array}{r}
.23 \\
15 \overline{)\ 3.45} \\
-30 \phantom{0} \\
\hline
45 \\
-45 \\
\hline
0
\end{array}
$$

Therefore, the cost is 23 cents per ounce.

A supermarket sells a 15 ounce box of oatmeal for $3.45. At the same rate, what would be the cost of a 26 ounce box of oatmeal?

This type of problem is what is known as a proportion problem. In a proportion problem, you are given the rate at which two quantities vary and asked to find the value of one of the quantities given the value of the other. A good way to approach a problem of this type is by first finding the unit rate and then multiplying. Note that in the preceding problem you found the unit rate of the oatmeal; it was 23 cents per ounce. The cost of 26 ounces, then, is 23 cents times 26:

$$
\begin{array}{r}
.23 \\
\times\ \ 26 \\
\hline
138 \\
+46 \phantom{0} \\
\hline
598
\end{array}
$$

Thus, 26 ounces costs $5.98.

A bus travels at a constant rate of 45 miles per hour. How far can the bus go in 5½ hours?

Previously, we saw that the rate of a vehicle is equal to its distance divided by its time. In the same way, the distance that the vehicle travels is equal to its rate multiplied by its time. You might remember from previous math classes that this formula is written $d = r \times t$, meaning distance = rate × time.

It is easier to solve this problem if you write 5 ½ as its decimal equivalent 5.5. Then, you simply need to multiply 45 by 5.5 to find the distance:

$$\begin{array}{r} 45 \\ \times\ 5.5 \\ \hline 225 \\ +225\phantom{.0} \\ \hline 247.5 \end{array}$$

Thus, the car goes 247.5 miles in 5½ hours.

## Measurement Problems

Some of the problems on the exams involve working with measurements and geometric shapes. Two concepts that you should be familiar with are *perimeter* and *area*.

The perimeter of a figure is the distance around it, that is, the sum of the lengths of its sides. Perimeter is measured is units of length, such as inches, feet, or meters. The area of a figure is the amount of surface contained within its boundaries. Area is measured in square units, such as square inches, square feet, or square meters.

Two important geometric figures that you should know how to find the perimeter and area of are the rectangle and the square.

A rectangle is a figure with four sides. The opposite sides are the same length. For example, the following figure depicts a rectangle with a measurement of four inches by three inches:

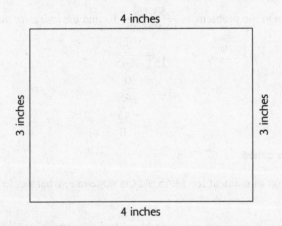

The perimeter of a rectangle is given by the formula $P = 2l + 2w$, which means that, to find the perimeter of a rectangle, you need to add together two lengths and two widths. If the rectangle is four inches by three inches, then its perimeter is $P = 3 + 3 + 4 + 4 = 14$ inches.

The area of a rectangle is given by the formula $A = l \times w$, which means that the area is the length times the width. In this case, the area would be 3 inches $\times$ 4 inches = 12 square inches. By the way, a square inch is simply a square that is an inch long on all 4 sides. If you look again at the preceding picture of the rectangle, you can see that it can be thought of as consisting of 12 squares that are each an inch on all sides. That is what is meant when we say that the area is 12 square inches.

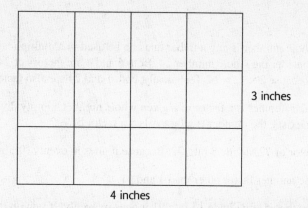

3 inches

4 inches

A square is a rectangle with 4 equal sides. In the case of a square, the formulas for the perimeter and the area of a rectangle take a simpler form. The perimeter of a square is $P = 4s$, where s is the length of the side, and the area is $A = s \times s$. For example, in a square with 4 sides of 5 feet, the perimeter is 20 feet because $4 \times 5$ feet = 20 feet. The area is 5 feet $\times$ 5 feet = 25 square feet.

It also helps to know some common measurement conversions, such as 12 inches are in a foot and 3 feet (or 36 inches) are in a yard.

The following examples are based on the concepts discussed previously.

A small bag of fertilizer covers 20 square feet of lawn. How many bags are needed to cover a lawn that is 4 yards by 3 yards?

The most direct way to handle this problem is to change the measurements of the lawn to feet because that is how the capacity of the bag of fertilizer is measured. A lawn that is 4 yards by 3 yards is 12 feet by 9 feet. Thus, its area is 12 feet $\times$ 9 feet = 108 square feet. Now, to determine the number of bags needed, we need to divide 20 into 108. When we do this division, we get the answer 5.4 bags. Because you obviously cannot purchase 5.4 bags, you would need 6 bags to cover the lawn.

A lot of land measures 50 meters by 40 meters. A house 24 meters by 18 meters is built on the land. How much area is left over?

Begin by finding the area of the lot and the house:

| Lot | *House* |
|:---:|:---:|
| 50 | 24 |
| $\times$ 40 | $\times$ 18 |
| 2000 | 432 |

Thus, the area of the lot is 2,000 square meters, and the area of the house is 432 square meters. To determine how much area is left, we need to subtract 432 square meters from 2,000 square meters:

$2{,}000 - 432 = 1{,}568$ square meters is left over.

# Number Theory

Remember that earlier we defined *whole numbers* as the set of numbers 0, 1, 2, 3, 4, 5 and so on. We are now going to look at some of the properties of whole numbers and then of the set of numbers called the *integers*.

# Factors

To begin, a *factor* of a given whole number is any number that can be used in a multiplication that results in the given whole number. For example, consider the whole number 24. Both 6 and 4 are factors of 24 because $6 \times 4 = 24$. Further, both 2 and 12 are factors of 24 because $2 \times 12 = 24$. Technically, both 1 and 24 are also factors of 24 because $1 \times 24 = 24$.

To determine whether a particular number is a factor of a given whole number, simply divide the number into the given whole number. If no remainder exists, the number is a factor. Is 8 a factor of 72?

To determine whether 8 is a factor of 72, divide 8 into 72. Because it goes in evenly (9 times), 8 is a factor of 72.

If 13 is a factor of 91, determine another factor other than 1 and 91.

If 13 is a factor of 91, you know that if you divide 13 into 91 it goes in evenly. If you do this division, you get:

$$13\overline{)91}^{\,7}$$

Thus, $13 \times 7 = 91$, so 7 is another factor of 91.

# Common Factors

A number that is a factor of two different whole numbers is called a *common factor,* or a *common divisor,* of those numbers. As the following examples show, two given whole numbers might have no common factors (other than, of course, 1), or they might have one or more. If two numbers have several common factors, the largest one is called the *greatest common factor.*

Find all the common factors and the greatest common factor of 36 and 48.

> The factors of 36 are 1, 2, 3, 4, 6, 9, 12, 18, and 36.
>
> The factors of 48 are 1, 2, 3, 4, 6, 8, 12, 16, 32, and 48.
>
> The common factors of 36 and 48 are 1, 2, 3, 4, 6, and 12.
>
> The greatest common factor is 12.

Find all the common factors of 35 and 66.

> The factors of 35 are 1, 5, 7, and 35.
>
> The factors of 66 are 1, 2, 3, 6, 11, 22, 33, and 66.
>
> The only common factor is 1.

# Prime Numbers

Obviously, every number has at least two factors: the number itself and 1. Some other numbers have additional factors as well. For example, the number 14 not only has 1 and 14 as factors, but also 2 and 7 because $2 \times 7 = 14$.

Numbers that have no additional factors other than themselves and 1 are known as *prime numbers.* An example of a prime number is 13. While 1 and 13 divide evenly into 13, no other whole numbers divide evenly into 13.

By definition, the smallest prime number is 2. The first 10 prime numbers are

> 2, 3, 5, 7, 11, 13, 17, 19, 23, 29

To determine whether a number is prime or not, you need to find out whether any whole numbers (other than the number itself and 1) divide evenly into the number.

Which of the following numbers are prime: 33, 37, 39, 42, and 43?

33 is not prime because $33 = 3 \times 11$.

37 is prime; it has no factors other than 1 and 37.

39 is not prime because $39 = 3 \times 13$.

42 is not prime because $42 = 2 \times 21$ or $6 \times 7$, and so on.

43 is prime; it has no factors other than 1 and 43.

A number that is not prime, is called a *composite* number. Any composite number can be *prime factored;* that is, it can be written as a product of prime numbers (excluding 1) in one and only one way. For example, 35 is a composite number and can be prime factored as $5 \times 7$. The number 12 is also composite. Note that $2 \times 6$ is a factorization of 12 but is not the prime factorization because 6 is not prime. The prime factorization of 12 would be $2 \times 2 \times 3$. The quickest way to prime factor a number is to break the number up as a product of two smaller numbers and then to break these two numbers up, until you are left with only prime numbers. The following example illustrates this process.

Prime factor the number 150.

By inspection, you can see that 150 can be factored as $15 \times 10$. This is not the prime factorization, however, as neither 15 nor 10 is prime. The number 15, however, can be further broken down as $15 = 3 \times 5$, and both 3 and 5 are prime. The number 10 can be further broken down as $10 = 2 \times 5$, and both 2 and 5 are prime. Therefore, the number 150 can be prime factored as $3 \times 5 \times 2 \times 5$. When prime factoring numbers, it is standard to rearrange the factors so that the numbers are in increasing order. Therefore, the prime factorization of 150 can best be expressed as $2 \times 3 \times 5 \times 5$.

What are the prime factors of 54?

You can begin by writing 54 as $2 \times 27$. The number 2 is prime, but 27 is not, so it can be further factored. Because 27 is $3 \times 9$, you get $54 = 2 \times 3 \times 9$. Now, 3 is prime, but 9 is not, so you need to factor the 9. The only way to do this is $9 = 3 \times 3$, so the prime factorization of 54 is $2 \times 3 \times 3 \times 3$. Thus, the prime factors of 54 are 2 and 3.

## Multiples

A multiple of a given whole number is a number that results from the multiplication of the given whole number by another whole number factor. For example, the multiples of 7 are 7, 14, 21, 28, 35, 42, 49, and so on because $7 = 7 \times 1$, $14 = 7 \times 2$, $21 = 7 \times 3$, and so on.

A *common multiple* of two numbers is a number that is a multiple of both of the numbers. For example, 32 is a common multiple of 8 and 16 because it is a multiple of both 8 and 16. Should you ever need to find a common multiple of two numbers, one quick way to find one is to multiply the two numbers together. For example, a common multiple of 4 and 10 would be $4 \times 10 = 40$. Note, however, that 40 is not the smallest common multiple of 4 and 10 because 20 is also a common multiple.

The smallest common multiple of two numbers is called the *least common multiple,* abbreviated LCM. A quick way to find the LCM of two numbers is to write out the first several multiples of each number and then find the smallest multiple that they have in common. The following examples show how to do this.

Find the first 8 multiples of 11.

To answer this question, you need to compute $11 \times 1$, $11 \times 2$, $11 \times 3$, and so on. The first 8 multiples would be 11, 22, 33, 44, 55, 66, 77, and 88.

Find the least common multiple of 3 and 8.

The first several multiples of 3 are 3, 6, 9, 12, 15, 18, 21, 24, and 27.

The first several multiples of 8 are 8, 16, 24, and 32.

Clearly, the LCM is 24, which in this case is the same as the product of 3 and 8.

Find the LCM of 6 and 9.

The first several multiples of 6 are 6, 12, 18, 24, and 30.

The first several multiples of 9 are 9, 18, 27, and 36.

Clearly, the LCM is 18, which in this case is less than $6 \times 9 = 54$.

# Exponents

As you saw previously, the numbers used in multiplication are called factors. Whenever the same factor is repeated more than once, a special shorthand, called *exponential notation,* can be used to simplify the expression. In this notation, the repeated factor is written only once; above and to the right of this number is written another number that is called the *exponent,* or *power,* indicating the number of times the base is repeated.

For example, instead of writing $7 \times 7$, you can write $7^2$. This expression is read "seven to the second power," or more simply, "seven squared," and it represents the fact that the seven is multiplied by itself two times. In the same way, $5 \times 5 \times 5 \times 5$ can be written as $5^4$, which is read "five to the fourth power," or simply "five to the fourth."

Recall that previously, you prime factored the number 150 and obtained $2 \times 3 \times 5 \times 5$. It is more common (and a bit simpler) to write this prime factorization using exponential notation as $2 \times 3 \times 5^2$.

What is the value of $3^5$?

Based on the preceding definition, $3^5$ represents $3 \times 3 \times 3 \times 3 \times 3 = 243$.

Simplify the expression $a \times a \times a \times a \times b \times b \times b \times b \times b \times b \times b$ by using exponential notation.

Because we have four factors of $a$ and seven factors of $b$, the expression is equal to $a^4 \times b^7$.

Prime factor the number 72 and write the prime factorization using exponential notation.

Begin by prime factoring the number 72. One way to do this is as follows:

$72 = 2 \times 36 = 2 \times 6 \times 6 = 2 \times 2 \times 3 \times 2 \times 3 = 2 \times 2 \times 2 \times 3 \times 3$. Then, writing this using exponents, you get $2^3 \times 3^2$.

# Square Roots

The *square root* of a given number is the number whose square is equal to the given number. For example, the square root of 25 is the number that yields 25 when multiplied by itself. Clearly, this number would be 5 because $5 \times 5 = 25$. The square root of 25 is denoted by the symbol $\sqrt{25}$.

The square roots of most numbers turn out to be messy, infinite nonrepeating decimal numbers. For example, $\sqrt{2}$ is equal to 1.414213562…. When such numbers appear on the test, you are able to leave them in what is known as *radical form;* that is, if the answer to a problem is $\sqrt{2}$, you can express the answer as $\sqrt{2}$, without worrying about its value.

Certain numbers, however, have nice whole-number square roots. Such numbers are called *perfect squares.* You should certainly be familiar with the square roots of the first 10 or so perfect squares. They are shown in the following table:

| Perfect Square | Square Root |
| --- | --- |
| 1 | $\sqrt{1} = 1$ |
| 4 | $\sqrt{4} = 2$ |
| 9 | $\sqrt{9} = 3$ |
| 16 | $\sqrt{16} = 4$ |
| 25 | $\sqrt{25} = 5$ |

| Perfect Square | Square Root |
|---|---|
| 36 | $\sqrt{36} = 6$ |
| 49 | $\sqrt{49} = 7$ |
| 64 | $\sqrt{64} = 8$ |
| 81 | $\sqrt{81} = 9$ |
| 100 | $\sqrt{100} = 10$ |

From time to time, you might be asked to find the *cube root* of a number. The cube root is defined in a way similar to that of the square root. For example, the cube root of eight is the number that when multiplied by itself twice is equal to eight. Clearly, the cube root of eight would be two because $2 \times 2 \times 2 = 8$. A special notation also exists for the cube root. The cube root of eight is written as $\sqrt[3]{8}$. Therefore, $\sqrt[3]{8} = 2$.

Just as perfect squares have nice whole-number square roots, *perfect cubes* have whole-number cube roots. You don't really have to learn many of these, as they become large very quickly, but it is helpful to know the cube roots of the first five perfect cubes. The following table gives the values for these numbers.

| Perfect Cube | Cube Root |
|---|---|
| 1 | $\sqrt[3]{1} = 1$ |
| 8 | $\sqrt[3]{8} = 2$ |
| 27 | $\sqrt[3]{27} = 9$ |
| 64 | $\sqrt[3]{64} = 4$ |
| 125 | $\sqrt[3]{125} = 5$ |

What is the value of $\sqrt{81} \times \sqrt{36}$?

Because $\sqrt{81} = 9$ and $\sqrt{36} = 6$, $\sqrt{81} \times \sqrt{36} = 9 \times 6 = 54$

What is the value of $12\sqrt{49}$?

To begin, you must know that $12\sqrt{49}$ is shorthand for $12 \times \sqrt{49}$. Because $\sqrt{49} = 7$, $12\sqrt{49} = 12 \times 7 = 84$.

# The Order of Operations

Whenever a numerical expression contains more than one mathematical operation, the order in which the operations are performed can affect the answer. For example, consider the simple expression $2 + 3 \times 5$. On one hand, if the addition is performed first, the expression becomes $5 \times 5 = 25$. On the other hand, if the multiplication is performed first, the expression becomes $2 + 15 = 17$. To eliminate this ambiguity, mathematicians have established a procedure that makes the order in which the operations need to be performed specific. This procedure is called the *Order of Operations*, and is stated here:

1. Perform all operations in parentheses or any other grouping symbol.
2. Evaluate all exponents and roots.
3. Perform all multiplications and divisions in the order they appear in the expression, from left to right.
4. Perform all additions and subtractions in the order they appear in the expression, from left to right.

Note that the Order of Operations consists of four steps. A common acronym to help you remember these steps is PEMDAS: parentheses, exponents, multiplication and division, addition and subtraction. If you choose to memorize this acronym, be careful. The expression PEMDAS might make it appear as if the Order of Operations has six steps, but it actually has only four. In the third step, all multiplications and divisions are done in the order they appear. In the fourth step, all additions and subtractions are done in the order they appear. The following examples make this clear.

> Evaluate the expression $18 - 6 \div 3 \times 7 + 4$.

Resist the temptation to begin by subtracting 6 from 18. Because this expression contains no parentheses and no roots, begin by starting on the left and performing all multiplications and divisions in the order they occur. This means that the division must be performed first. Because $6 \div 3 = 2$, you obtain:

$18 - 6 \div 3 \times 7 + 4 = 18 - 2 \times 7 + 4$

Next, do the multiplication:

$18 - 2 \times 7 + 4 = 18 - 14 + 4$

Finally, subtract and then add:

$18 - 14 + 4 = 4 - 4 = 0$

> Evaluate $14 - 2(1 + 5)$.

To begin, the operation in parentheses must be performed. This makes the expression $14 - 2(6)$. Now, remember that a number written next to another number in parentheses, such as 2(6), is a way of indicating multiplication. Because multiplication comes before subtraction in the Order of Operations, multiply 2(6) to get 12. Finally, $14 - 12 = 2$.

> Evaluate $5^3 - 3(8 - 2)^2$.

The first operation to perform is the one in parentheses, which yields $5^3 - 3(6)^2$.

Next, evaluate the two exponents: $125 - 3(36)$. Now multiply and then finish by subtracting: $125 - 108 = 17$.

## Operations with Integers

When you include the negatives of the whole numbers along with the whole numbers, you obtain the set of numbers called the *integers*. Therefore, the integers are the set of numbers:

$$\ldots -4, -3, -2, -1, 0, 1, 2, 3, 4, \ldots$$

The ellipses to the left and right indicate that the numbers continue forever in both directions.

Up to this point, when we have talked about adding, subtracting, multiplying, and dividing, we have always been working with positive numbers. However, on one of these tests, you are just as likely to have to compute with negative numbers as positive numbers. Therefore, take a look at how mathematical operations are performed on positive *and* negative numbers; that is, how mathematical operations are performed on *signed* numbers.

## Adding Positive and Negative Numbers

Two different circumstances must be considered as you add positive and negative numbers. The first circumstance is how to add two signed numbers with the same sign. If the numbers that you are adding have the same sign, add the numbers in the usual way. The sum, then, has the same sign as the numbers you have added. For example, $(+4) + (+7) = +11$. This, of course, is the usual positive number addition you are used to.

Consider $(-5) + (-9) = -14$.

In this problem, because the signs of the two numbers you are adding are the same, simply add them $(5 + 9 = 14)$. The result is negative because both numbers are negative. It might help to think of positive numbers as representing a gain and negative numbers as representing a loss. In this case, $(-5) + (-9)$ represents a loss of 5 followed by a loss 9, which, of course, is a loss of 14.

Now, what if you have to add two numbers with different signs? Again, the rule is simple. Begin by ignoring the signs and subtract the two numbers—the smaller from the larger. The sign of the answer is the same as the sign of the number with the larger size.

For example, to compute $(+9) + (-5)$, begin by computing $9 - 5 = 4$. Because 9 is bigger than 5, the answer is positive, or $+4$. You can think of the problem in this way: A gain of 9 followed by a loss of 5 is equivalent to a gain of 4.

On the other hand, to compute $(-9) + (+5)$, begin in the same way by computing $9 - 5 = 4$. This time, however, the larger number is negative, so the answer is $-4$. In other words, a loss of 9 followed by a gain of 5 is equivalent to a loss of 4.

Consider $(+6) + (-8) + (+12) + (-4)$.

Two ways can be used to evaluate this expression. One way is to simply perform the additions in order from left to right. To begin, $(+6) + (-8) = -2$. Then, $(-2) + (+12) = +10$. Finally, $(+10) + (-4) = +6$.

The other way to solve the problem, which might be a bit faster, is to add the positive numbers, add the negative numbers, and then combine the result. In this case, $(+6) + (+12) = +18$; $(-8) + (-4) = -12$, and finally, $(+18) + (-12) = +6$.

## Subtracting Positive and Negative Numbers

The easiest way to perform a subtraction on two signed numbers is to change the problem to an equivalent addition problem, that is, an addition problem with the same answer. To do this, you need to change the sign of the second number and add instead of subtract. For example, suppose that you need to compute $(+7) - (-2)$. This problem has the same solution as the addition problem $(+7) + (+2)$ and is, therefore, equal to $+9$. Take a look at the following samples that help clarify this procedure:

Determine the value of $(-7) - (+2)$.

To evaluate this, make it into an equivalent addition problem by changing the sign of the second number. Therefore, $(-7) - (+2) = (-7) + (-2) = -9$.

In the same way, you can see that $(-7) - (-2) = (-7) + (+2) = -5$.

Find the value of $(-7) - (+4) - (-3) + (-1)$.

Begin by rewriting the problem with all subtractions expressed as additions:

$(-7) - (+4) - (-3) + (-1) = (-7) + (-4) + (+3) + (-1)$

Now, just add the four numbers in the usual way:

$(-7) + (-4) + (+3) + (-1) = (-11) + (+3) + (-1) = -8 + (-1) = -9$.

## Multiplying and Dividing Positive and Negative Numbers

An easy way to multiply (or divide) signed numbers is to begin by ignoring the signs and multiply (or divide) in the usual way. Then, to determine the sign of the answer, count up the number of negative signs in the original problem. If the number of negative signs is even, the answer is positive; if the number of negative signs is odd, the answer is negative. For example, $(-2) \times (+3) = -6$ because the original problem has one negative sign. However, $(-2) \times (-3) = +6$ because the original problem has two negative signs.

What about the problem $(-4) \times (-2) \times (-1) \times (+3)$? First of all, ignoring the signs and multiplying the four numbers, you get 24. Because the problem has a total of three negative signs, the answer must be negative. Therefore, the answer is $-24$.

Division works in exactly the same way. For example, $(-24) \div (+6) = -4$, but $(-24) \div (-6) = +4$.

Find the value of $\dfrac{(-6)(+10)}{(-2)(-5)}$.

The easiest way to proceed with this problem is to evaluate the number on the top and the number on the bottom separately and then divide them. Because $(-6)(+10) = -60$ and $(-2)(-5) = +10$, you have $\dfrac{(-6)(+10)}{(-2)(-5)} = \dfrac{-60}{+10} = -6$.

$(-5)(-2)(+4) - 6(-3) =$

The multiplications in this problem must be done before the subtractions. Because

$(-5)(-2)(+4) = 40$, and $6(-3) = -18$, you have

$$(-5)(-2)(+4) - 6(-3) = 40 - (-18) = 40 + 18 = 58.$$

## Negative Numbers and Exponents

Be a little bit careful when evaluating negative numbers raised to powers. For example, if you are asked to find the value of $(-2)^8$, the answer is positive because you are technically multiplying eight $-2$s. For a similar reason, the value of $(-2)^9$ is negative.

Also, you must be careful to distinguish between an expression like $(-3)^2$ and one like $-3^2$. The expression $(-3)^2$ means $-3 \times -3$ and is equal to $+9$, but $-3^2$ means $-(3^2)$, which is equal to $-9$.

Evaluate $-2^4 - (-2)^2$.

Evaluating the exponents first, you get $-2^4 - (-2)^2 = -16 - (4) = -16 + -4 = -20$.

Find the value of $\dfrac{(-3)^3 + (-2)(-6)}{-5^2 + (-19)(-1)}$.

Again, determine the values of the top and bottom separately and then divide. To begin, $(-3)^3 = -27$, and $(-2)(-6) = +12$, so the value on the top is $-27 + 12 = -15$. On the bottom, you have $-25 + 19 = -6$. Therefore,

$$\frac{(-3)^3 + (-2)(-6)}{-5^2 + (-19)(-1)} = \frac{-15}{-6} = \frac{15}{6} = 2.5$$

## Operations with Fractions

In the "Arithmetic Reasoning" section, we discussed how to write a fraction as a decimal and vice versa. One thing that we did not discuss in that section was how to perform arithmetic operations on fractions. It is now time to review how to do this.

You probably remember learning a procedure called *reducing* or *simplifying* fractions. Simplifying a fraction refers to rewriting it in an equivalent form, with smaller numbers. As an easy example, consider the fraction $\frac{5}{10}$. This fraction can be simplified by dividing the top and bottom by the number 5. If you do this division, you get $\frac{5}{10} = \frac{5 \div 5}{10 \div 5} = \frac{1}{2}$. Thus, $\frac{5}{10}$ and $\frac{1}{2}$ have the same value, but $\frac{1}{2}$ is in simpler form.

In general, to simplify a fraction, you need to find a number that divides evenly into both the top and bottom, and then do this division. Sometimes, after you divide by one number, you might notice another number you can further divide by. As an example, suppose that you want to simplify $\frac{12}{18}$. The first thing that you might notice is that the top and bottom can be divided by 2. If you do this division, you get the fraction $\frac{6}{9}$. Now, this fraction can be further divided by 3, and if you do this division, you get the fraction $\frac{2}{3}$. Because no other numbers (except 1, of course) can divide evenly into the top and bottom, you have reduced the fraction to its *lowest terms*. If a problem on one of the tests has a fractional answer, you should always reduce the answer to its lowest terms.

Just as you can reduce a fraction to lower terms by dividing the top and bottom by the same number, you can raise a fraction to *higher terms* by multiplying the top and bottom by the same number. For example, consider the fraction $\frac{3}{4}$. If you multiply the top and bottom by 2, you get $\frac{6}{8}$. If instead, you multiply the top and bottom by 5, you get $\frac{15}{20}$. The fractions $\frac{6}{8}$ and $\frac{15}{20}$ are two different ways to write $\frac{3}{4}$ in higher terms. As you see in the next section, it is often necessary to raise fractions to higher terms to add and subtract them.

Express the fraction $\frac{12}{15}$ in lowest terms.

It is easy to see that the number 3 can be divided evenly into both the numerator and the denominator. Performing this division, you get $\frac{12}{15} = \frac{12 \div 3}{15 \div 3} = \frac{4}{5}$, which is in lowest terms.

Rewrite the fraction $\frac{2}{3}$ as an equivalent fraction with a denominator of 21.

To change the denominator of 3 to 21, you need to multiply by 7. Because you need to perform the same operation to the numerator as well, you would get $\frac{2}{3} = \frac{2 \times 7}{3 \times 7} = \frac{14}{21}$.

## Adding and Subtracting Fractions

You probably recall that the number on the top of a fraction is called the *numerator* and the number on the bottom of a fraction is called the *denominator*. If two fractions have the same denominator, they are said to have *common denominators*.

Adding or subtracting two fractions with common denominators is easy. Simply add the numerators and retain the common denominator. For example,

$$\frac{2}{9} + \frac{5}{9} = \frac{7}{9} \quad \text{and} \quad \frac{7}{8} - \frac{5}{8} = \frac{2}{8} = \frac{1}{4}$$

Note that, in the subtraction problem, you get a fraction that can be simplified, and you perform the simplification before finishing.

If you need to add or subtract two fractions that do not have the same denominator, you need to begin by raising them to higher terms so that they do have a common denominator. The first step in this process is determining a common denominator for the two fractions. For example, suppose that you are asked to add $\frac{3}{4} + \frac{1}{3}$. You need to find a common denominator for 4 and 3. Actually, an infinite number of common denominators exist for 4 and 3. Some of them would be 24, 36, and 48. Although you can work with any of these denominators, it is easiest to work with the smallest one, which in this case is 12. This number is called the *least common denominator* of 4 and 3, and it is actually the same number as the least common multiple (LCM), which has already been discussed. Thus, the least common denominator can be found by using the same process you used to find the LCM previously.

When you know the least common denominator (LCD), you simply need to multiply the top and bottom of each fraction by the appropriate number to raise the denominators to the LCD. For example,

$$\frac{3}{4} + \frac{1}{3} = \frac{3}{3} \times \frac{3}{4} + \frac{4}{4} \times \frac{1}{3} = \frac{9}{12} + \frac{4}{12} = \frac{13}{12}$$

Note that the answer, $\frac{13}{12}$, is an improper fraction. Any improper fraction can also be written as a mixed number by dividing the denominator into the numerator and writing the remainder as the numerator of a fraction with the original denominator. In this case, 12 goes into 13 one time with a remainder of one, so $\frac{13}{12} = 1\frac{1}{12}$, which is another way to write the answer to the question.

Note that this process can also be reversed. So, for example, the mixed number $2\frac{1}{5}$ can be written as an improper fraction. The denominator is the same, that is, 5, and the numerator is the denominator times the whole number plus the numerator; that is, $5 \times 2 + 1 = 11$. Therefore, $2\frac{1}{5} = \frac{11}{5}$. Often, when performing operations on mixed numbers, it is helpful to write them as improper fractions. The upcoming examples illustrate this.

Add $2\frac{3}{5} + 3\frac{1}{7}$.

You can proceed in two ways. You can write both mixed numbers as improper fractions and add, but it is quicker to just add the whole number part ($2 + 3 = 5$) and the fractional part: $\frac{3}{5} + \frac{1}{7} = \frac{21}{35} + \frac{5}{35} = \frac{26}{35}$. The answer, then, is $5\frac{26}{35}$.

Find the value of $\frac{3}{7} - \frac{1}{2}$.

The LCD is 14. Thus, $\frac{3}{7} - \frac{1}{2} = \frac{6}{14} - \frac{7}{14} = \frac{-1}{14}$.

## Multiplying and Dividing Fractions

Multiplying fractions is actually a bit easier than adding or subtracting them. When multiplying, you don't need to worry about common denominators. Just multiply the numerators, multiply the denominators, and then simplify if possible. For example, $\frac{2}{3} \times \frac{4}{5} = \frac{2 \times 4}{3 \times 5} = \frac{8}{15}$. That's all you need to do!

To understand the procedure for dividing fractions, you first need to define a term. The *reciprocal* of a number is the number that is obtained by switching the numerator and the denominator of the number. For example, the reciprocal of $\frac{3}{8}$ is simply $\frac{8}{3}$. To find the reciprocal of a whole number, such as 7, visualize the 7 as the fraction $\frac{7}{1}$. The reciprocal, then, is $\frac{1}{7}$.

Now, the easiest way to divide two fractions is to change the division to a multiplication with the same answer. In fact, if you change the second fraction to its reciprocal and multiply, you get the correct answer! For example, $\frac{4}{5} \div \frac{3}{4} = \frac{4}{5} \times \frac{4}{3} = \frac{16}{15} = 1\frac{1}{15}$.

What is the value of $2\frac{2}{3} \times 1\frac{4}{5}$?

Before you can multiply these mixed numbers, you need to write them as improper fractions:

$$2\frac{2}{3} \times 1\frac{4}{5} = \frac{8}{3} \times \frac{9}{5} = \frac{72}{15} = 4\frac{12}{15} = 4\frac{4}{5}$$

Evaluate $2\frac{2}{5} \div 6$

Begin by writing the problem as $\frac{12}{5} \div \frac{6}{1}$. Then

$$\frac{12}{5} \div \frac{6}{1} = \frac{12}{5} \times \frac{1}{6} = \frac{12}{30} = \frac{2}{5}$$

# Algebraic Operations and Equations

## Numerical Evaluation

Algebra is a generalization of arithmetic. In arithmetic, you learned how to perform mathematical operations (such as addition, subtraction, multiplication, and division) on different types of numbers, such as whole numbers, decimals, percents, and fractions. Algebra extends these concepts by considering how to perform mathematical operations on symbols standing for numbers and how to use these techniques to solve a variety of practical word problems.

In algebra, you refer to numbers that have a definite value as *constants*. For example, the numbers $17, -3, \frac{2}{3}, \sqrt{41}$, 5.123, and 12% are constants. Symbols standing for numbers are called *variables* because, until you specify further, they can take on any value. For example, in the expression $3x + 13y + 29$, the numbers 3, 13, and 29 are constants, and the symbols $x$ and $y$ are variables. As the following examples show, when you are given the values of all variables in an expression, you can find the value of the expression.

If $a = 4$ and $b = -3$, find the value of the expression $a^3 - b$.

When evaluating numerical expressions, it is crucial to remember the Order of Operations, and to pay careful attention to plus and minus signs. Begin by substituting the values of $a$ and $b$ in the given expression, and then carefully evaluate as in the previous section:

$$a^3 - b = (4)^3 - (-3) = 64 + 3 = 67$$

If $x = 3$, and $y = 2$, find the value of $\frac{24 - 2x}{-6y}$.

$$\frac{24 - 2x}{-6y} = \frac{24 - 2(3)}{-6(2)} = \frac{24 - 6}{-12} = \frac{18}{-12} = \frac{-3}{2}$$

The formula for the perimeter of a rectangle is $P = 2l + 2w$, where $l$ represents the length of the rectangle and $w$ represents the width. What is the perimeter of a rectangle with length 21 and width 15?

$$P = 2l + 2w = 2(21) + 2(15) = 42 + 30 = 72$$

## Solving Equations

An *equation* is simply a mathematical expression that contains an equal sign. For example, $10 = 4 + 6$ is an equation and is always true. Alternately, $10 = 5 + 4$ is also an equation, but it is always false.

An equation that contains a variable, such as $2x + 1 = 7$, might or might not be true depending on the value of $x$. *Solving an equation* refers to finding the value of the unknown that makes both sides of the equation equal. Note that the number three makes both sides of the equation equal. Therefore, you say that three *solves* the equation, or that three is the *solution* of the equation.

Some equations, like the preceding one, are easy to solve by just looking at them. Others are so complicated that you need an organized series of steps to solve them. In this section, we examine how to do this.

The principal for solving equations is, essentially, to rewrite the equation in simpler and simpler forms (without, of course, changing the solution), until the solution becomes obvious. The simplest equation of all, of course, would be an equation of the form $x = a$, where $x$ is the variable and $a$ is some number. Whenever you are given an equation that is more complicated than $x = a$, the idea is to change the equation so that it eventually looks like $x = a$, and you can read the answer right off.

Now, what can you do to change an equation? The answer is simple: almost anything you want as long as you do the same thing to both sides. To start, you can add or subtract the same number to or from both sides, multiply both sides by the same number, or divide both sides by the same number (as long as that number isn't zero). The following examples demonstrate this procedure with some very simple equations; after this, we will look at some more complicated ones.

Solve for $x$: $x + 7 = 20$.

Even though you can easily solve this equation in your head, pay attention to the procedure, as it will help you when we get to more complicated equations. Remember that the easiest possible type of equation is one of the form $x = a$. This equation isn't quite like that; it has a +7 on the left side that you would like to get rid of. Now, how can you get rid of an addition of 7? Easy; just subtract 7 from both sides:

$$
\begin{array}{rl}
x + 7 = & 20 \\
\underline{-7} & \underline{-7} \\
x = & 13
\end{array}
$$

So, the solution to this equation is $x = 13$.

Solve for $y$: $9y = 72$.

In this equation, you have a 9 multiplying the $y$ that we would like to get rid of. Now, how can you undo a multiplication by 9? Clearly, you need to divide both sides by 9:

$$\frac{9y}{9} = \frac{72}{9}$$

$y = 8$ is the solution.

The equations in the two preceding examples are called one-step equations because they can be solved in one step. Some examples of equations that require more than one step to solve follow. The procedure is the same; keep doing the same thing to both sides of the equation until it looks like $x = a$.

Solve for $t$: $4t - 3 = 9$.

In this equation, you have a few things on the left hand side that you would like to get rid of. First of all, let's undo the subtraction of 3 by adding 3 to both sides.

$$\begin{array}{rcl} 4t - 3 = & 9 \\ \underline{+3} & \underline{+3} \\ 4t & 12 \end{array}$$

Now, you need to undo the multiplication by four, which can be done by dividing both sides by 4:

$$\frac{4t}{4} = \frac{12}{4}, \text{ or, } t = 3$$

Note that you can check your answer to any equation by substituting the answer back into the equation and making certain that both sides are equal. For example, you know that you did the preceding problem correctly because

$4(3) - 3 = 9$

$12 - 3 = 9$

$9 = 9$

Solve for $p$: $15p = 3p + 24$.

This problem puts you in a situation that you have yet to encounter. The variable $p$ appears on both sides of the equation, but you only want it on one side. To get this into the form you want, subtract $3p$ from both sides:

$$\begin{array}{rcl} 15p = & 3p + 24 \\ \underline{-3p} & \underline{-3p} \\ 12p & 24 \end{array}$$

Now, you have an equation that looks a bit better. It is easy to see that if you divide both sides by 12, you end up with the answer $p = 2$.

A few more examples for you to practice with follow. Before you get to them, it will be helpful if you refamiliarize yourself with a very important mathematical property called the *Distributive Property*.

Consider, for example, the expression $7(2 + 3)$. According to the Order of Operations, you should do the work in parentheses first and, therefore, $7(2 + 3) = 7(5) = 35$. However, note that you get the same answer if you "distribute" the 7 to the 2 and the 3 and add afterward:

$7(2 + 3) = 7(2) + 7(3) = 14 + 21 = 35$

The Distributive Property tells you that you can always use this distribution as a way of evaluating an expression. Algebraically, the Distributive Property tells you that $a(b + c) = ab + ac$. The following examples incorporate the Distributive Property into the solving of equations.

Solve for $c$: $3(c - 5) = 9$.

Before you can get the $c$ by itself on the left, you need to get it out of the parentheses, so distribute:

$3c - 15 = 9$

The rest is similar to what you have already done. Add 15 to both sides to get:

$3c = 24$

Now divide by 3 to get:

$c = 8$

Solve for $q$: $5q - 64 = -2(3q - 1)$.

As in the preceding example, you must begin by eliminating the parentheses, using the Distributive Property:

$5q - 64 = -6q + 2$

Now, add $6q$ to both sides:

$11q - 64 = +2$

Next, add 64 to both sides:

$11q = 66$.

Finally, dividing both sides by 11 gives us the answer: $q = 6$.

# Solving Word Problems

Many problems that deal with practical applications of mathematics are expressed in words. To solve such problems, it is necessary to translate the words into an equation that then can be solved. The following table lists some common words and the mathematical symbols that they represent:

| Words | Mathematical Representation |
|---|---|
| a equals 9, a is 9, a is the same as 9 | $a = 9$ |
| a plus 9, the sum of a and 9, a added to 9, a increased by 9, a more than 9 | $a + 9$ |
| 9 less than a, a minus 9, a decreased by 9, the difference of a and 9, a less 9 | $a - 9$ |
| 9 times a, the product of 9 and a, 9 multiplied by a | $9a$ (or $9 \times a$) |
| The quotient of a and 9, a divided by 9, 9 divided into a | $a/9$ |
| ½ of $a$ | $½ \times a$ |
| 50% of $a$ | $50\% \times a$ |

Now, when you are given a word problem to solve, begin by translating the words into an equation and then solve the equation to find the solution.

If 5 increased by 3 times a number is 21, what is the number? Let's call the number $x$. Then, the problem statement tells us that:

$5 + 3x = 21$

Subtract 5 from both sides:

$3x = 15$

Divide by 3:

$x = 5$

Thus, the number is 5.

Brian needs $54 more to buy new hockey gloves. If new gloves cost $115, how much money does he already have to spend on the gloves?

Let $m$ represent the amount of money that Brian has to spend on the gloves. Then, you have an easy equation: $m + 54 = 115$. If you subtract 54 from both sides, you get $m = 61$. Brian already has $61 to spend on the gloves.

Edgar bought a portable compact disc player for $69 and a number of discs for $14 each. If the total cost of his purchases (before tax) was $167, how many compact discs did he buy?

Let's start by letting $d$ represent the number of discs he bought. Then the cost of the player plus $d$ discs at $14 each must add up to $167. Therefore, $14d + 69 = 167$.

Subtract 69 from both sides: $14d = 98$

Divide both sides by 14: $d = 7$

Edgar bought 7 discs.

## Multiplication with Exponents

Consider the problem $x^3 \times x^5 = ?$ If you think about it, you realize that if you compute $x^3 \times x^5$, you end up with eight $x$s multiplied together. Therefore, $x^3 \times x^5 = x^8$. This indicates the general rule for multiplication of numbers with exponents: $x^n \times x^m = xm^{+n}$. In other words, to multiply two numbers with exponents, simply add the exponents and keep the common base.

This rule can be extended to other types of multiplication. For example, if you need to multiply $x(x + 3)$, you can use the distributive property to obtain:

$x(x + 3) = x^2 + 3x$

Now, how would you multiply something like $(x + 2)(x + 5)$? Basically, you need to take each of the terms in the first expression—that is, the $x$ and the 2—and distribute them to both of the terms in the second expression. Doing this, you end up with:

$(x + 2)(x + 5) = x^2 + 5x + 2x + 10 = x^2 + 7x + 10.$

Multiply $2x(x^2 - 3x)$. Begin by distributing as you did previously:

$2x(x^2 - 3x) = 2x(x^2) - 2x(3x)$

Now, perform the indicated multiplications:

$2x(x^2) - 2x(3x) = 2x^3 - 6x^2$

Multiply $(2x + 7)(3x - 4)$.

As in the preceding example, begin by distributing the $2x$ and the 7 to the other terms:

$(2x + 7)(3x - 4) = 2x(3x) - 2x(4) + 7(3x) - 7(4)$

Now, perform the multiplications and combine terms where possible:

$2x(3x) - 2x(4) + 7(3x) - 7(4) = 6x^2 - 8x + 21x - 28 = 6x^2 - 13x - 28$

# Factoring

Earlier in this chapter, we talked about factoring whole numbers; for example, 35 can be factored as $35 = 5 \times 7$. As you can see, the word *factoring* refers to taking a mathematical quantity and breaking it down into a product of other quantities.

Certain algebraic expressions can be factored, too. Earlier in this chapter, you saw how to perform two types of multiplication. In the first, you used the distributive property to perform multiplications such as $x(x + 3) = x^2 + 3x$. To use the correct vocabulary, the $x$ at the front of this expression is called a *monomial* (one term), whereas the expression $x + 3$ is called a *binomial* (two terms). Thus, you have used the distributive property to help multiply a monomial by a binomial. You also saw how to multiply two binomials, for example:

$$(2x + 7)(3x - 4) = 6x^2 - 13x - 28$$

The process of taking the results of these multiplications and breaking them back down into their component factors is also called factoring. It is not difficult to factor, but it does often require a bit of trial and error.

For example, if you are asked to multiply the expression $2x(x - 7)$, you would get:

$$2x^2 - 14x$$

If you were given $2x^2 - 14x$ and asked to factor it, you would basically need to undo the distribution process and get the expression back to what it originally was.

To do this, begin by looking at the expression $2x^2 - 14x$ and try to find the largest common monomial factor—that is, the largest monomial that divides into both $2x^2$ and $14x$ evenly. Clearly, in this problem, the largest common factor is $2x$. You then place the $2x$ outside a set of parentheses. Finish by dividing the $2x$ into each of the two terms ($2x^2$ and $14x$) and write the resulting terms inside the parentheses. This leaves you with

$$2x(x - 7)$$

You have successfully factored the expression.

Factor $2a^2b - 8ab$.

The largest common monomial factor in this expression is $2ab$. If you divide $2a^2b$ by $2ab$, you get $a$. If you divide $8ab$ by $2ab$, you get 4. Thus, putting the $2ab$ outside of the parentheses and the $a$ and 4 on the inside, you get $2ab(a - 4)$.

Note that it is easy to check whether you have factored correctly or not by multiplying the expression and seeing whether you get the original expression back.

It is also possible to factor certain *trinomial* (three-term) expressions into two binomials. Consider a simple example: If you were asked to multiply $(x + 2)(x + 3)$, you would get $x^2 + 5x + 6$. Now, what if you were given the expression $x^2 + 5x + 6$ and asked to factor it back down to the two binomials it came from?

To begin, make two sets of parentheses, and note that you can position $x$s in the first position of each set because the first terms of each binomial multiply to give the $x^2$ in $x^2 + 5x + 6$. Therefore, to begin

$$x^2 + 5x + 6 = (x \quad)(x \quad)$$

Because both signs in $x^2 + 5x + 6$ are positive, you can position plus signs within the parentheses:

$$x^2 + 5x + 6 = (x + \quad)(x + \quad)$$

Now, what are the last entries in each binomial? Well, you know that whatever you put in these spots must multiply to get six, so the possibilities would be one and six, or two and three. The correct entries, however, must add up to five to get the correct middle term. Thus, it must be two and three, and you get $x^2 + 5x + 6 = (x + 2)(x + 3)$. You can check the answer by multiplying:

$$(x + 2)(x + 3) = x^2 + 3x + 2x + 6 = x^2 + 5x + 6$$

As you can see, factoring a trinomial into two binomials requires a bit of trial and error. The following examples give you a bit more practice with this.

Factor $x^2 - 8x + 12$.

You begin as before, by making two sets of parentheses and entering first terms of $x$ in each:

$$x^2 - 8x + 12 = (x \qquad)(x \qquad)$$

Now, the two last entries must multiply to get +12, but add to get −8, so that you get the correct middle term. Proceed by trial and error, and it does not take long to determine that the two numbers that work are −2 and −6. The factorization is $x^2 - 8x + 12 = (x - 2)(x - 6)$.

Factor $x^2 - 49$.

This one might look at bit tricky, but actually it is rather easy. Begin, as before, by writing:

$$x^2 - 49 = (x \quad)(x \quad)$$

Now, the last two entries must multiply to get 49 and add to get 0, so that the middle term is, essentially, 0. Clearly, this works with +7 and −7. Thus, $x^2 - 49 = (x + 7)(x - 7)$.

# Simplifying Algebraic Expressions

Earlier in this chapter, we talked about simplifying fractions. If, for example, the answer to a problem turns out to be $\frac{15}{20}$, it should be simplified to $\frac{3}{4}$. In the same way, certain algebraic expressions can be simplified as well. For example, consider the algebraic fraction $\frac{x^2 - 16}{3x + 12}$. To simplify this expression, begin by factoring the expressions on the top and on the bottom: $\frac{x^2 - 16}{3x + 12} = \frac{(x + 4)(x - 4)}{3(x + 4)}$. Now, the common factor of $x + 4$ can be divided from the top and bottom, yielding a simplified fraction of $\frac{x - 4}{3}$.

Mathematical operations can be performed on algebraic fractions in much the same way as they can be performed on fractions that contain only numbers. Consider this example:

Add $\frac{x + 1}{4x + 6} + \frac{x + 2}{4x + 6}$.

Because these two fractions have the same denominator, they can be added in the usual way:

$$\frac{x + 1}{4x + 6} + \frac{x + 2}{4x + 6} = \frac{x + 1 + x + 2}{4x + 6} = \frac{2x + 3}{4x + 6}$$

Now, finish by factoring the expression on the bottom and dividing:

$$\frac{x + 1}{4x + 6} + \frac{x + 2}{4x + 6} = \frac{x + 1 + x + 2}{4x + 6} = \frac{2x + 3}{4x + 6} = \frac{2x + 3}{2(2x + 3)} = \frac{1}{2}$$

Multiply $\frac{x^2 - 7x + 6}{x^2 - 1} \times \frac{x + 1}{x - 6}$.

Begin by factoring as much as possible, then multiply and cancel:

$$\frac{x^2 - 7x + 6}{x^2 - 1} \times \frac{x + 1}{x - 6} = \frac{(x - 6)(x - 1)}{(x - 1)(x + 1)} = \frac{x + 1}{x - 6} = \frac{(x - 6)(x - 1)(x + 1)}{(x - 1)(x + 1)(x - 6)} = 1$$

Divide $\frac{a^2 - b^2}{5} \div \frac{a^2 + ab}{5a - 5}$.

Begin by changing this to a multiplication problem by reciprocating the second fraction. Then factor and cancel:

$$\frac{a^2-b^2}{5} \div \frac{a^2+ab}{5a-5} = \frac{a^2-b^2}{5} \times \frac{5a-5}{a^2+ab} = \frac{(a+b)(a-b)}{5} \times \frac{5(a-1)}{a(a+b)} = \frac{(a+b)(a-b)5(a-1)}{5a(a+b)} = \frac{(a-b)(a-1)}{a}$$

# Geometry and Measurement

Although geometry is not prevalent on most of the nursing entrance exams, you may be asked some questions that require a basic knowledge of the subject. These facts are presented in the following section.

## Angle Measurement

You measure angles in degrees, which you indicate with the symbol °. By definition, the amount of rotation needed to go completely around a circle one time is 360°.

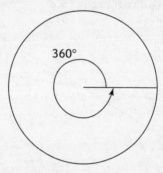

You can measure every angle by determining what fraction of a complete rotation around a circle it represents. For example, an angle that represents ¼ of a rotation around a circle would have a measurement of ¼ of 360° = 90°. The following diagram depicts a 90° angle. AB and AC are the sides of the angle, and the point A is the vertex.

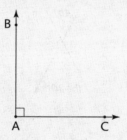

Angles that measure less than 90° are called *acute* angles, and angles that measure more than 90° are called *obtuse* angles. The following diagram depicts an acute angle of 60° as well as an obtuse angle of 120°.

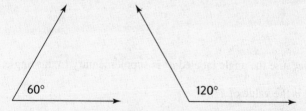

Note that an angle with the size of ½ a revolution around the circle has a measure of 180°. In other words, a straight line can be thought of as an angle of 180°.

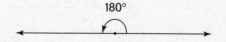

Two angles whose measures add up to 90° are called *complementary* angles, and two angles whose measures add up to 180° are called *supplementary* angles. In the following diagram, angles 1 and 2 are complementary, and angles 3 and 4 are supplementary. As the diagram shows, whenever a straight angle is partitioned into two angles, the angles are supplementary.

Another very important fact about angles relates to what are known as *vertical* angles. As the following diagram shows, when two lines intersect, four angles are formed. In this situation, the angles that are across from each other are called *vertical* angles. All vertical angles are equal, so $a° = b°$, and $c° = d°$.

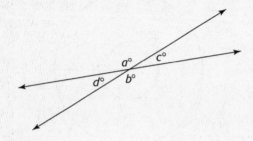

In the following diagram, what is the value of $a$?

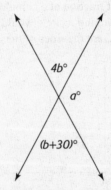

Begin by noting that the angles labeled $4b$ and $b + 30$ are vertical angles and therefore have the same measure. In this case, you can set the two angles equal and solve the resulting equation for $b$:

$4b = b + 30$

$3b = 30$

$b = 10$

Now, if $b = 10$, then $4b = 40$. Because the angle labeled $a°$ is supplementary to this angle, $a$ must be equal to 140°.

In the following diagram, what is the value of $x$?

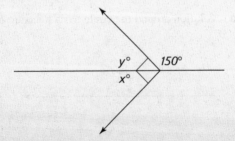

Begin by noting that the angle labeled $y$ is supplementary to the angle labeled 150° and is, therefore, equal to 30°. Next, note that the angle labeled $x$ is complementary to that 30° angle and is, therefore, equal to 60°.

# Properties of Triangles

A triangle is a geometric figure having three straight sides. One of the most important facts about a triangle is that, regardless of its shape, the sum of the measures of the three angles it contains is always 180°. Of course, then, if you know the measures of two of the angles of a triangle, you can determine the measure of the third angle by adding the two angles you are given and subtracting from 180.

Some triangles have special properties that you should know about. To begin, an *isosceles* triangle is a triangle that has two sides of the same length. In an isosceles triangle, the two angles opposite the equal sides have the same measurement. For example, in the following figure, $AB = BC$, and, therefore, the two angles opposite these sides, labeled $x°$, have the same measure.

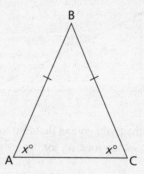

A triangle that has all three sides the same length is called an *equilateral* triangle. In an equilateral triangle, all three angles also have the same measure. Because the sum of the three angles must be 180°, each angle in an equilateral triangle must measure 180° ÷ 3 = 60°. Therefore, in the following equilateral triangle, all three angles are 60°.

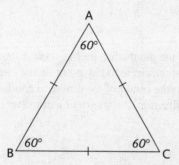

Another extremely important triangle property relates to what are known as *right* triangles, that is, triangles containing a right angle. In such triangles, the side opposite the right angle is called the *hypotenuse* and must be the longest side of the triangle. The other two sides of the triangle are called its legs. Therefore, in the following right triangle, the side labeled $c$ is the hypotenuse, and sides $a$ and $b$ are the legs.

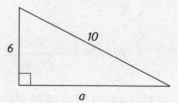

The three sides of a right triangle are related by a formula known as the Pythagorean theorem. The Pythagorean theorem states that the square of the hypotenuse is equal to the sum of the squares of the legs of the triangle, or, using the notation in the preceding diagram, $a^2 + b^2 = c^2$.

The importance of this result is that it enables you, given the lengths of two of the sides of a right triangle, to find the length of the third side.

In triangle $XYZ$, angle $X$ is twice as big as angle $Y$, and angle $Z$ is equal to angle $Y$. What is the measure of angle $X$?

Because the measure of angle $X$ is twice as big as angle $Y$, you can say that the measure of angle $X$ is equal to $2Y$. Because it must be true that $X + Y + Z = 180$, you can write:

$$2Y + Y + Y = 180$$
$$4Y = 180$$
$$Y = 45$$

If the measure of angle $Y$ is 45°, the measure of angle $X$, which is twice as big, must be 90°.

In the following triangle, what is the length of $a$?

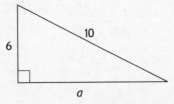

The triangle is a right triangle, so you can use the Pythagorean theorem to find the length of the missing side. Note that the hypotenuse is 10; one of the legs is 6; and you are looking for the length of the other leg. Therefore:

$$a^2 + 6^2 = 10^2$$
$$a^2 + 36 = 100$$
$$a^2 = 64$$
$$a = 8$$

## Properties of Circles

A circle is a closed figure, consisting of all the points that are the same distance from a fixed point called the *center* of the circle. A line segment from the center of the circle to any point on the circle is called a *radius* of the circle. A line segment from one point on a circle, through the center of the circle, to another point on the circle is called a *diameter* of the circle. As you can see in the following diagram, the length of a diameter of a circle is always twice the length of a radius of a circle.

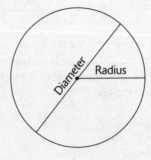

## Perimeter and Area

To find the perimeter of a triangle, you need to add together the lengths of the three sides. The area of a triangle is given by the formula Area $= \frac{1}{2}\, bh$, where $b$ represents the length of the base of the triangle, and $h$ represents the height of the triangle. The height of a triangle is defined as the length of a line segment drawn from a *vertex* (corner) of the triangle to the base, so that it hits the base at a right angle.

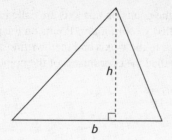

Formulas for the perimeter, which is more commonly known as the *circumference,* and the area of circles are based on the length of the radius and include the symbol $\pi$, which represents a number that is approximately equal to 3.14.

The circumference of a circle is given by the formula $C = 2\pi r$, where $r$ is the radius of the circle. The area of the circle is given by the formula $A = \pi r^2$. Unless you are told otherwise, when answering problems involving the circumference or area of a circle, you can leave the answer in terms of $\pi$, as in the following problem.

What is the circumference of a circle whose area is $36\pi$?

The area of a circle is $\pi r^2$, so you have $\pi r^2 = 36\pi$. This means that $r^2 = 36$, so $r = 6$.

Now, the circumference of a circle is $2\pi r$, so the circumference in this case would be $2\pi(6) = 12\pi$?

What is the area of the shaded part of the following rectangle?

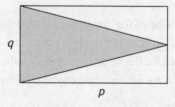

The shaded area is a triangle, so we can use the formula $A = \frac{1}{2} bh$ to find its area. The width of the rectangle, labeled $q$, is also the base of the triangle. You can see that the length of the rectangle, labeled $p$, is equal to the height of the triangle. Therefore, the area of the shaded region is $\frac{1}{2} pq$.

# Coordinates and Slope

Points in a plane can be located by means of a reference system called the coordinate system. Two number lines are drawn at right angles to each other, and the point where the lines cross is considered to have a value of zero for both lines. Then, positive and negative numbers are positioned on the lines.

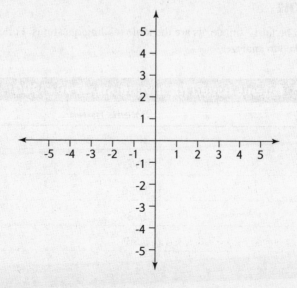

The horizontal line is called the *x-axis,* and the points on this axis are called *x-coordinates.* The vertical line is called the *y-axis,* and the points on this axis are called *y-coordinates.* Points on the plane are identified by first writing a number that represents where they lie in reference to the *x*-axis and then writing a number that expresses where they lie in reference to the *y*-axis. These numbers are called the coordinates of the point. The coordinates of a variety of points are shown in the following diagram:

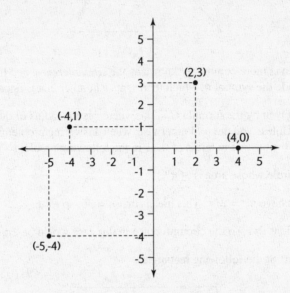

Any two points on a plane determine a line. One of the important characteristics of a line is its steepness, or *slope.* The slope of a line can be determined from the coordinates of the two points that determine the line. If the coordinates of the two points are $(x_1, y_1)$ and $(x_2, y_2)$, the formula for the slope is $\frac{y_2 - y_1}{x_2 - x_1}$. In other words, to find the slope of a line, find two points on the line and divide the difference of the *y*-coordinates by the difference of the *x*-coordinates.

Find the slope of the line that goes through the points (9, 5) and (3, −2).

The slope of the line can be computed as $\frac{y_2 - y_1}{x_2 - x_1} = \frac{5 - (-2)}{9 - 3} = \frac{5 + 2}{6} = \frac{7}{6}$.

# Data Interpretation and Table Reading

Data interpretation involves reading and analyzing tables, charts and graphs, and table reading tests your ability to select appropriate material by rows and columns. Let's analyze each of them one at a time.

## Data Interpretation

These types of questions should be fairly simple, as are the table reading questions. Following are some examples of the types of data you will be asked to analyze.

| Patents Issued for Inventions, 1790–1900 | |
|---|---|
| *Period* | *Patents Issued* |
| 1790–1800 | 309 |
| 1801–10 | 1,093 |
| 1811–20 | 1,930 |
| 1821–30 | 3,086 |
| 1831–40 | 5,519 |

| Period | Patents Issued |
| --- | --- |
| 1841–50 | 5,933 |
| 1851–60 | 23,065 |
| 1861–70 | 79,459 |
| 1871–80 | 125,438 |
| 1881–90 | 207,514 |
| 1891–1900 | 220,608 |

**1.** In what period was the greatest increase in the number of patents issued over the previous period?

    **A.** 1790–1800
    **B.** 1801–10
    **C.** 1831–40
    **D.** 1841–50
    **E.** 1851–60

The correct answer is **E**. Do you understand why that is correct? If you analyze each of the answers, you should be able to determine the correct answer. Choice **A** is incorrect because you have no information before 1790–1800. You cannot, therefore, determine the increase from the previous period. Choice **B** shows an increase of about three times the previous period. (You don't always have to perform mathematics in these tables or graphs. You can often determine the answer just by looking at the choices.) Choice **C** also is incorrect. The growth from the previous period is less than double. Choice **D** does not indicate much growth at all from the previous period. And, choice **E**, the correct answer, is almost four times the previous period.

Let's answer another question based on this table.

**2.** In what period was there the least amount of growth from the previous period?

    **A.** 1801–10
    **B.** 1811–20
    **C.** 1821–30
    **D.** 1831–40
    **E.** 1841–50

Again, let's analyze each answer. To find the answers, subtract the previous period from the current period. We are only going to estimate here.

    **A.** From 1790–1800 to the next period, about 700 more patents were issued. ($1,093 - 309 = 784$)
    **B.** From 1801–10 to the next period, just over 800 more patents were issued. ($1,930 - 1,093 = 837$).
    **C.** From 1811–20 to the next period, over 1,100 more patents were issued. ($3,086 - 1,930 = 1,156$)
    **D.** From 1821–30 to the next period, about 2,400 more patents were issued. ($5,519 - 3,086 = 2,433$)
    **E.** From 1831–40 to the next period, about 400 more patents were issued. ($5,933 - 5,519 = 414$)

The correct answer, therefore, is **E**.

Line graphs and bar graphs are essentially comparisons. In a line graph, you are asked to read and analyze the information based on different styles or widths of lines. The information is present on the horizontal and vertical axes. A bar graph is not as accurate as a table, but it gives you a quick, visual comparison of the data.

The following is an example of another type of question you will encounter.

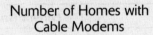

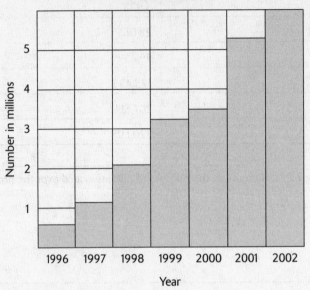

Number of Homes with Cable Modems

---

**3.** In what year was there the greatest amount of growth over the previous year?

    **A.** 1997

    **B.** 1998

    **C.** 2000

    **D.** 2001

    **E.** 2002

---

A quick look at the graph shows that the greatest amount of growth was from 2000 to 2001. You can see that visually by the bars. At the same time, by looking along the left, you can also see that about 3.2 million homes had cable modems in 2000 and 5.2 million homes had cable modems in 2001. This is an increase of 2 million. None of the other bars indicate that type of growth.

Let's look at one other type of graph—a line graph.

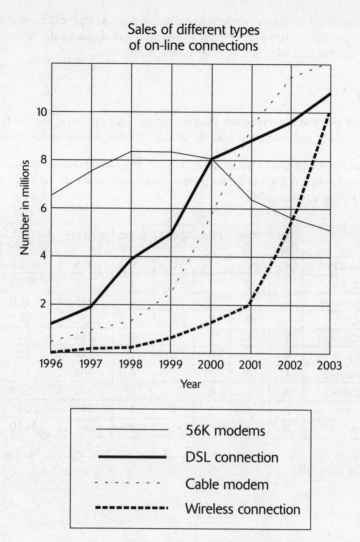

Sales of different types
of on-line connections

Number in millions

1996  1997  1998  1999  2000  2001  2002  2003

Year

———————— 56K modems

———————— DSL connection

- - - - - - - Cable modem

-------- Wireless connection

---

**4.** In what year were the most 56K modems installed?

    **A.** 1996
    **B.** 1997
    **C.** 1998
    **D.** 1999
    **E.** 2000

If you follow the thin line that indicates 56K modems on the scale and then trace it across the graph, starting at about 6.8 million, you'll see that sales peaked in 1998 with a little over 8 million sold. The correct answer is **C**.

---

**5.** How many more DSL connections were sold in 2001 compared to cable modems?

    **A.** 1 million
    **B.** 1.5 million
    **C.** 2 million
    **D.** 2.5 million
    **E.** 3 million

The correct answer is **C**, 2 million. Find the number of cable modems sold in 2000. Trace the light dotted line to 2000. It ends on 6 million. Now find the DSL connections, which is indicated by the bold line. That ends at 8 million. The difference is 2 million.

Answering these types of questions involves some arithmetic and requires strong reading skills. You have to know what the question is asking, and you have to be aware of what is being illustrated graphically. When you find the bars, numbers or lines that you are asked to deal with, you can then do the math.

## Table Reading

The second type of question that you may encounter is table reading. This portion of the test is designed to measure your ability to read tables quickly and accurately. Like the earlier material, it involves less mathematics.

Tables normally present you with columns of information, and the data corresponds to the rows and columns. There are always units such as numbers, years, dollars, and even people. You have to compare the items on both the X and Y axes to find the answers. Let's look at a typical table.

| Player | At Bats | Runs | Hits | Walks | Strike Outs | Average | Annual Salary (millions $) |
|---|---|---|---|---|---|---|---|
| Johnson rf | 4 | 0 | 1 | 0 | 0 | .255 | $2.7 |
| Smith 3b | 3 | 0 | 0 | 0 | 1 | .231 | $5.6 |
| Hernando cf | 3 | 0 | 0 | 1 | 1 | .255 | $6.0 |
| Lubitz 1b | 4 | 0 | 1 | 0 | 1 | .291 | $8.8 |
| MacDonald lf | 3 | 3 | 2 | 1 | 0 | .294 | $5.5 |
| Philips dh | 4 | 0 | 0 | 0 | 1 | .246 | $8.0 |
| Auerhaan 2b | 4 | 0 | 1 | 0 | 0 | .306 | $2.0 |
| Augustine c | 3 | 0 | 0 | 1 | 0 | .275 | $3.3 |
| Borger ss | 3 | 1 | 1 | 0 | 1 | .248 | $4.1 |
| **Totals** | 31 | 4 | 6 | 3 | 5 | | $46.0 |

6. Which player had the most hits?

   A. Johnson
   B. Lubitz
   C. MacDonald
   D. Auerhaan
   E. Borger

Find the Hits column along the top and match it to the player along the left side. The correct answer is MacDonald, with 2 hits—choice **C**. All the other players given as choices had only one hit.

7. Of those players who had hits, which player has the highest average?

   A. Johnson
   B. Lubitz
   C. MacDonald
   D. Auerhaan
   E. Borger

This time you have to analyze each player. Find the players with hits, and follow across to the Average column to find the answer.

Johnson's average is .255.

Lubitz's average is .291.

MacDonald's average is .294.

Auerhaan's average is .306.

Borger's average is .248.

Thus, the correct answer is Auerhaan, choice **D**.

A second form of table reading question might appear on the tests. In these questions, you are presented with a table of numbers, with X values running along the top and Y values running along the side. You will be asked to select the answer that occurs where the two axes intersect.

|  | | X-Values | | | | | | | | |
|---|---|---|---|---|---|---|---|---|---|---|
|  |  | -4 | -3 | -2 | -1 | 0 | +1 | +2 | +3 | +4 |
|  | +4 | 16 | 18 | 20 | 22 | 24 | 27 | 29 | 31 | 33 |
|  | +3 | 17 | 19 | 21 | 23 | 25 | 26 | 28 | 30 | 32 |
|  | +2 | 18 | 20 | 22 | 24 | 26 | 28 | 30 | 32 | 34 |
| Y-Values | +1 | 19 | 21 | 23 | 25 | 27 | 29 | 30 | 33 | 35 |
|  | 0 | 20 | 22 | 24 | 27 | 29 | 31 | 33 | 35 | 36 |
|  | -1 | 22 | 23 | 25 | 28 | 30 | 32 | 34 | 36 | 37 |
|  | -2 | 24 | 25 | 26 | 29 | 31 | 33 | 36 | 37 | 38 |
|  | -3 | 26 | 27 | 28 | 30 | 32 | 34 | 37 | 39 | 40 |
|  | -4 | 28 | 29 | 30 | 31 | 33 | 36 | 38 | 40 | 42 |

For each question, determine the number that can be found at the intersection of the row and column.

This is how the questions will appear. Try the first one and analyze it.

|  | **X** | **Y** | **A** | **B** | **C** | **D** | **E** |
|---|---|---|---|---|---|---|---|
| **1.** | −1 | +2 | 22 | 23 | 24 | 25 | 26 |

To find the answer, locate the X values along the top and find −1. Then trace down the column until you find +2 in the Y-value row. Where they intersect, you'll find the number 24. That is the correct answer. You will have an answer sheet in which you can fill in the choice, **C**. Try the following and circle the correct answer.

|  | **X** | **Y** | **A** | **B** | **C** | **D** | **E** |
|---|---|---|---|---|---|---|---|
| **2.** | +1 | −2 | 31 | **33** | 35 | 37 | 40 |
| **3.** | +2 | +4 | 18 | 22 | 25 | **29** | 30 |
| **4.** | −4 | −3 | **26** | 27 | 28 | 30 | 32 |
| **5.** | 0 | −2 | 29 | 30 | **31** | 32 | 33 |

The correct answers are

  **2. B**, 33

  **3. D**, 29

  **4. A**, 26

  **5. C**, 31

Now that you have an idea of the types of questions you'll encounter, take the time to answer all the following practice questions. If you have any problems with them, go back and reread this chapter. Make sure that you read the questions carefully so that you don't misinterpret what is being asked of you, and as a result, misread the tables or charts.

# Practice Questions

*Answer questions 1–5 based on the following table showing the number of games won by each of five teams in each month of a seven-month season.*

## Number of Games Won

| Month | Team 1 | Team 2 | Team 3 | Team 4 | Team 5 |
|---|---|---|---|---|---|
| April | 11 | 10 | 10 | 12 | 16 |
| May | 12 | 12 | 17 | 15 | 11 |
| June | 15 | 13 | 13 | 14 | 13 |
| July | 10 | 17 | 13 | 14 | 10 |
| August | 11 | 12 | 14 | 12 | 15 |
| Sept. | 14 | 11 | 12 | 11 | 16 |
| Oct. | 14 | 16 | 12 | 13 | 17 |

1. How many games did team 4 win in the first three months of the season?

   A. 38
   B. 40
   C. 41
   D. 43
   E. 44

2. In the month of August, team 5 won how many more games than team 1?

   A. 4
   B. 5
   C. 6
   D. 11
   E. 15

3. In which month did team 3 win one game more than team 4?

   A. May
   B. June
   C. August
   D. September
   E. October

4. If there are no ties and team 1 played 28 games each month, in which month did team 1 win more games than they lost?

   A. June
   B. July
   C. August
   D. September
   E. October

5. What was the total number of games won by all five teams in June?

   A. 59
   B. 64
   C. 68
   D. 72
   E. 73

*Answer questions 6–10 based on the following table of earned interest.*

### Interest Earned in One Year

| | Principal in Dollars | | | | | |
|---|---|---|---|---|---|---|
| | 1000 | 1100 | 1200 | 1300 | 1400 | 1500 |
| 1 1/4 | 12.50 | 13.75 | 15.00 | 16.25 | 17.50 | 18.75 |
| 1 3/4 | 17.50 | 19.25 | 21.00 | 22.75 | 24.50 | 26.25 |
| 2 1/4 | 22.50 | 24.75 | 27.00 | 29.25 | 31.50 | 33.75 |
| 2 3/4 | 27.50 | 30.25 | 33.00 | 35.75 | 38.50 | 41.25 |
| 3 1/4 | 32.50 | 35.75 | 39.00 | 42.25 | 45.50 | 48.75 |
| 3 3/4 | 37.50 | 41.25 | 45.00 | 48.75 | 52.50 | 56.25 |
| 4 1/4 | 42.50 | 46.75 | 51.00 | 55.25 | 59.50 | 63.75 |

Interest Rate in Percent (row labels)

6. If Lauren invested $1,400 at 2 1/4% and Evan invested $1,200 at 3 1/4%, what would be the combined earnings of Lauren and Evan in one year?

   A. $57.50
   B. $63.00
   C. $70.50
   D. $80.00
   E. $82.50

7. How much more interest is earned on $1,500 invested at 2 1/4% than on $1,000 invested at 2 3/4%?

   A. $6.25
   B. $6.50
   C. $6.75
   D. $7.00
   E. $7.25

8. John, a senior citizen, withdraws his interest earnings at the end of each year. He deposits $1,000 for one year at 4 1/4% and withdraws the $42.50 interest at the end of the year. The following year he is only able to get a rate of 3 1/4% on his $1,000. How much money does he earn that year?

   A. $9.75
   B. $32.50
   C. $42.25
   D. $50.00
   E. $74.75

9. What is the minimum interest rate you could get on $1,300 to be sure of earning at least $36.00 in interest?

   A. 2 1/4%
   B. 2 3/4%
   C. 3 1/4%
   D. 3 3/4%
   E. 4 1/4%

10. How much interest is earned in one year on $4,800 at 2 3/4%?

    A. $33.00
    B. $50.00
    C. $66.00
    D. $103.00
    E. $132.00

*Answer questions 11–15 based on the following circle graph showing the breakdown of elementary school students by grade level.*

Percent of Students by Grade Based
on a Total of 750 Students

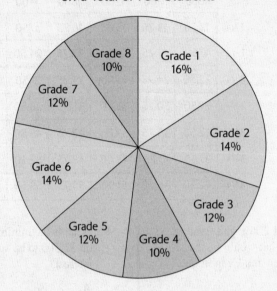

11. How many students are in grade 5?

    A. 12
    B. 63
    C. 87
    D. 90
    E. 150

12. The total number of students in grades 1 and 3 is the same as the total number of students in which of the following grades?

    A. 2 and 7
    B. 4, 7, and 8
    C. 4, 5, and 7
    D. 2 and 6
    E. 5 and 6

13. How many more students are in grade 2 than in grade 8?

    A. 4
    B. 24
    C. 30
    D. 46
    E. 48

14. How many students are in grades 5 and 6 combined?

    A. 195
    B. 260
    C. 305
    D. 350
    E. 375

15. If 30 students in grade 1 transfer to a different school and no other students enter or leave any of the other grades, what is the new percent of students in grade 3?

    A. 9%
    B. 9.5%
    C. 10%
    D. 12%
    E. 12.5%

*Answer questions 16–20 based on the following bar graph showing the distances covered by the drivers of the ABC Taxi Company in a one-week period.*

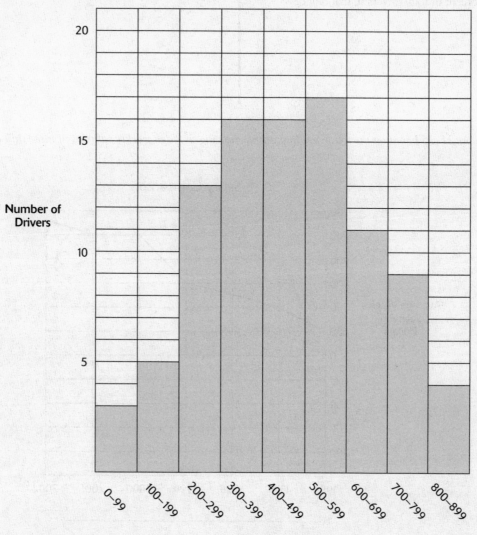

**Number of Miles**

**16.** What is the total number of drivers?

  A. 17
  B. 45
  C. 63
  D. 94
  E. 99

**17.** How many drivers drove at least 700 miles?

  A. 4
  B. 5
  C. 9
  D. 11
  E. 13

**18.** How many drivers drove less than 300 miles?

  A. 13
  B. 16
  C. 21
  D. 28
  E. 32

**19.** How many drivers drove at least 600 but less than 700 miles?

  A. 11
  B. 9
  C. 8
  D. 4
  E. 2

**20.** If the records of six more drivers are discovered and they belong in the 100–199 range, what would be the percent of total drivers in that range?

    **A.**  5
    **B.**  11
    **C.**  13
    **D.**  16
    **E.**  17

*Answer questions 21–25 based on the following line graph showing average weekly salaries at three different companies.*

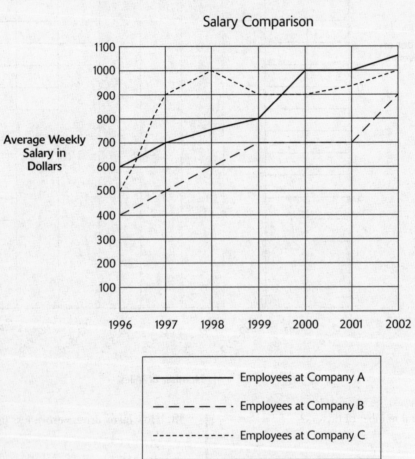

Salary Comparison

**21.** Which of the following statements is true for the time period from 1997–1999?

    **A.**  The average salary at Company C was less than at Company A.
    **B.**  The average salary at Company B was greater than at Company A.
    **C.**  The average salary at Company B was greater than at Company C.
    **D.**  The average salary at Company C was greater than at Company B.
    **E.**  The average salary at Company A was greater than at Company C.

**22.** In which time period was there no increase in the average salary at Company A?

    **A.**  1999–2000
    **B.**  1999–2001
    **C.**  2000–2001
    **D.**  2000–2002
    **E.**  2001–2002

**23.** When was the average salary at Company B greater than at Company A?

    **A.** 1996–1998
    **B.** 1997–1999
    **C.** 1998–2000
    **D.** 1999–2002
    **E.** Never

**24.** What is the difference between the average salaries at Company A and Company B in 1999?

    **A.** $100
    **B.** $300
    **C.** $500
    **D.** $700
    **E.** $800

**25.** The greatest one-year increase in salary occurred at which company and in which time period?

    **A.** At Company A from 1999–2000
    **B.** At Company A from 2001–2002
    **C.** At Company C from 1996–1997
    **D.** At Company C from 1997–1998
    **E.** At Company B from 1998–1999

# Answers and Explanations

**1. C.** The number of games won by team 4 in April, May, and June: $12 + 15 + 14 = 41$.

**2. A.** In August, team 5 won 15 games and team 1 won 11 games. $15 - 11 = 4$.

**3. D.** In May, team 3 won 17 games and team 4 won 15 games. $17 - 15 = 2$. In June, team 3 won 13 games and team 4 won 14 games. You cannot subtract 14 from 13. In August, team 3 won 14 games and team 4 won 12 games. $14 - 12 = 2$. In September, team 3 won 12 games and team 4 won 11 games. $12 - 11 = 1$. This is the correct answer.

**4. A.** If 28 games are played in a month and team 1 won 15 games in June, they lost $28 - 15 = 13$ games. Because 15 is greater than 13, June is the correct answer.

**5. C.** The total number of games won by all 5 teams in June $= 15 + 13 + 13 + 14 + 13 = 68$.

**6. C.** If Lauren invested $1,400 at 2 ¼%, she would earn $31.50. If Evan invested $1,200 at 3 ¼%, he would earn $39.00. $31.50 + $39.00 = $70.50.

**7. A.** The interest earned on $1,500 at 2 ¼% is $33.75. The interest earned on $1,000 at 2 ¾% is $27.50. $33.75 – $27.50 = $6.25.

**8. B.** John's earnings the first year do not affect his earnings in subsequent years. $1,000 invested at 3 ¼% earns $32.50.

**9. C.** Any interest rate higher than 2 ¾% earns more than $36.00 on a principal investment of $1,300. The question asks for the minimum rate, which is 3 ¼%.

**10. E.** $4,800 is four times as much as $1,200 and, therefore, earns four times as much interest. $4 \times $33.00 = $132.00.

**11. D.** The school has 750 students and 12% of them are in grade 5. 12% of 750 $= .12 \times 750 = 90$.

**12. D.** Sixteen percent of the students are in grade 1, and 12% of the students are in grade 3. Therefore, $16\% + 12\% = 28\%$ of the students are in grades 1 and 3. For choice **A** you need to add the percentages for grades 2 and 7: $14\% + 12\% = 26\%$. For choice **B** you need to add the percentages for grades 4, 7, and 8: $10\% + 12\% + 10\% = 32\%$. For choice **C** you need to add the percentages for grades 4, 5 and 7: $10\% + 12\% + 12\% = 34\%$. For choice **D** you need to add the percentages for grades 2 and 6: $14\% + 14\% = 28\%$. This is the correct answer.

**13. C.** The school has 750 students and 14% of them are in grade 2. 14% of 750 $= .14 \times 750 = 105$. Ten percent of the students are in grade 8. 10% of 750 $= .10 \times 750 = 75$. To determine how many more students are in grade 2, subtract: $105 - 75 = 30$.

**14. A.** Twelve percent of students are in grade 5 and 14% of students are in grade 6. 12% + 14% = 26%. Because 750 students are in the school, we need to calculate 26% of 750 = .26 × 750 = 195.

**15. E.** The school has 750 students, and 12% of them are in grade 3. 12% of 750 = .12 × 750 = 90. After 30 students leave the school, 750 − 30 = 720 students remain. We need to determine what percent 90 is of 720: 90 ÷ 720 = .125 = 12.5%.

**16. D.** The number of drivers who drove 0–99 miles is 3. The number of drivers who drove 100–199 miles is 5. The number of drivers who drove 200–299 miles is 13, and so on. 3 + 5 + 13 + 16 + 16 + 17 + 11 + 9 + 4 = 94.

**17. E.** At least 700 miles means 700 or more miles. 9 + 4 = 13.

**18. C.** Less than 300 miles includes the first three bars of the graph. 3 + 5 + 13 = 21.

**19. A.** At least 600 but less than 700 means the 600–699 bar. The correct answer is 11.

**20. B.** The total number of drivers indicated on the graph is 94, as explained in question 16. If 6 more drivers are added to the graph, there are 94 + 6 = 100 drivers. If all 6 are added in the 100–199 range, there are 5 + 6 = 11 drivers in this range. You need to determine what percent 11 is of 100: 11 ÷ 100 = .11 = 11%.

**21. D.** In the time period from 1997–1999, the line representing the average salary at Company C is higher on the graph than the lines representing either of the other 2 companies. Therefore, the average salary at Company C was greater than at Company B and choice **D** is the correct answer.

**22. C.** No increase in average salary is indicated when the line in the line graph is horizontal. For Company A this occurs from 2000–2001.

**23. E.** For the average salary at Company B to be greater than the average salary at Company A, the line representing Company B has to be higher than the line representing Company A. This never happens.

**24. A.** In 1999, the average salary at Company A was $800, and the average salary at Company B was $700. $800 − $700 = $100.

**25. C.** The increase at Company A from 1999–2000 is $1,000 − $800 = $200. Choice **A** = $200. The increase at Company A from 2001–2002 is $1,050 − $1,000 = $50. Choice **B** = $50. The increase at Company C from 1996–1997 is $900 − $500 = $400. Choice **C** = $400. The increase at Company C from 1997–1998 is $1,000 − $900 = $100. Choice **D** = $100. The increase at Company B from 1998–1999 is $700 − $600 = $100. Choice **E** = $100. The largest value is $400, choice **C**.

# Scale Reading

While "Scale Reading" may not be important on most of the nursing entrance tests you'll take, the ability to read various types of scales (that is, thermometer, blood pressure, and so on) will be important in the future. In this review section, you are given a variety of scales with various points indicated on them by numbered arrows. You are to estimate the numerical value indicated by each arrow and then choose your answer.

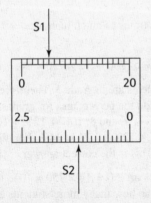

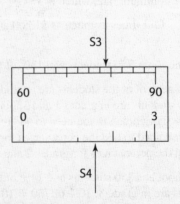

**S1.**

    A.  6.00
    B.  5.00
    C.  4.25
    D.  2.25
    E.  1.25

**S2.**

    A.  13.0
    B.  12.0
    C.  10.2
    D.  1.30
    E.  1.20

**S3.**

    A.  81.75
    B.  79.50
    C.  78.75
    D.  77.60
    E.  67.50

**S4.**

    A.  1.75
    B.  1.65
    C.  1.50
    D.  0.75
    E.  0.65

In S1 there are five subdivisions of four steps each between 0 and 20. The arrow points between the long subdivision markers representing 4 and 8. Because it points to the marker that is one step to the right of subdivision marker 4, it points to 5.00. This is choice **B** in sample item S1.

In S2 the scale runs from right to left. There are five subdivisions of five steps each, so each step represents .1, and the arrow points to the marker representing 1.20. This is choice **E** in sample item S2.

In S3 the arrow points between two markers. You must estimate the fractional part of the step as accurately as possible. Because the arrow points halfway between the markers representing 77.5 and 80.0, it points to 78.75. This is choice **C** in sample item S3.

In S4 each step represents .5, but the steps are of unequal width with each step being two-thirds as wide as the preceding one. Therefore, the scale is compressed as the values increase. The arrow is pointing to a position halfway between the marker representing .5 and 1.0, but because of the compression of the scale, the value of this point must be less than 0.75. Actually it is 0.65, which is choice **E** in sample item S4.

All that's required of you is to read the scales and determine which selection is the correct one. You have 10 minutes in which to answer 40 questions. As with all tests, the more you practice, the better you become. Keep in mind, also, that your score is based on the number of correct answers. Because you do not lose any points for incorrect answers, answer all the questions, whether you think you know the answer or not.

## Practice Questions

Following are several more questions that will help you review for these types of questions. Time yourself. It should only take a couple of minutes to answer all 10 questions.

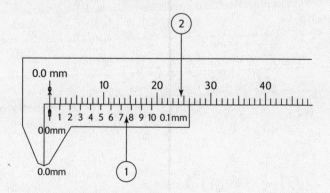

**1.**

    A.   7.5mm
    B.   7.8mm
    C.   8.5mm
    D.   17.5mm
    E.   107.5mm

**2.**

    A.   240mm
    B.   245mm
    C.   24mm
    D.   24.5mm
    E.   25.5mm

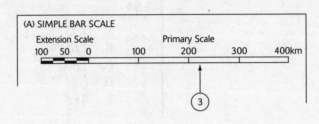

**3.**

    A.   200km
    B.   225km
    C.   250km
    D.   300km
    E.   375km

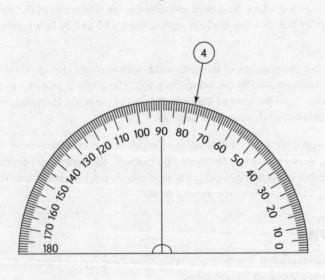

**4.**

    A.   80.5
    B.   80.4
    C.   77.0
    D.   75.7
    E.   75.2

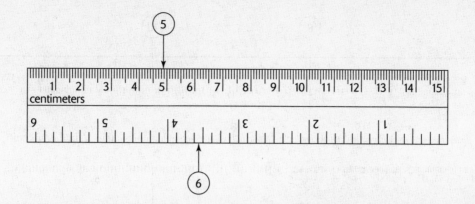

**5.**

    **A.**   4.7 cm
    **B.**   48.0 cm
    **C.**   4.85 cm
    **D.**   50.2 cm
    **E.**   5.2 cm

**6.**

    **A.**   3.45
    **B.**   3.50
    **C.**   3.80
    **D.**   3.55
    **E.**   3.95

**7.**

    **A.**   172
    **B.**   173
    **C.**   17.3
    **D.**   1.73
    **E.**   .173

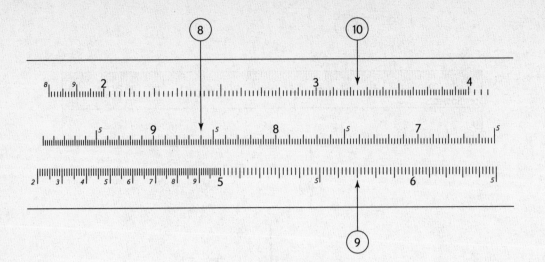

**8.**

    A.  9.40

    B.  8.52

    C.  8.70

    D.  5.10

    E.  5.00

**9.**

    A.  5.2

    B.  5.7

    C.  52.0

    D.  55.2

    E.  57.0

**10.**

    A.  322

    B.  47.60

    C.  32.20

    D.  8.40

    E.  3.22

# Answers

1. A
2. D
3. B
4. C
5. C
6. D
7. D
8. C
9. B
10. E

How did you do on these? Were you able to "read between the lines?" Always look to see in which directions the numbers run. Sometimes, they run from left to right, and sometimes they run from right to left, depending on the scale. In addition, the spacing between the numbers is not always even, as it is on a standard ruler. On many gauges and other types of scales, the hash marks between numbers might not be equal. Furthermore, some gauges might have several different scales running in different directions. Just pay attention to them, and you should have very little trouble.

# Quantitative Comparison Review

## Overview

If you have never seen a Quantitative Comparison question before, you may be in for a surprise. To begin, Quantitative Comparison questions are not followed by a series of possible answer choices like most standard multiple choice questions. It may not even be obvious what question you are supposed to answer. All you see are two columns, Column A and Column B, each of which contains some sort of mathematical or verbal entry.

Quantitative Comparison questions are special format questions. They have their own unique set of rules, and their own answer choice *code*. To be able to successfully answer these questions, you must understand the rules, memorize the answer choice code, and know all of the strategies.

Although it may take a while to become familiar with the format, the code, and the strategies, after you master this information, Quantitative Comparison questions are frequently easier to answer than regular multiple choice questions. In this section, we will look at the directions for the questions, discuss the answer choice code, and examine all of the strategies.

Each Quantitative Comparison question consists of an entry in Column A and an entry in Column B. These entries might be arithmetic, algebraic, or geometric, or they may just contain words. Your job is to examine the entry in Column A and the entry in Column B and determine which one is larger. If, after examining the entries in both columns, you determine that the entry is Column A is *always* bigger, then the answer is **A**. If, on the other hand, you determine that the entry in Column B is *always* bigger, the answer is **B**. Should you conclude that both entries always are of the same size, then the answer is **C**. There is only one other possibility, and that is that you do not have enough information to determine which quantity is bigger. In this case, you would answer **D**.

Thus, the answer code is actually rather straightforward. An answer of **A** means that the entry in Column A is larger, and an answer of **B** means that the entry in Column B is larger. Choice **C** means that the entries are equal, and **D** means that it is not possible to tell. You should have this code memorized so that you do not have to waste valuable test-taking time trying to learn it while you are taking the test.

There is only one other aspect of these questions that you need to know about. Some questions give you additional information to help you to determine which of the quantities is bigger. This common information is centered above the entries in Columns A and B.

In order to become more familiar with these questions, take a look at the directions as they appear on the test and then consider four sample problems that will be used to illustrate the four answer choices:

*Directions:* For each of the following questions, two quantities are given, one in each of Column A and Column B. You are to compare the two quantities and mark your answer sheet with the correct choice, based on the following:

> Select A if the quantity in Column A is the greater;
>
> Select B is the quantity in Column B is the greater;
>
> Select C if the two quantities are equal
>
> Select D if the relationship cannot be determined from the information provided.

| Column A | Column B |
|---|---|
| **1.** 63% | $\frac{5}{8}$ |

The entry in Column A is a percent, and the entry in Column B is a fraction. In order to determine which is larger, it is perhaps easiest to express them both as decimals. To begin, $63\% = 0.63$. Then, $\frac{5}{8} = 0.625$. Based on this, it is clear that the entry in Column A is larger. Thus, the answer is **A**.

| Column A | Column B |
|---|---|
| **2.** $\left(4 - \sqrt{11}\right)\left(4 + \sqrt{11}\right)$ | $\sqrt{25}$ |

Here, we will need to evaluate the two given expressions. To begin, $\left(4 - \sqrt{11}\right)\left(4 + \sqrt{11}\right) = 16 - 4\sqrt{11} + 4\sqrt{11} - 11 = 16 - 11 = 5$. Then, simply note that $\sqrt{25} = 5$, and it will be clear that the answer is **C**. (Although the square root of 25 could be argued as $+$ or $-5$, a common convention is that the radical sign is considered the $+$ root.)

| Column A | Column B |
|---|---|
| **3.** $x^2 + y^2$ | $(x + y)^2$ |

Begin with the entry in Column B. Note that $(x + y)^2 = x^2 + 2xy + y^2$. Therefore, you have $x^2 + y^2$ in Column A and $x^2 + 2xy + y^2$ in Column B. Note that the only difference between these two entries is that the entry in Column B has an extra term of $2xy$. Based on this, many people will select **B** as the answer, feeling that the "extra" $2xy$ makes the entry in Column B bigger. However, it is also possible that $2xy$ could be negative, which would make the entry in Column B smaller. Because you have no way of knowing the size of $2xy$, you cannot say which quantity is bigger. The answer is **D**.

Now, consider the strategies that will help you to solve these questions.

In general terms, two main categories of questions appear in the Quantitative Comparison section of the test. The first category is the "purely numerical question." Such questions contain arithmetic numbers only and do not involve variables. The second category of quantitative comparison questions is the question that *does* involve working with variables, or letters standing for numbers, such as $x$, $y$, or $a$. There are very useful distinct strategies for each of these two question types. Before you examine these strategies, however, begin by considering some extremely important strategies that should always be in your mind regardless of the category of question you are trying to solve.

Perhaps the most important thing to be aware of at all times when solving Quantitative Comparison questions is the type of number that is being used in the problem. As an example, consider the four questions that follow. Note that all of these questions have the same entries in Column A and Column B, and yet the answers vary from question to question.

| Column A | Column B |
| --- | --- |
| **4.** $x$ | $x^3$ |

At first glance, this appears to be a very straightforward question. The question is simply asking you to determine which is bigger: $x^2$ or $x^3$. Common intuition is that when you square a number it gets bigger and when you cube it, it gets bigger still. For example, if you start with $x = 3$, then $x^2 = 3^2 = 9$, and $x^3 = 3^3 = 27$. Thus, the answer seems as if it should be **B**.

The answer, however, is not **B**, and the thinking that leads to the selection of this answer choice reflects one of the most common reasoning flaws in attempting to solve Quantitative Comparison questions. The intuition that squaring a number makes it bigger, and cubing it makes it bigger still, is only true for numbers that are bigger than 1. What if, for example, $x$ was equal to 1? After all, there is no reason why it couldn't be 1. In such a case, $x^2 = 1^2 = 1$, and $x^3 = 1^3 = 1$. Thus, if $x = 1$, the entries in Column A and Column B are equal. This means that the size relationship is indeterminate, and the actual correct answer is **D**.

It is extremely important, when solving a Quantitative Comparison question, that you are aware of what types of numbers are being used in the problem. Frequently, as in this example, test-takers only think in terms of positive whole numbers, and this gets them into trouble. Look at several other variations of this problem.

| Column A | Column B |
| --- | --- |
| **5.** | |
| $x > 1$ | |
| $x^2$ | $x^3$ |

Now, this is the question that you might initially thought that you were answering in Example 5. Note here that the common information tells us that $x > 1$. In this case, common intuition holds true, and the answer to this question *would be* **B**.

| Column A | Column B |
| --- | --- |
| **6.** | |
| $0 < x < 1$ | |
| $x^2$ | $x^3$ |

This question looks the same as the preceding one, only now you are told that the value of $x$ is between 0 and 1. Remember the intuition that told you that squaring a number made it bigger, and cubing it made it bigger still? Well, see what happens if the number is between 0 and 1. Work with the fraction $\frac{1}{2}$ as an example. Note that $\left(\frac{1}{2}\right)^2 = \frac{1}{4}$, and that $\left(\frac{1}{2}\right)^3 = \frac{1}{8}$. These examples illustrate another general property of numbers. When a number that is between 0 and 1 is squared, it gets *smaller.* If you cube such a number, it gets smaller still. Thus, the answer to this question is **A**.

Note that you have now looked at three different versions of the same question, and you have obtained three different answers. Let's take the problem one step further.

| Column A | Column B |
| --- | --- |
| **7.** | |
| $x < 0$ | |
| $x^2$ | $x^3$ |

In this problem, you are told that $x$ is less than 0, that is to say, that $x$ is negative. What is the answer now? Well, you know that when you square any negative number, the result is positive. For example, $(-4)^2 = +16$. However, when a negative number is cubed, the result is negative, as in $(-4)^3 = -64$. Thus, the entry in Column A is always positive, and the entry in Column B is always negative. Since any positive number is bigger than any negative number, the answer to this question is **A**.

To summarize what the example problems have shown, remember at all times to *consider all possible types of numbers in a problem.* Do not assume that the properties of positive integers also hold for other types of numbers. Fractions, negative numbers, and the numbers 1 and 0 sometimes behave in different ways. This realization is so important in Quantitative Comparison problems, that it makes sense to consider a variety of other situations where the type of number makes a difference. Following are additional questions for you to use as practice. Remembering the preceding discussion, try to answer all of them before reading the solutions.

## Practice Questions

| Column A | Column B |
|---|---|
| | |

**1.**

$$x > 1$$

| $\sqrt{x}$ | $x$ |
|---|---|

**2.**

$$0 < x < 1$$

| $\sqrt{x}$ | $x$ |
|---|---|

**3.** $\sqrt{x}$         $x$

**4.**

$$a^2 = b^2$$

| $a$ | $b$ |
|---|---|

**5.**

$$a^3 = b^3$$

| $a$ | $b$ |
|---|---|

**6.**

$$a > 1$$

| $8a$ | $\dfrac{8}{a}$ |
|---|---|

**7.**

$$0 < a < 1$$

| $8a$ | $\dfrac{8}{a}$ |
|---|---|

**8.** $8a$         $\dfrac{8}{a}$

**9.**

$$\frac{a}{b} = \frac{3}{4}$$

$$a > 0, b > 0$$

| $a$ | $b$ |
|---|---|

**10.**

$$\frac{a}{b} = \frac{3}{4}$$

| $a$ | $b$ |
|---|---|

## Answers and Solutions

1. **B.** The common information tells you that $x > 1$, and therefore, your intuition regarding the relative sizes of numbers and their square roots is correct. In particular, the square root of a number greater than one is *less than* the number itself.

2. **A.** When you are dealing with numbers that are between 0 and 1, however, the common intuition regarding the relative sizes of numbers and their square roots reverses. Note, for example, that $\sqrt{\frac{1}{4}} = \frac{1}{2}$. In general, the square root of a number between 0 and 1 is larger than the number itself.

3. **D.** With no information regarding the size of $x$, you simply cannot tell which entry is bigger.

4. **D.** The common mistake is to look at the given information, $a^2 = b^2$, and to conclude that $a$ and $b$ must be the same size, leading to the answer **C**. The faulty reasoning is to think that, if two numbers "square out" to the same number, then the numbers had to be the same to begin with. What if, however, $a = 5$, and $b = -5$? The squares of both of these numbers would be the same, 25; however, the two entries are not the same. Because the entries might or might not be negative, there is no way to tell which one is bigger.

5. **C.** Note that, if $a = 5$ and $b = -5$, then $a^3$ does not equal $b^3$. Specifically, $a^3 = 5^3 = 125$, but $b^3 = (-5)^3 = -125$, so such a selection violates the common information. In fact, the only way that $a^3$ can equal $b^3$ would be if $a$ and $b$ were the same.

6. **A.** Common intuition says that if you multiply by a number, the result is bigger than what you would obtain if you divided by the number. As you will see in the next problem, however, this intuition is only true for numbers larger than 1. Since here you are told that $a > 1$, common intuition holds.

7. **B.** In this problem, however, common intuition reverses. As an example, say that $a = \frac{1}{2}$. In this case, $8a = 8\left(\frac{1}{2}\right) = 4$, but $\frac{8}{a} = \frac{8}{\frac{1}{2}} = 8 \times 2 = 16$. Thus, the product of 8 by a number between 0 and 1 is less than 8, but the quotient of 8 and a number between 0 and 1 is larger than 8.

8. **D.** Here, of course, with no information about the size of $a$, we cannot reach any conclusion regarding the relative sizes of the two entries.

9. **B.** Common intuition tells us that a fraction is less than 1 only if the numerator is less than the denominator. In this problem, note that $a$ is not necessarily 3 and $b$ is not necessarily 4. However, $a$ and $b$ must be in a 3 to 4 ratio. For example, $a$ could be 30 and $b$ could be 40, or $a$ could be 6 and $b$ could be 8. In every case, though, $b$ is bigger than $a$, so the answer is **B**. However, this is only true, as you will see in the next problem, if $a$ and $b$ are positive.

10. **B.** In this problem, there's an open possibility that $a$ and $b$ are negative. Note that if, for example, $a = -3$ and $b = -4$, then the ratio is still 3 to 4, but $a$ is larger than $b$.

These problems, once again, illustrate one of the most important strategies regarding Quantitative Comparison questions—the fact that you must be very careful regarding the types of numbers that are permitted in a problem. If applicable, always ask yourself what would happen if the numbers in the problem were positive, negative, between 1 and 0, or 1, or 0.

## Strategies

Another very useful strategy can be applied to Quantitative Comparison questions. When you studied algebra, you learned how to solve algebraic equations and inequalities. Recall that an algebraic equation or inequality is a statement that tells you that two quantities are either equal, or that one is less than or greater than the other. For example, $3a + 7 = 12$ is an equation, and $3a + 7 > 12$ is an equality.

Equations and inequalities can be simplified by either adding or subtracting the same quantity from both sides. In addition, you can also multiply or divide both sides by the same number as long as (in the case of an inequality) you do not multiply or divide both sides by a negative number.

Now, if you think about it, any Quantitative Comparison question can be viewed as an inequality or an equation. You have a quantity on the left side (the quantity in Column A), and a quantity on the right hand side (the quantity in

Column B). Although you do not know, at least initially, the correct inequality sign to position between these two quantities, you still can treat them as inequalities or equations. That means that you can add or subtract the same quantity to both columns in a Quantitative Comparison question. You can also multiply or divide both columns by the same **non-negative** number. You can also perform other operations on both columns that are permitted to be performed on inequalities. For example, as long as both sides are positive, you can square both sides.

The value of this strategy is that it allows you to simplify the quantities in Column A and Column B, so that it is easier to tell which one is bigger. Using this strategy, you can always change, for example, subtractions and divisions, to the relatively less confusing operations of addition and subtraction. The following examples illustrate the effective use of this strategy.

| Column A | Column B |
|---|---|
| $8\sqrt{3}$ | $\dfrac{24}{\sqrt{3}}$ |

Instead of trying to estimate the size of $\sqrt{3}$, and, in order to avoid the division, multiply both columns by $\sqrt{3}$. The entry in Column A, then, becomes $8\sqrt{3} \times \sqrt{3} = 8 \times 3 = 24$, and the entry in Column B becomes $\dfrac{24}{\sqrt{3}} \times \sqrt{3} = 24$. The answer is **C**.

| | |
|---|---|
| $12.9 - \dfrac{5}{6}$ | $11.8 + \dfrac{1}{6}$ |

This problem becomes much easier if you eliminate the subtraction by adding $\dfrac{5}{6}$ to both sides. If you do this, Column A becomes $12.9 - \dfrac{5}{6} + \dfrac{5}{6} = 12.9$, and Column B becomes $11.8 + \dfrac{1}{6} + \dfrac{5}{6} = 11.8 + 1 = 12.8$. Thus, you easily see the answer is **A**.

| | |
|---|---|
| $\sqrt[3]{2,197}$ | $12$ |

To simplify, cube the entries in both columns. The quantity in Column A, then, becomes 2,197, and the quantity in Column B becomes $12 \times 12 \times 12 = 1,728$. The answer is **A**.

| $p \neq 0$ | |
|---|---|
| $-3p$ | $\dfrac{p^4 - 6p}{2}$ |

Begin by trying to simplify the quantity in Column B. Multiply both quantities by 2. If you do this, you obtain $-6p$ in Column A, and $p^4 - 6p$ in Column B. Now, eliminate the subtraction by adding $-6p$ to both sides. You end up with 0 in Column A and $p^4$ in Column B. You have, thus, taken this complicated problem and simplified it to a comparison between 0 and $p^4$. To finish, note that you are told that $p$ does not equal 0, which means that $p^4$ must be positive. Thus, the entry in Column B is larger, and the answer is **B**.

The two strategies that you have just considered are, perhaps, the two most useful strategies for Quantitative Comparison questions. These two strategies can be summarized as follows:

**Strategy #1:** Consider all possible values for the numbers in a Quantitative Comparison question.

**Strategy #2:** Treat the Quantitative Comparison question as an algebraic inequality.

There are a number of other useful strategies that will help you as you approach these questions. These strategies are summarized in the following discussion and examples are given.

**Strategy #3:** Do as little work as possible to determine which quantity is bigger.

Always remember, your goal is to determine which quantity is larger. You do not need to determine the actual values of the quantities; all you need to do is determine the size relationship.

| The number of minutes in a week | The number of seconds in a day |
|---|---|

This problem might initially seem as if it is going to be rather messy. However, if you remember that you only need to determine which quantity is larger, it is quite easy. The number of minutes in a week is $60 \times 24 \times 7$. The number of seconds in a day is $60 \times 60 \times 24$. Which of these is bigger? Well, since each product has a 60 and a 24, it is the product that has the other 60 instead of the 7 that will be bigger. There is no reason to actually evaluate the expressions. The answer is **B**.

**Strategy #4:** Estimate

Sometimes, a few quick estimates will enable you to determine which quantity is larger.

| $\sqrt{26} + \sqrt{11}$ | $\sqrt{37}$ |
|---|---|

Let's try to determine the approximate sizes of each entry. In Column A, note that $\sqrt{26}$ is a little bit bigger than 5, and that $\sqrt{11}$ is a bit bigger than 3. Thus, overall, the entry in Column A is a bit bigger than 8. However, $\sqrt{37}$ is only a bit bigger than 6. Thus, the answer is **A**.

**Strategy #5:** Compare terms and factors

This strategy follows from Strategy 2. When comparing Column A to Column B, note that sums and products can often be compared term by term or factor by factor.

| $\frac{2}{3} \times \frac{5}{6} \times \frac{11}{12}$ | $\frac{2}{3} \times \frac{2}{3} \times \frac{5}{6}$ |
|---|---|

Compare these quantities factor by factor. To begin, each quantity begins with a factor of $\frac{2}{3}$. Since these factors are the same, they will impact both quantities in the same way and can, therefore, be ignored. In fact, it may help to cross them out. Now, compare the $\frac{5}{6}$ in Column A to the $\frac{2}{3}$ (the second factor) in Column B. Since $\frac{2}{3} = \frac{4}{6}$, the quantity in Column A is bigger. Similarly, $\frac{11}{12}$ is bigger than $\frac{5}{6} = \frac{10}{12}$. Thus, the result of the comparison is that two of the factors in Column A are larger than the corresponding two factors in Column B, and the other factors are the same. No need to do any arithmetic; the quantity in Column A is bigger. The answer is **A**.

**Strategy #6:** Reduce or Factor

Lengthy computations often can be simplified by factoring or reducing an expression. Remember, the test-makers know that you do not have a calculator. If you find yourself faced with a difficult computation, you have likely missed a shorter way of answering the question.

| $13(12^{50})$ | $12^{51} - 12^{50}$ |
|---|---|

There is no way that you can be expected to evaluate these expressions by hand. Instead, note that the expression in Column B can be simplified by removing the largest common factor from both terms: $12^{51} - 12^{50} = 12^{50}(12 - 1) = 11(12^{50})$. Thus, you are actually comparing $13(12^{50})$ in Column A to $11(12^{50})$ in Column B. If you cross out the common factor of $12^{50}$ from both expressions, you can see that you are actually comparing 13 to 11. The answer is **A**.

**Strategy #7:** If there are equations in the common information that can be easily solved, solve them.

Often, as a way of testing your knowledge of algebra, you will be given equations to solve in the common information. Once you have solved them, the answer will be obvious.

| $x + 2y = 22$ |
|---|
| $2x = 20$ |

| $x$ | $y$ |
|---|---|

The second equation, $2x = 20$, can be easily solved to obtain $x = 10$. If 10 is substituted into the first equation, it can be solved to obtain $y = 6$. The answer is **A**.

**Strategy #8:** Manipulate the Common Information

There is a very tricky type of question that is frequently used in Quantitative Comparison sections. Take a look at the problem that follows and think about how you would answer it.

| | |
|---|---|
| | $5a - 2b = 18$ |
| $\dfrac{10a - 4b}{9}$ | 4 |

It probably appears, at least initially, as if the answer to this question is **D**. After all, the common information only contains one equation in two unknowns, and this is not enough information to determine the values of $a$ and $b$, which would be needed to evaluate the entry in Column A. However, note that if you multiply both sides of the equation given in the common information by 2, you will obtain the equation $10a - 4b = 36$. And, the value of $10a - 4b$ is exactly the numerator of the entry in Column A. Therefore, the entry in Column A is equal to $\dfrac{10a - 4b}{9} = \dfrac{36}{9} = 4$. The answer is **C**. The only way to get a question like this correct is to be looking for this type of a shortcut. Sometimes, the common information can be directly used to evaluate an entry without first finding the values of the variables.

**Strategy #9:** Pick Values for the Variables

This is a strategy that will often enable you to find the answer to a tricky problem, or at least limit the answer down to two possible choices, after which you can at least make an educated guess. In a problem involving a variable(s), select a value for the variable(s) and evaluate the entries in the Columns. Let's say that, in doing this, the entry in Column A is larger. This means that the answer cannot possibly be **B** or **C** and is either **A** or **D**.

In order to determine whether **A** or **B** is correct, select some other values for the variable(s). Try to use a variety of values, such as 1, 0, a fraction, and a negative number. If, at any time, the entry in Column B turns out to be larger than in Column A, or if they become equal, you can eliminate **A** as the answer, and the answer must by **D**. If, on the other hand, **A** turns out to be larger every time you test it, you can be reasonably certain that the answer is **A**.

| | |
|---|---|
| | $a$ is a positive integer |
| $a^3$ | $3a$ |

Let's try a value for $a$, say $a = 1$. In this case, the value of the quantity in Column A becomes $a^3 = 1^3 = 1$, while the value of the quantity in Column B is $3a = 3^1 = 3$. Since the quantity in Column B is larger in this case, the answer is either **B** or **D**.

If, however, you let $a = 3$, both quantities become $3^3$ and are thus equal. This means that the answer must be **D**.

**Strategy #10:** In purely numerical questions, the answer is never **D**.

This is a very obvious strategy, but it doesn't hurt to state it before wrapping up this list of strategies. If both entries are purely numerical (all numbers, no variables), then each has a definite size, and thus one of them is bigger, or else they are equal. In such questions, the answer cannot be **D**, and so, particularly if you are uncertain and want to try to guess the answer, do not pick **D**.

The more you practice Quantitative Comparison questions, the better you will become at using the strategies and the faster and easier the questions will become. There are three practice tests in this book; you should solve all of the problems carefully and read all of the solutions.

# Life Science Review

## Abilities Tested

One of the most important areas of your education in nursing school will be your understanding of science—and especially life science. This section presents an in-depth overview of material that you will not only encounter in school but will surely find on any nursing entrance exam you plan to take.

This section is designed to evaluate your understanding of the basic concepts studied in the Life Sciences, including "The Cellular Basis of Life;" "Classical (Mendelian) Genetics;" "Gene Expression (Molecular Biology);" "Principles of Evolution;" "Taxonomy (Classification of Life);" "Human Anatomy and Physiology" (The Digestive System, The Respiratory System, The Circulatory System, The Excretory System, The Endocrine System, The Nervous System, and The Reproductive System); and "Ecology."

## General Science

This section provides an overview of general life science topics including cells, the plasma membrane, and photosynthesis. Use this information as a basic review only. If you struggle on the practice questions, you may want to further review the life sciences before taking a nursing entrance exam.

## The Cellular Basis of Life

All living organisms are composed of cells. Some organisms consist of a single cell, and others are composed of multiple cells organized into tissues and organs. Tissues are composed of groups of cells that share a common function and are, in turn, organized into organs.

All cells share two basic features: a **plasma membrane** (the outer boundary of the cell) and **cytoplasm** (a semi-liquid substance that composes the foundation of the cell). Living organisms are classified as either prokaryotes or eukaryotes, based on their cellular structure and complexity.

**Prokaryotic cells** are relatively simple, lacking membrane-bound internal cellular bodies (organelles). Prokaryote cells have ribosomes. Their DNA is found in a circular chromosome that exists freely in the cytoplasm. **Eukaryotic cells**, however, are compartmentalized into membrane bound organelles—internal cellular bodies that carry out specialized functions.

One of the most important facts about prokaryotes is their lack of an organized nucleus. Among the organelles found in eukaryotic cells are the nucleus, mitochondria, chloroplasts (in plants), and the endoplasmic reticulum.

The following illustrates the components of an idealized eukaryotic cell. Such a cell may not exist, but the diagram shows the relative sizes and locations of the various cell parts.

The nucleus of eukaryotic cells is composed primarily of protein and deoxyribonucleic acid (DNA). The DNA is organized into linear units called chromosomes. The functional segments of chromosomes that determine the characteristics of an organism are **genes**.

The mitochondria (singular, mitochondrion) play a role in the release of energy to the cell in the form of adenosine triphosphate (ATP). Because they are involved in the release and storage of energy, the mitochondria often are referred to as the "powerhouses" of the cells.

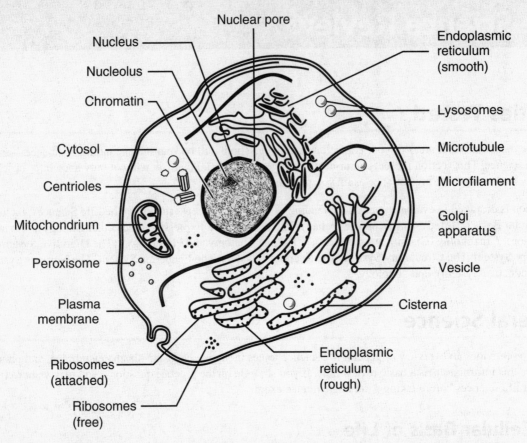

Many plant cells (those found in green plant tissues) contain chloroplasts. These organelles carry out the process of photosynthesis in which plants absorb radiant energy from the sun and use it in the production of glucose from carbon dioxide and water. The glucose then is broken down in the mitochondria to produce energy for use in cell metabolism, or the glucose is converted to starch (a long chain of glucose molecules held together by chemical bonds) and stored until energy is needed. Animal cells do not contain chloroplasts.

The endoplasmic reticulum is a series of membranes extending throughout the cytoplasm of eukaryotic cells. Some of the membranes (rough endoplasmic reticulum) are studded with small bodies called ribosomes and serve as sites for protein synthesis. Other membranes of the endoplasmic reticulum are smooth. These membranes lack ribosomes and serve as sites for lipid and fatty acid synthesis.

## Movement through the Plasma Membrane

In order for the cytoplasm to communicate with the external environment, materials must be able to move through the plasma membrane. One method of movement through the membrane is diffusion. Diffusion is the movement of molecules from a region of higher concentration to a region of lower concentration. This movement occurs because the molecules are constantly colliding with one another, and the net movement of molecules is from regions of high concentration to regions of low concentration. In other words, diffusion is a random, passive movement of molecules down a concentration gradient. A type of diffusion involving water molecules is known as osmosis. Osmosis is the movement of water across a semipermeable membrane from a region of higher concentration to a region of lower concentration.

A third mechanism for movement across the plasma membrane is facilitated diffusion. Certain proteins in the membrane assist facilitated diffusion by permitting only certain molecules to pass through. The proteins encourage movement in the direction the molecules would normally move, from a region of higher concentration to a region of lower concentration.

A fourth method for movement across the membrane is active transport, in which a protein moves certain molecules across the membrane from a region of lower concentration to a region of higher concentration (against a concentration gradient). Active transport requires an expenditure of energy by the cell for this type of movement to occur.

# Photosynthesis

Some living organisms, including all green plants, synthesize their own food from simple molecules such as carbon dioxide and water. This process requires energy, which is obtained from sunlight in the form of radiant energy. Radiant (light) energy is captured by the specialized pigments (primarily chlorophyll) in the chloroplasts of cells and is converted to chemical energy through the synthesis of glucose molecules from carbon dioxide and water. In the process, oxygen is released as a by-product. The process can be summarized by the following equation:

$$6CO_2 + 12H_2O \longrightarrow C_6H_{12}O_6 + 6O_2 + 6H_2O$$

The wavelengths of light used in photosynthesis are primarily those in the red and blue ranges. Chlorophyll molecules typically reflect green light, which is why most plants' leaves appear green.

# Cellular Respiration and Fermentation

Animals, plants, and microorganisms obtain the energy they need through the process of cellular respiration. In cellular respiration, carbohydrates (primarily glucose) are broken down in the cell to produce water and carbon dioxide. In the process, energy is released and stored in the form of adenosine triphosphate (ATP). When energy is needed by the cell, the bonds in ATP molecules are broken down and the energy stored in them can be utilized in metabolism. The process of cellular respiration, which requires the presence of oxygen, can be summarized by the following equation:

$$C_6H_{12}O_6 + 6O_2 \longrightarrow 6H_2O + 6CO_2 + energy \ (ATP)$$

When no oxygen is present, the cells of some organisms (for example, yeast) carry out a form of anaerobic respiration called fermentation. The products of fermentation are carbon dioxide and ethanol.

# Cell Division

One distinguishing feature of living organisms is that they can reproduce themselves independently of other organisms. This reproduction takes place at the cellular level as part of what's known as the cell cycle. Eukaryotic cells go through the cell cycle, but not all prokaryotic cells follow the steps of mitosis.

Cell division is essential to life. It allows for the growth of multicellular organisms as well as the replacement of worn out and damaged cells. For single-celled organisms, cell division increases the population of the species. Cellular reproduction at the cellular level is called the cell cycle.

The cell cycle is divided into two phases: interphase and mitosis. During interphase, the cell carries out its specific metabolic functions that make it unique. During mitosis, the cell divides into two new cells (called daughter cells). It is through cell division, combined with cell expansion, that growth of an organism occurs.

Interphase is divided into three distinct phases: G1, S, and G2. During the G1 phase, the cell carries out its typical functions. During this phase, the chromosomes consist of single units of DNA. In humans, there are 46 chromosomes in each cell. During the S phase, the DNA within each chromosome replicates itself, such that each chromosome now has two copies of the hereditary information it carries. These copies are referred to as sister chromatids. In the G2 phase, the cell prepares for mitosis and a series of fibers, called the spindle, forms. The spindle is involved in the movement of chromosomes during mitosis.

Mitosis is a continuous process, however, for convenience in explaining the processes that occur during cell division, scientists divide mitosis into a series of phases: prophase, metaphase, anaphase, and telophase.

In prophase, the chromosomes condense and become visible. The two copies of each chromosome (sister chromatids) can be distinguished. The chromatids are held together at a region called the centromere. As prophase continues, the spindle forms and the chromosomes attach to the spindle fibers in the region of the centromere.

In metaphase, the chromosomes are pulled along the spindle fibers until they are lined up along a region at the center of the cell called the equatorial plate.

During anaphase, the centromere holding sister chromatids together splits, and the chromatids are pulled to opposite ends of the cell (opposite poles). The result of anaphase is an equal separation and distribution of the chromosomes to opposite poles of the cell.

In telophase, the chromosomes again become diffuse, two daughter nuclei are formed, and the spindle fibers break down.

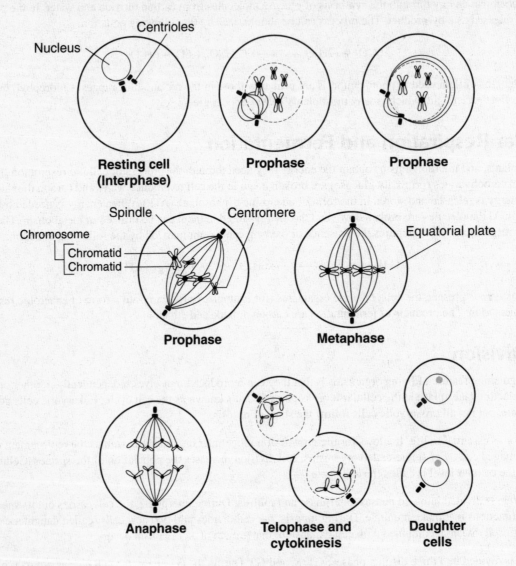

The process of mitosis.

Cell division is not complete unless mitosis (nuclear division) is accompanied by cytokinesis (division of the cytoplasm). In animals, cytokinesis begins with the formation of a cleavage furrow in the center of the cell and the membrane pinches into the cytoplasm until the two cells are pinched apart. In plants, which have rigid cell walls surrounding their plasma membranes, the process is a bit more complex. A cell plate is assembled between the two daughter cells, and cell wall material is secreted on each side of the cell plate until the two daughter cells are separated from one another.

Most plant and animal cells are diploid, meaning they have two sets of chromosomes. In human cells, there are 46 chromosomes organized into 23 pairs. In order for sexual reproduction to occur, sex cells (gametes) from two individuals must unite.

For this to occur successfully, while maintaining the normal number of chromosomes in an organism from generation to generation, a different form of cell division occurs in specialized cells that give rise to gametes (eggs and sperm in humans). In order to successfully maintain the normal number of chromosomes in an organism from generation to generation, a different form of cell division occurs. This type of cell division gives rise to gametes (eggs and sperm in humans) and occurs in specialized cells called sex cells.

This specialized form of cell division is known as meiosis and gives rise to gametes with half the number of chromosomes as was present in the parent cell. Because the gametes only contain one copy of each chromosome, they are said to be haploid. Meiosis in humans gives rise to egg cells and sperm cells that each contains 23 chromosomes—one member of each chromosome pair. When the gametes unite at fertilization, the "normal" (diploid) chromosome number is re-established in the resulting zygote.

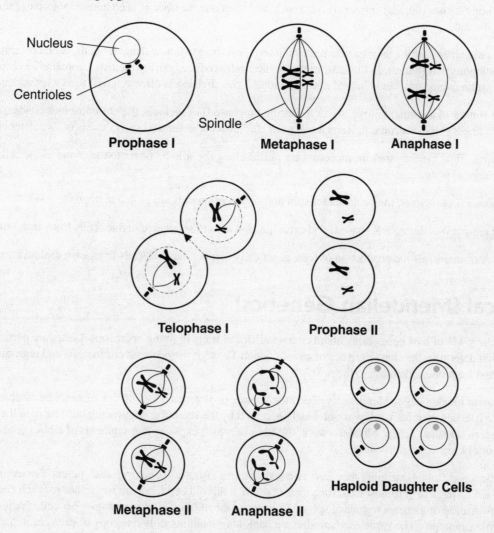

The process of meiosis.

The two members of each chromosome pair are called homologues (or homologous chromosomes). Homologous chromosomes are similar to each other in that they carry copies of the same genes; however, they may carry different versions of the genes (different alleles). For example, both members of a homologous pair may carry genetic information for hair color, however, one member of the homologous pair may carry information for blond hair while the other member of the pair carries information coding for brown hair.

Meiosis occurs through a series of phases that results in two separate cell division events. These phases are divided up into those that occur during meiosis I (the first division) and those that occur during meiosis II (the second division). Meiosis I and meiosis II each consist of the same phases: prophase, metaphase, anaphase, and telophase as observed in mitosis.

Prophase I of meiosis is similar in many ways to prophase of mitosis. The chromosomes have already passed through the S stage of interphase and, therefore, each chromosome has been duplicated and consists of two sister chromatids attached to each other at the centromere. In addition, the chromosomes have shortened and condensed and are now visible under the microscope. One very important difference between prophase I of meiosis and prophase of mitosis is that homologous chromosomes pair up with each other to form tetrads in a process known as synapsis. After synapsis has taken place, the chromatids paired together may physically cross over each other. When that happens, the chromatids often break and reattach to the broken segment of the opposite chromatid in a process known as crossing over. As a result of crossing over, the chromatids now contain new combinations of genetic information than previously existed. Crossing over is an important source of genetic variation, making it a driving force in evolution.

In metaphase I of meiosis, the homologous pairs line up together in tetrads at the equatorial plate. During anaphase I of meiosis, the homologues (tetrads) split apart from each other and one member of each homologous pair moves to opposite poles of the cell.

The nucleus reorganizes during telophase I, and cytokinesis results in two new daughter cells, each containing one half of each homologous pair (tetrad). In humans, each daughter cell produced during meiosis I contains 23 chromosomes. Because the chromosome number is halved during meiosis I, this division is often referred to as a reduction division.

Meiosis II is similar to a normal mitotic division. During prophase II of meiosis, the chromosomes condense and attach to the spindle fibers at the centromere. Remember, each chromosome in the cell still consists of two sister chromatids.

During metapase II of meiosis, the chromosomes are pulled along the spindle fibers to the center of the cell and line up along the equatorial plate.

During anaphase II of meiosis, the centromeres split and sister chromatids are pulled to opposite poles.

The nucleus reorganizes during telophase II and cytokinesis occurs to separate daughter cells from each other.

The end result of meiosis is the production of four, genetically distinct, haploid cells from each diploid parent cell.

# Classical (Mendelian Genetics)

Genetics is the study of how genes bring about characteristics or traits in living organisms. Genes are portions of DNA molecules that determine the characteristics of an individual. Through the processes of meiosis and reproduction, genes are transmitted from one generation to the next.

The Augustinian monk, Gregor Mendel, developed the science of genetics based on experiments he conducted in the 1860s and 1870s, however, his work was not widely accepted by the scientific community until early in the twentieth century. Modern scientists accept Mendel's work, the basis of which explains that segments of DNA (genes) control the inheritance of discrete characteristics.

Most organisms are diploid, meaning they have two sets of chromosomes—one from each parent. For example, human cells each have 23 pairs of chromosomes, for a total of 46. In a diploid cell there are two genes for each characteristic. During the formation of gametes (eggs and sperm) in meiosis, the number of chromosomes per cell is reduced by half (to 23 in human gametes). The gametes, therefore, are haploid (containing only one copy of each chromosome). When the gametes unite during fertilization, the diploid number of chromosomes (46 in humans) is re-established in the zygote. As such, the gametes receive one copy of each gene from the maternal parent (mother) and one copy of each gene from the paternal parent (father).

Genes come in various forms called alleles. For example, in humans there are two alleles controlling earlobe type. One allele codes for earlobes that are attached, while the other allele codes for earlobes that hang free. The type of earlobes a person has is determined by the alleles inherited from their parents.

The gene composition of an individual is referred to as its genotype, while the expression of the genes is referred to as an individual's phenotype. There are three possible genotypes for earlobe structure: a person may have two alleles for attached earlobes, two alleles for free earlobes, or one allele for attached and one allele for free earlobes. When both alleles for a gene are the same in an individual, we say that individual is homozygous for that trait (for example, two alleles for attached earlobes or two alleles for free earlobes). When an individual has two different alleles for a trait (for example one allele for attached earlobes and one allele for free earlobes), that individual is considered heterozygous for that trait.

The phenotype of an individual (for example, whether they have attached or free earlobes) depends on the relationship between the alleles governing that trait. In the case of earlobe structure, when at least one allele for free earlobes is present, the individual will have free earlobes. The presence of the allele for free earlobes overshadows the presence of the allele for attached earlobes when both are present together in an individual (heterozygous condition). Thus, free earlobes is said to be dominant over attached earlobes. As a result, an individual with one allele for attached earlobes and one allele for free earlobes will express free earlobes in their phenotype, as will an individual with two alleles for free earlobes. Only individuals with two alleles for attached earlobes will express that trait. Dominant alleles always express themselves, while recessive alleles express themselves only when there are two of them together (no dominant allele present).

Mendel developed a method for predicting the outcome of inheritance patterns by conducting genetic experiments on pea plants. Pea plants pollinate themselves, and after several generations of self-pollination, individuals that are homozygous for particular traits will be produced. These individuals are considered true-breeding or pure lines.

In his work, Mendel took several pure lines of peas and cross-pollinated them with other pure lines and followed the inheritance patterns of different traits through several generations. Mendel called the pure lines he started with the parental generation. One thing he noticed was that when he crossed pure-line tall plants with pure-line short plants, all of the offspring plants were tall. Mendel called this first generation of offspring the first filial or $F_1$ generation. Next, Mendel crossed several of the $F_1$ plants together to produce the second filial, or $F_2$ generation. In the $F_2$ generation, he observed that three-fourths of the plants were tall and one-fourth of the plants were short.

To predict the possibility of a particular trait being inherited by offspring, several steps are followed. First, a symbol is designated for each allele of the gene. The dominant allele is represented by a capital letter and the recessive allele by the corresponding lowercase letter. In keeping with our previous example, we could designate the allele for free earlobes 'E' and the allele for attached earlobes 'e'. For a homozygous dominant individual, the genotype would be 'EE'; for a heterozygous individual, the genotype would be 'Ee'; and for a homozygous recessive individual, the genotype would be 'ee'.

The next step in performing a genetic cross is determining the genotypes of the parents and the genotypes of the gametes. If two heterozygous parents are crossed (Ee × Ee), each parent could produce gametes containing a dominant allele (E) or a recessive allele (e), and each type of gamete would be produced in roughly equal frequency. To predict the genotypes and phenotypes of the offspring between these two parents, a Punnett square could be used. The possible gametes produced by the female parent are indicated at the top of the square and the possible gametes produced by the male parent are indicated to the left of the square. Thus, for the cross between two heterozygous parents, Ee × Ee, the Punnett square would be as follows:

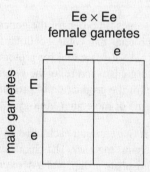

To determine the possible genotypes of the offspring, all possible combinations of gametes must be considered. This is done by combing the gamete at the top of each cell of the square with the gamete to the left of the cell, as illustrated here:

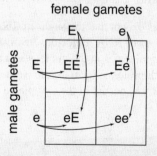

From the Punnett square, we can see that 1/4 of the offspring will be homozygous dominant ('EE'), 1/2 of the offspring will be heterozygous ('Ee'), and 1/4 of the offspring will be homozygous recessive ('ee'). Therefore, the offspring from the cross between the two heterozygotes would produce offspring with a genotypic ratio of 1:2:1 (1 EE : 2 Ee : 1 ee). Because free earlobes are dominant over attached earlobes, the heterozygous individuals, as well as the homozygous dominant individuals will have free earlobes, and only the homozygous recessive individuals will have attached earlobes. Therefore, the phenotypic ratio among the offspring is 3:1 (3 with free earlobes : 1 with attached earlobes).

Mendel conducted several more experiments following the inheritance of various traits—either one trait at a time or pairs of traits simultaneously. Over many years of conducting such experiments, Mendel developed several principles of inheritance that are known today as Mendel's laws of genetics:

1. Mendel's law of dominance: When an organism has two different alleles for a trait, one allele dominates.
2. Mendel's law of segregation: During gamete formation by a diploid organism, the pair of alleles for a particular trait separate, or segregate (as in meiosis).
3. Mendel's law of independent assortment: The members of a gene pair separate from one another independent of the members of other gene pairs. (These separations occur during the formation of gametes in meiosis).

Using Mendel's principles, scientists can predict the probability of inherited traits among offspring by performing controlled crosses. Not all traits fall neatly into the patterns of inheritance described by Mendel. For some traits, one allele does not display dominance over another allele. Instead, the two characters blend to give an intermediate phenotype in the hetreozygote. For example, in snapdragons, there are two alleles for flower color: one red and one white. Heterozygous individuals, which contain one red allele and one white allele, are pink. When neither allele shows dominance over the other, the alleles are said to display incomplete dominance. When two pink snapdragons are crossed, the phenotypic ratio among the offspring is one red, two pink, and one white. These results show that the two genes remain independent of each other and only the expression of the genes (phenotypes) blend.

Many traits are controlled by multiple genes on one or more chromosomes. This condition is known as polygenic inheritance. Other genes are located so close together on the same chromosome that crossing over rarely occurs between them during meiosis. As a result, the genes are usually inherited together as a unit. The inheritance of more than one gene together as a unit is known as gene linkage.

# Gene Expression (Molecular Biology)

The genetic material is packaged into chromosomes. In order for the genetic information contained in the chromosomes to be expressed, it must be processed into the proteins that control cellular functions. Two types of nucleic acids, deoxyribonucleic acid (DNA) and ribonucleic acid (RNA) are essential for protein synthesis to occur. DNA molecules in the nucleus contain the genetic information of an organism and relay the genetic information they contain to messenger RNA (mRNA) molecules, which in turn, code for the production of proteins. The flow of information from DNA to mRNA to protein is known as the Central Dogma of molecular biology.

DNA molecules consist of two long strands that twist around each other to form a double helix, a shape that resembles a spiral staircase. Chemical bonds hold the two chains together. The chains are composed of nucleotides. Each nucleotide consists of three parts: a nitrogenous base, a phosphate group, and a deoxyribose sugar. The nitrogenous bases found in DNA are adenine (A), guanine (G), cytosine (C), and thymine (T). The backbone of the DNA molecule consists of alternating sugars and phosphate groups, with the nitrogenous bases facing inward, like rungs on a ladder. Chemical bonds between the bases hold the molecule loosely together. Adenine is always opposite (and pairs with) thymine on the ladder, while cytosine is always opposite (and pairs with) guanine. This is known as complementary base pairing.

RNA molecules are similar to DNA molecules except that the sugar in RNA is ribose, and the RNA nucleotides include uracil in place of thymine. There are three types of RNA molecules involved in protein synthesis. Messenger RNA (mRNA) copies the genetic code from DNA molecules in the nucleus and transports the message to the cytoplasm. Ribosomal RNA (rRNA), in combination with proteins, form the ribosomes. These organelles are the sites of protein synthesis in the cytoplasm. Transfer RNA (tRNA) occurs in the cytoplasm and carries amino acids to the ribosomes as protein synthesis takes place.

The basis of protein structure is how its amino acid components are linked together. The sequence of amino acids in a protein is determined by the sequence of nucleotides on the DNA molecule that encodes that protein. The linking together of the amino acids into a protein occurs in the cytoplasm of the cell. In order for the amino acids to be linked together in the proper order, the message encoded by the DNA molecule must move out of the nucleus and into the cytoplasm. This is accomplished through the formation of mRNA molecules.

A mRNA strand complementary to the base sequence on the DNA molecule is synthesized in the nucleus. The DNA molecule opens up allowing an enzyme, RNA polymerase, to bind to one of the strands of DNA. The polymerase enzyme moves along the DNA molecule reading the bases one at a time. As the enzyme moves along the DNA molecule, nucelotide bases of RNA are incorporated into a mRNA molecule according to the principle of complementary base pairing. This process of making a mRNA molecule complementary to the base sequence on the DNA molecule is known as transcription. The nucleotides on the DNA molecule are read in groups of three. Each group of three bases is referred to as a codon. The RNA polymerase will continue along the DNA molecule until it reaches a specific sequence of three bases on the DNA molecule that signals it to stop. These "stop" messages typically occur at the ends of gene-coding sequences on the DNA.

After a complementary mRNA molecule is made from the DNA molecule in the nucleus, it moves through the nuclear envelope into the cytoplasm where it attaches to a ribosome. The ribosome holds the mRNA molecule in place while tRNA molecules carry amino acids to the ribosome. Each tRNA molecule recognizes a specific amino acid that it captures and carries to the ribosome. The amino acid it recognizes corresponds to a series of three bases found on the opposite end of the tRNA molecule. The bases on the tRNA molecules are complementary to codons on the mRNA molecule and, thus, are referred to as anticodons. As the anticodon on the tRNA molecule pairs with its complementary codon on the mRNA molecule, the amino acid carried by the tRNA will be placed into position according to the original code on the DNA molecule. As each tRNA molecule brings its corresponding amino acid to the ribosome, the amino acid will link up with the amino acids brought by previous tRNA molecules through the formation of a peptide bond. When a tRNA molecule has released its amino acid, it will leave the ribosome and be recycled in the cytoplasm where it is free to connect with another amino acid.

The ribosome moves along the mRNA exposing one codon at a time. As each new codon is exposed, tRNA will bring in the corresponding amino acid and add it to the growing polypeptide chain. The conversion of the genetic message encoded on the mRNA molecule into a polypeptide is known as translation. When the ribosome reaches the end of the mRNA molecule (the "stop" signal) the mRNA will be released from the ribosome and become degraded in the cytoplasm, and the completed polypeptide chain (protein) will be released.

# Biotechnology

Biotechnology is an industrial process that uses scientific research on DNA for practical applications. In biotechnology, including genetic engineering, the genes of an organism are changed and often combined with genes from other organisms. The resulting DNA is referred to as recombinant DNA. Biotechnology can, therefore, be used to produce proteins not normally found in the cells of particular organism by inserting genes from one organism into another to create transgenic plants and animals. Biotechnology also is used to produce drugs or vaccines, to produce treatments for human disorders, to identify individuals from evidence left at a crime scene (forensics), and to determine the likelihood of paternity.

# Ecology

Ecology is the discipline of biology concerned primarily with the interaction between organisms and their environments. There are many levels of organization among living organisms: populations, communities, ecosystems, and the biosphere.

A population is a group of individuals belonging to one species occupying a defined area. Populations of living things interact with other populations of their own kind, populations of other species, and with physical aspects of their environment. A population's growth proceeds until reaching certain environmental limits. When a population has reached the maximum size that the environment can support, the environment is said to have reached its carrying capacity. The growth of a population passes through stages. There is an initial lag period, followed by a period of exponential growth.

The curbs that limit population growth may include crowding of a population, an example of a density-dependent population. Other density-dependent curbs include disease, competition, predation, and territoriality. Curbs that take place in density-independent populations include external limiting factors such as climatic fluctuations and catastrophic events such as floods, fires, and tornadoes.

Communities of plants, animals, and other organisms may be found in such places as deserts, salt marshes, or forests. A community includes all populations in a given environment. Within a community, each population of organisms has a habitat and a niche. The habitat is the physical place where the organism lives, and the niche is the role that organism plays in the life of the community.

Organisms living together in a community will interact with each other in various ways. If the relationship between two organisms is mutually beneficial, such as the relationship between fungi and cyanobacteria in lichens, it is known as mutualism. If the relationship benefits one organism but does not affect the other organism, the relationship is known as commensalism and is illustrated by the bacteria living in the guts of humans. Another type of relationship, in which one organism benefits while the other is harmed, is known as parasitism. The microorganisms that cause human diseases are parasites. Predation occurs when one organism feeds on another organism. In this type of relationship, again, one organism benefits and the other is harmed.

In a community, the orderly and predictable replacement of populations over a given period of time in a given area is called succession. In each succession, certain populations dominate and then decline, to be superseded by a new dominant population. A community in the last stage of succession is known as a climax community.

Interactions between communities and their physical environments form ecosystems. One of the major phenomena underlying an ecosystem is the flow of energy within it. Because photosynthesizing organisms trap the energy from the sun to make their own food, they are referred to as the producers. Organisms that meet their energy needs by feeding on these producers are called primary consumers. Primary consumers are herbivores, feeding directly on plants (producers); whereas, secondary consumers are carnivores, feeding on animals that eat plants (the primary consumers).

Transfer of energy from producers to consumers is called a food chain. Many food chains interacting in a complex manner form a food web. Decomposers, the organisms responsible for breaking down organic matter, are present at each level of food chains and food webs. The decomposers are primarily bacteria and fungi.

The food pyramid is a way of expressing the availability of food in an ecosystem at successive levels, called trophic levels. The number of producers, which are always at the base of the pyramid, is high, and the number of consumers at the top of the pyramid is low. The difference in numbers of individuals at each trophic level occurs because only a small percentage of the food energy available at one trophic level can be passed on to the next, as much of the energy is used up carrying out metabolic functions in the organisms at each level. The total dry weight of food available at each trophic level is called *biomass*.

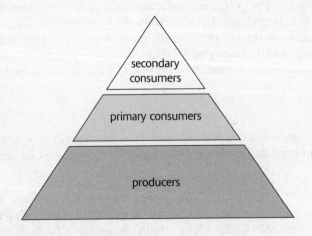

Hypothetical food pyramid.

Another phenomenon of an ecosystem is the recycling of nutrients and minerals. Carbon, nitrogen, and phosphorus are examples of substances that are recycled through ecosystems. Some of the carbon is recycled through respiration; however, the majority is recycled through decomposition.

Nitrogen, which is vital for the synthesis of proteins and nucleic acids, is released to the atmosphere as waste products by bacteria. Much of the nitrogen that is released as waste (ammonium) from bacteria is released into the soil where it is converted into a usable form by soil bacteria.

The biosphere is composed of the living organisms and the physical environment that blankets the earth. The physical environment includes the rocky material of the earth's surface, the water on or near the earth's surface, and the blanket of gases surrounding the earth. All of life is confined to a five-mile vertical space around the surface of the earth.

Ecologists study the living components of the biosphere in subunits called biomes. A biome is a group of communities dominated by a particular climax community. Each biome is also characterized by the climatic conditions present. Each type of living organism is adapted to its own habitat and niche within a biome. Examples of biomes include deserts, tropical forests, temperate forests, prairies, tundra, and taiga (the southern edge of the tundra). The general composition of a biome remains uniform; however, local differences arise as a result of population fluctuations, floods, fires, and other ecological factors.

# Principles of Evolution

Evolution implies a change in one or more characteristics of a population of organisms over time. In the mid-1800s, two researchers—Charles Darwin and Alfred Wallace—independently developed the theory of evolution based on extensive research and observation.

The basis for evolution is the presence of genetic variation among living organisms and the selection of those individuals that are best able to survive and reproduce. The method by which individuals are selected is called natural selection.

Two essential points underlie natural selection. First, the genetic variation that occurs among individuals is random. Second, the genetic variation among individuals is subtle and has little effect on the population as a whole.

The main ideas usually taught with natural selection are as follows:

1. Individuals of a population have random genetic variations.
2. More individuals are produced than live to grow up and reproduce.
3. Some characteristics allow organisms to be more likely to survive and reproduce.

Traits that allow an individual to survive and reproduce will be passed on to the individual's offspring. Therefore, individuals that are better adapted to their environment will be more likely to reproduce and preferentially pass on those genes to the next generation. The ability to survive and reproduce is referred to as reproductive fitness. Thus, if certain inherited traits provide an advantage of one individual over another in a given environment, that trait would provide a reproductive advantage to the individual. This concept is sometimes referred to as survival of the fittest.

Evolution does not occur in individuals; it takes place in populations. A population is an interbreeding group of individuals of the same species occupying a given geographic area. The collection of genes present in the population is known as the gene pool for that population. As changes occur in the gene pool, for example as the most reproductively fit individuals contribute a higher percentage of alleles, the population gradually evolves. In addition to natural selection, several other mechanisms contribute to changes in the gene pool of a population including mutation, migration (gene flow), and genetic drift.

Mutation is an important force driving evolution. Mutations give rise to new alleles and result in random changes to the gene pool of a population. As such, mutations are an important source of genetic variation in a population. Mutations may be harmful and selected against, or they may be beneficial and confer a selective advantage for an individual. In this case, the individuals with the mutation will show greater reproductive fitness than those without the mutation.

Migration of individuals into or out of a population results in gene flow between two or more populations. When migrating individuals mate with native individuals, they contribute their genes to the gene pool of the local population. The migrating individuals often bring in new traits that were not previously present in the local population.

Genetic drift occurs when a small group of individuals leaves the population and establishes a new population in a geographically isolated region. This small group of individuals typically represents only a small portion of the original gene pool, and the genetic variability in this "new" population is usually quite low. Over time these individuals may become reproductively isolated from the original population and develop into a separate species.

Several pieces of evidence strongly support evolution. One piece of evidence comes from paleontology—the study of fossils.

The fossil record shows that over time, organisms have changed in a variety of ways, both in size and form. This information can be used to deduce a descent of modern organisms from common ancestors.

More evidence for evolution comes from the study of comparative anatomy. For example, the forelimbs of such diverse animals as humans, porpoises, cats, birds, and bats are strikingly similar, even though the forelimbs are used for very different purposes (lifting, swimming, flying, etc.). The various modifications are thought to be adaptations to the specific needs of modern organisms that all arose from a common ancestor. Also, many organisms have structures they don't use. Often, these structures are degenerate and undersized compared with similar structures in other organisms. The useless structures are called vestigial organs. In humans, they include the appendix, the fused tail vertebrae, and the wisdom teeth. It's possible that environmental changes made the organs unnecessary, and the structures gradually became nonfunctional and reduced in size.

The following illustrates the forelimbs of a human and two other animals showing the similarities in construction. These anatomical similarities are considered evidence for evolution.

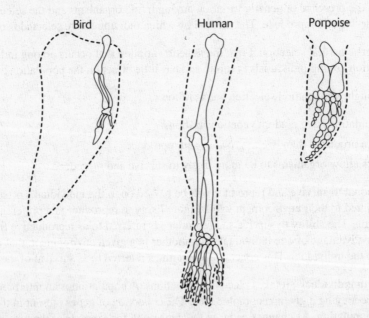

Embryology offers additional evidence for evolution. The embryos of fish, reptiles, chickens, rabbits, and humans share many similarities. For example, all have gill slits, a two-chambered heart, and a tail with muscles. This uniformity provides evidence of evolutionary relationships in that diverse organisms have all inherited the developmental mechanisms of a common ancestor. In the later stages of embryo development, the organisms appear less and less similar.

Studies in modern biochemistry indicate there are biochemical similarities among all living organisms. For example, the mechanisms for transferring energy and building proteins from amino acids are nearly identical in all organisms. DNA and RNA serve as the basis for inheritance in all living organisms, and the structure of the genetic code is virtually identical in all living systems. The uniformity in biochemical organization points to evolutionary relationships among organisms.

# The Origin and Evolution of Life

The universe is thought to have come into existence about 15 billion years ago with a colossal explosion known as the big bang. The gases and dust from the explosion produced the earliest stars, and over a period of years, the stars exploded, and their debris formed other stars and planets. Our solar system is thought to have formed this way 4–5 billion years ago. During the next billion years, the earth cooled and formed a hardened outer crust, and the first living organisms came into being approximately 3.5 billion years ago.

The early atmosphere of the earth consisted largely of nitrogen, hydrogen, sulfur, sodium, and carbon. Some of these elements combined to form hydrogen sulfide, methane, water, and ammonia. Water vapor in the early atmosphere probably caused millions of years of torrential rains, during which time the oceans formed. Gas and water from the earth's core came to the surface through volcanoes. Ultraviolet radiation bathed the earth, and the elements and compounds interacted with one another to form complex molecules.

Scientists believe that the first cells lived within the organic environment of the earth and used organic compounds to obtain energy. However, organic materials would soon be used up if they were the sole source of nutrition and energy. The evolution of a pigment system that could capture energy from the sun and store it in chemical bonds was an essential breakthrough in the evolution of living things. The first organisms to possess these pigments were photosynthetic bacteria, ancestors of modern cyanobacteria. Oxygen, which is produced as a byproduct of photosynthesis, enriched the atmosphere.

Approximately 1.5 billion years ago, in an oxygen-rich environment, the first eukaryotic cells came into being. One theory explaining the development of eukaryotic cells is the endosymbiotic theory, which suggests that bacteria were engulfed by larger cells. The bacteria remained in the larger cells and assumed specific functions, such as energy production or photosynthesis. This would explain the origin of mitochondria and chloroplasts, for example. The cells were then able to carry out more complex metabolic functions and eventually came to be the dominant life forms.

For billions of years, the only life on earth existed in the nutrient-rich environments of the oceans, lakes, and rivers. About 600 million years ago, as the atmosphere became rich in oxygen, living organisms began to colonize land. The first multicellular organisms were probably marine invertebrates (animals that lack backbones), followed by wormlike animals with stiff rods in their backs. These organisms, now called chordates, were the ancestors of the amphibians, reptiles, birds, and mammals.

# Human Evolution

Fossils and fragments of jaws suggest to scientists that the ancestors of monkeys, apes, and humans began their evolution approximately 50 million years ago. Additional evidence comes from studies of biochemistry and changes that occur in the DNA of cells.

Scientific evidence indicates that the first hominids (human-like organisms) belonged to a group called *Australopithecus*. Members of this group displayed a critical step in human evolution: the ability to walk upright on two feet. Although members of this group are considered the first hominids, they are not considered the first humans. Their brains were small in comparison with humans, and they had long, monkey-like arms. Members of this group eventually died out about one million years ago.

Fossils dating back to two million years ago have been found with brain capacities much larger than any *Australopithecus* fossil. On the basis of brain size, these fossils were called *Homo habilis*. *Homo habilis* is regarded as the first human. Members of this species were able to make tools, build shelters, and fashion protective clothing. They also walked upright on two feet. *Homo habilis* eventually became extinct approximately 35,000 years ago.

The first hominid to leave Africa for Europe and Asia was *Homo erectus*. Members of this species were about the same size as modern humans and were fully adapted for upright walking. Their brains were much larger than those of their ancestors, and they are believed to have developed the concept of language.

The earliest fossils of *Homo sapiens* date to about 200,000 years ago. Modern humans are classified in this species. The evolution from *Homo erectus* to *Homo sapiens* is thought to have taken place in Africa. Fossil evidence shows a gradual change in *Homo sapiens* over the last 200,000 years, but no new species have emerged.

# Biology

## Classification of Life (Taxonomy)

The earth is home to more than 300,000 species of plants and more than one million species of animals. Biologists have developed a scheme for organizing and classifying this diversity of living organisms. The classification scheme is based on the work of Carolus Linnaeus, a Swedish physician and botanist who published several books describing thousands of plants and animals. Linnaeus developed the two-part binomial taxonomy system of categorizing organisms according to genus and species. The work of Linnaeus has been combined with the work of Charles Darwin in the field of evolution to form the foundation of modern taxonomy.

Taxonomists classify organisms in a way that reflects their ancestral relationships. All living organisms are named according to an international system in which the organism is given a binomial name. The first name reflects the genus in which the organism is classified, while the second name is the species modifier. For example, humans are assigned the name *Homo sapiens*. The generally accepted criterion for defining a species is that organisms of the same species interbreed under natural conditions to yield fertile offspring. Individuals of different species usually do not mate. If they are forced to mate, their offspring are usually sterile. For example, a horse (*Equus caballus*) can be mated with a donkey (*Equus assinus*); however, the offspring (a mule) is sterile and cannot reproduce.

The standard classification scheme provides a mechanism for bringing together various species into progressively larger groups. Taxonomists can classify two or more species together in the same genus. Similar genera are classified together within an order. Families are groups of similar orders.

Orders with similar characteristics are grouped into a class. Related classes are grouped together as divisions or phyla (divisions are used for plants and fungi, while phyla are used for animals and animal-like organisms). Divisions or phyla are grouped into kingdoms, while the broadest level of classification is the domain.

The classification scheme that is currently most widely accepted recognizes three domains: Domain Archaea, Domain Eubacteria, and Domain Eukarya. Domain Eukarya is subdivided into four kingdoms: Protista, Fungi, Plantae, and Animalia.

## Domain Archaea

Members of the domain Archaea are primitive bacteria, most of which are prokaryotic anaerobic organisms that use methane production in their energy metabolism. They are primarily found in marshes and swamps. This domain also includes the bacteria that thrive under extreme conditions, such as in hydrothermal vents and hot springs.

## Domain Eubacteria

Members of the Eubacteria are prokaryotic organisms. They can be found in virtually all environments on earth, including soil, water, and air. Most species of eubacteria are heterotrophic; they acquire their food from organic matter. The majority are saprobic, meaning they feed on dead and decaying organic matter. Some are parasitic, living within a host organism and causing disease. There also are several species of eubacteria that are autotrophic; they have the ability to synthesize their own food. Most of the autotrophic eubacteria use pigments to absorb light energy and make food through the process of photosynthesis. Some autotropic bacteria are chemosynthetic; they use chemical reactions as a source of energy from which they synthesize their own food.

Many eubacteria species are beneficial to the environment. Some are responsible for the decay of organic matter in natural ecosystems and thus, serve an important role as recylers of organic matter in an ecosystem. Other species are responsible for the decay of organic matter in landfills.

In the food industry, certain species of eubacteria are used to prepare many products, including cheeses, fermented dairy products, sauerkraut, and pickles. In other industries, eubacteria are used to produce antibiotics, chemicals, dyes, vitamins, and insecticides. In the human intestine, eubacteria are responsible for the synthesis of several vitamins that are not readily obtainable from food, especially vitamin K.

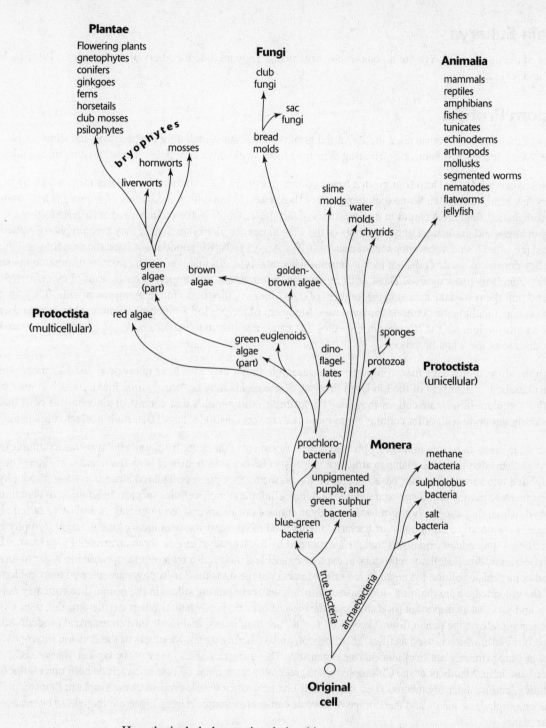

Hypothetical phylogenetic relationships among organisms.

Unfortunately, many eubacteria are pathogenic, causing diseases in plants, animals, and humans. Such diseases as tuberculosis, gonorrhea, syphilis, pneumonia, and food poisoning are causes by eubacterial organisms.

The cyanobacteria are photosynthetic members of the eubacteria. As autotrophs, they are important components of the plankton found in oceans, and they contribute a significant amount of oxygen to the atmosphere. Scientists believe the cyanobacteria were among the first photosynthetic organisms to colonize the earth's surface, playing a large role in oxygenating the atmosphere, which in turn, made possible the development of all life-forms that use oxygen in their metabolism.

# Domain Eukarya

Members of the domain Eukarya are all eukaryotic organisms. They include members of the kingdoms Protista, Fungi, Plantae, and Animalia.

# Kingdom Protista

Members of the kingdom Protista are a highly varied group of organisms, including the protozoa, the slime molds, and the algae. Many species are autotrophs, creating their own food, while others are heterotrophs, feeding on organic matter.

The protozoa are subdivided into four groups based on their method of locomotion. Flagellates move about by using one or more whip-like flagella. Some members are zooflagellates, living within the bodies of animals. These include the wood-digesting flagellates found in the intestines of termites, as well as the pathogenic zooflagellates that cause sleeping sickness and giardiaia. Other members of the Flagellates are phytoflagellates; they contain photosynthetic pigments and are often found as components of plankton. The Amoeboids (Rhizopoda) contains the amoebas and their relatives. They consist of single cells that lack a definite shape and typically feed on small particles of organic matter, which they engulf by phagocytosis. These cells move using pseudopods, or temporary extensions of cytoplasm that anchor and pull the rest of the cell along. Members of the Ciliates (Ciliophora) move by means of cilia. They are all heterotrophic and include the common *Paramecium*. Members of the phylim Apicomplexa are exclusively parasites. Included in this phylum are the *Plasmodium* species that cause malaria and *Toxoplasma gondii*, which causes toxoplasmosis, a disease of the white blood cells.

Although the slime molds have many properties that resemble fungi, they also have many protozoa-like properties and, thus, are classified as members of the kingdom Protista. Slime molds may be "true" slime molds, which consist of a single, flat, large, multinucleate cell, or they may be "cellular" slime molds that consist of amoeba-like cells that live independently but unite with other cellular slime mold cells to form a single, large, flat, multinucleate organism.

The term algae refers to a large number of photosynthetic organisms that range from unicellular forms to complex, multicellular organisms that resemble plants in structure. Algal species occur in bodies of both fresh and salt water. The algae are subdivided into several divisions based in part on the pigments they possess. The red algae (Division Rhodophyta) are almost exclusively marine organisms and include both unicellular and multicellular species. In addition to containing chlorophyll, which they use in photosynthesis, red algae contain one of several red pigments. A derivative of red algae called agar is commonly a component of bacterial media used in laboratories. Members of the division Pyrophyta are dinoflagellates—unicellular organisms that are surrounded by thick plates that give them an armored appearance. Under optimal conditions, dinoflagellates reproduce at explosive rates and their red-brown pigments cause the water to turn a blood-red color. This condition is known as red tide. Members of the division Chrysophyta are referred to as golden algae. Most of the golden algae are diatoms—organisms with cell walls containing silica. In the ocean, diatoms carry out photosynthesis and serve as an important food source at the base of oceanic food chains. When the diatoms die, their silica "shells" accumulate on the ocean floor. The silica "shells" are then mined and made into commercial products such as diatomaceous earth, which is used as filler, an absorbent, and a filtering agent. Members of the division Phaeophyta, the brown algae, are primarily multicellular marine organisms. This group includes many of the typical "seaweeds" such as rock-weed and kelp. Members of the Chlorophyta, the green algae, are quite diverse and include both unicellular forms and complex, multicellular organisms. They share many characteristics with members of the kingdom Plantae, including the same chlorophyll pigments and the storage of starch as an energy source. Green algae are thought to be the ancestors of higher plants.

# Kingdom Fungi

Fungi, together with eubacteria and some protists, are the major decomposers of organic matter on earth. Most fungi are saprobes, digesting nonliving organic matter such as wood, leaves, and dead animals. However, some fungi are parasitic, living off other living organisms. Parasitic fungi cause many diseases affecting plants, animals, and humans.

A unique physical structure and the method by which they obtain nutrients distinguishes fungi from the other kingdoms. Fungi secrete enzymes into the environment that break down organic matter, and then they absorb the nutrients through their cell membranes. This process is referred to as extracellular digestion.

A fungal organism consists primarily of cells joined in filaments. The filaments, called hyphae (singular, hypha), become intertwined, forming a large network called a mycelium (plural mycelia). The fungi are subdivided into four phyla based on their structure and mode of reproduction.

Members of the Phylum Zygomycota typically have multinucleate hyphae without cross walls between cells. Sexual reproduction in these organisms occurs when sexual hyphae of opposite mating types fuse and form spores called zygospores. A common member of the Zygomycota is the black bread mold *Rhizopus stolonifer*. This species forms a white or gray mass of mycelium on bread, fruits, or vegetables. Sporangia, containing asexual spores, develop on the mycelia and can be seen as black balls extending into the air on small stalk-like structures.

Members of the Ascomycota are quite diverse in structure. They range from unicellular yeasts to powdery mildews to large cup fungi and morels. During sexual reproduction, members of the Ascomycota form a sac-like structure called an ascus, where hyphae of two mating types meet. Within the sac, several ascospores develop, each of which can reproduce an entire fungal organism.

Members of the Basidiomycota are known as club fungi. They include the common mushroom, the shelf fungi, and puffballs, as well as the rusts and smuts. When hyphae from two mating types fuse, a fruiting body called the basidiocarp develops. The basidiocarp is what we typically think of as a "mushroom."

Some fungal organisms have lost the ability to reproduce sexually and only reproduce through the production of asexual spores. These fungi are referred to as imperfect fungi and are classified in the phylum Deuteromycota. Members of this phylum include species of the genera *Penicillium* and *Aspergillus*. *Penicillum notaum* is the original source of the antibiotic penicillin, and *P. camembertii* is used in the production of camembert cheese.

Lichens are associations between a fungal organism and a cyanobacteria or a green alga. The cyanobacteria (or alga) photosynthesizes, providing nutrients for themselves and the fungus, while the fungal organism provides water and minerals to both organisms. Lichens exist in many environments, including several environments that are considered harsh or extreme.

# Kingdom Plantae

Plants are multicellular eukaryotic organisms with the ability to produce their own food through the process of photosynthesis. They are divided into two main groups: the nonvascular plants and the vascular plants. Nonvascular plants do not have specialized tissues for transporting water and nutrients, while vascular plants do have such tissues.

The life cycle of plants has both a multicelluar diploid phase and a multicellular haploid phase. Because both phases of the life cycle are multicellular, plants are said to go through an alternation of generations. In contrast, animal life cycles typically have a multicellular diploid phase and a unicellular haploid phase. The alternating generations of plants are the sporophyte (diploid) generation and the gametophyte (haploid) generation. Individuals in the gametophyte generation produce gametes, haploid sex cells that contain one set of chromosomes. Haploid gametes fuse during fertilization to produce diploid zygotes with two sets of chromosomes. The plants that develop from the zygotes represent the sporophyte generation. Individuals in the sporophyte generation undergo meiosis to produce haploid spores that develop into gametophytes. Plants produce their gametes in specialized structures. The egg cells are formed in structures called archegonia, and sperm cells are produced in structures called antheridia.

## Nonvascular Plants

Nonvascular plants belong to the division Bryophyta, which includes the mosses, liverworts, and hornworts. Because these plants lack vascular tissue, they cannot grow very large and cannot retain water for extended periods of time. This is why bryophytes are typically found in moist areas. They also must rely on the presence of water for fertilization to occur. The male gametophytes produce numerous sperm that swim in drops of rainwater or dew into the neck of the archegonia on female gametophytes and fertilize egg cells at the base of the archegonia. The zygotes that result from fertilization develop into young sporophytes within the archegonia. The sporophytes grow out of the archegonia, obtaining nourishment from the gametophytes. The sporophytes spend their entire existence attached to and nourished by the gametophyte. Each sporophyte consists of a slender stalk with a spore capsule on the end. Haploid spores are produced as meiosis occurs in cells within the spore capsule and are dispersed when the capsule dries and breaks open. The spores settle onto the soil, where they germinate and grow into new gametophyte plants. In the bryophytes, the gametophyte generation is the larger and most commonly observed stage of the life cycle.

## Vascular Plants

The vascular plants encompass several divisions of plants and are collectively referred to as Trachyophytes. They are characterized by the presence of two types of specialized tissue, the xylem and the phloem. Xylem conducts water and minerals upward through the plant, while phloem transports sugars from the leaves, where they are made during photosynthesis, to other parts of the plant body. The vascular tissue also serves as a means of support in the plant, so vascular plants are capable of maintaining a much larger size than nonvascular plants.

In all vascular plants, the sporophyte generation is the dominant form in the life cycle. In some plants, seeds are the structures through which the sporophyte generation emerges, while other plant species do not form seeds during their life cycle. Among the seed-producing vascular plants are those that produce unprotected seeds (the gymnosperms) and those that produce seeds enclosed in protective fruit tissue (angiosperms).

### Seedless Vascular Plants

Among the seedless vascular plants are the ferns and fern allies. A mature fern sporophyte produces spores through meiosis. The spores are stored in small structures called sori (singular sorus) on the undersides of the fern leaves (fronds). The sori resemble small yellow-orange fuzzy dots. After the spores are dispersed, they germinate into small heart-shaped gametophytes called prothallia. Each prothallus contains both antheridia and archegonia. Sperm produced in the antheridia swim through moisture on the gametophyte plants to the egg cells contained in the archegonia, where fertilization occurs. The zygote produced in fertilization develops into a young sporophyte. As the sporophyte continues to develop into a mature fern plant, the gametophyte breaks down and disintegrates. Other seedless vascular plants include the whisk ferns, the club mosses, and the horsetails. Most of these groups represent extant specimens of ancient species that have mostly gone extinct.

### Vascular Plants with Unprotected Seeds

The vascular plants that produce unprotected ("naked") seeds are known as gymnosperms. Their seeds are not enclosed within tissues of the female parent. There are four divisions of gymnosperms: Cycadophyta (cycads), Ginkgophyta (*Ginkgo*), Gnetophyta (*Ephedra* and *Welwhitchia*), and Coniferophyta (conifers).

The conifers are the largest and most familiar group of gymnosperms and include the pines, spruces, and firs. The mature trees (sporophyte generation) bear male and female cones. Meiosis occurs in spores within the cones to produce male and female gametophytes. The male gametophytes (also called microgametophytes) are the pollen grains, which produce sperm, while the female gametophytes (megagametophytes) produce two or three egg cells that develop within the ovules.

In the spring, the male cones release pollen, which is blown about by the wind, and ultimately some will land on female cones of the same species. The pollen grains germinate inside the female cones and form pollen tubes that grow down to the ovule. The sperm cells migrate through the pollen tube to fertilize the egg. The zygote produced in fertilization develops into an embryo within the ovule. In time, the ovule develops into a mature seed, which germinates and grows into a new mature sporophyte. Both male and female gametophytes are very tiny, reduced to nothing more than a reproductive mechanism in the gymnosperms. The gametophytes are entirely dependent on the dominant sporophyte generation for survival.

### Vascular Plants with Protected Seeds

The angiosperms are the most developed and complex of the vascular plants. They are the flowering plants, of which more than a quarter of a million species have been identified. The seeds of angiosperms develop within protective tissues of the female parent. The flower of the angiosperm consists of a ring of modified leaves called sepals that enclose and protect the developing flower bud. In some species the sepals are small and green, while in others they become colored and resemble petals, the next ring of modified leaves found in the flower. Flower petals are usually colorful and serve to attract pollinators. Within the petals are two sets of modified leaves that serve as the reproductive structures. The stamens (male reproductive structures) consist of a stalk called the filament with a bulbous structure at the end called the anther. Cells in the anther undergo meiosis to produce pollen grains (the male gametophytes). The pistil (female reproductive structure) consists of a tubular structure called the style, with a sticky surface called the stigma at the top and an enlarged region (the ovary) at the base.

Within the ovary, the megagametophtye (also known as the embryo sac) develops through meiosis within a megaspore mother cell, followed by three mitotic divisions. The mature embryo sac consists of eight nuclei. Cells walls form around six of the nuclei individually, leaving two nuclei in the center cell. Thus, a mature female gametophyte consists of only seven cells and eight nuclei. One of those cells is the egg cell, which sits between two other cells called synergids. At the opposite end of the embryo sac are three cells called antipodals. The two nuclei in the center cell are referred to as polar nuclei.

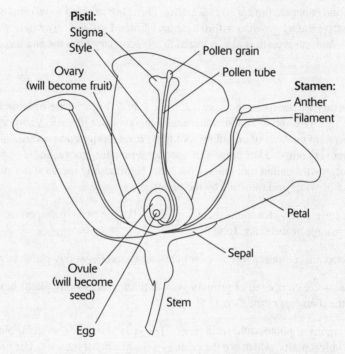

The structural features of a typical flower.

During pollination, pollen grains land on the stigma where they germinate and form a pollen tube. The pollen tube grows down the style and into an opening in the ovary called the micropyle. When the pollen tube reaches the ovary, two sperm cells are released. One sperm cell unites with the egg cell in the embryo sac to form a diploid zygote, while the second sperm unites with both polar nuclei to form a triploid endosperm. The synergids and antipodals disintegrate.

Within the ovule, the zygote develops into an embryo surrounded by the endosperm, which serves as nutritive tissue for the developing embryo. The ovary tissue expands, forming a fruit, which serves as a protective covering for the developing seed. Thus, a fertilized ovule becomes a seed, while the ovary tissue surrounding the ovule develops into a fruit. The protective fruit tissue also serves as an important dispersal mechanism. Fleshy fruits are often eaten by animals, and the seeds "travel" inside the animal to another location where they will be "dispersed" when the animal defecates. Some fruits have barbs or hooks on the outer fruit that attach to the fur of animals and are dispersed in that manner. Other fruits are dry upon maturity. Some of these split open quite forcefully, ejecting their seeds great distances, while other dry fruits have thin paper tissue attached to them that serve as "wings" for dispersal by wind.

## Structure and Function of Vascular Plants

Vascular plants have four types of tissue: vascular tissue, ground tissue, dermal tissue, and meristematic tissue. Vascular tissues include xylem, which conducts water and minerals from the roots upward throughout the plant, and phloem, which transports dissolved foods in all directions throughout the plant.

The ground tissue of the vascular plant is responsible for storing carbohydrates produced by the plant. It comprises the majority of the young plant body and is located between the vascular tissue and the dermal tissue. The ground tissue in leaves contains the majority of the chloroplasts found in the plant body and is responsible for making food for the plant through photosynthesis.

The dermal tissue functions to protect the plant from injury and water loss. Dermal tissue covers the outside of the plant and consists primarily of epidermal cells in herbaceous (non-woody) plants and periderm in woody plants. Other cells in the dermal tissue include guard cells that surround stomata. The stomata are pores in leaves and young stems through which gases and water vapor are exchanged with the atmosphere.

Meristematic tissue is the location of most of the cell division that occurs in the plant. The meristematic cells give rise to cells that differentiate into vascular tissue, ground tissue, and dermal tissue. Growth generally occurs in meristematic tissues. At the tips of stems and roots are the apical meristems. These are referred to as primary meristems and are responsible for growth in length (primary growth) within the plant. Lateral growth (growth in width) occurs through cell division in lateral meristems. Lateral growth is also referred to as secondary growths and takes place in woody plants.

## Plant Organs

The three organs found in plants are the roots, the stems, and the leaves. Flowers are modified leaves. The roots function to anchor the plant to a substrate and to take in water and minerals from the soil. Various plants have different types of root systems. A tap root system consists of one main root that grows straight downward, with lateral roots growing out of it. A fibrous root system is composed of numerous, slender, branching roots. Some of the epidermal cells of roots are modified into slender outgrowths called root hairs. Root hairs significantly increase the surface area of the root, greatly enhancing the uptake of water and minerals by the plant.

The stems of vascular plants have several functions including support of the plant, transport of water, minerals, and sugars by the vascular system, and storage of water and food.

In herbaceous plants, the stems are composed mostly of primary tissue, while woody plants have much secondary growth.

The stems of herbaceous plants are composed of primary growth tissue, and woody plants have secondary growth tissue that causes a thickening of the diameter of the stem.

The leaves are the principal organs of photosynthesis in plants. The ground tissue in vascular plant leaves contains numerous cells that are filled with chloroplasts, which are the primary sites of photosynthesis. The presence of stomata on the leaves of vascular plant allows for gas exchange (mainly carbon dioxide and oxygen) between the plants' cells and the atmosphere. Stomatas also allow for evaporation of water vapor from the surfaces of the leaves. Evaporation of water from the leaves causes a tension in the cells of the xylem, which in turn causes the roots of the plant to take up additional water from the soil.

## Kingdom Animalia

Animals are multicellular eukaryotic organisms. They differ from plants in that they are heterotrophic; they take in food and digest it into smaller components. The primary mode of reproduction in animals is sexual. Two major groups of animals exist: the invertebrates and the vertebrates.

## Invertebrates

Invertebrates are animals that do not have a backbone, and vertebrates are animals with backbones. The invertebrates are represented by numerous phyla and comprise approximately 95 percent of all animal species.

The phylum Porifera includes a number of simple animals commonly referred to as sponges. Sponges filter and consume fine particles of food through their pores. Cells lining the body cavity digest suspended food particles, and waste is excreted through a central opening. Sponges are typically asymmetrical and have a relatively simple cellular organization. The body wall contains a protective layer of flat cells on the outside and an inner layer of flagellated cells, with a gelatinous filling in between. The cells of sponges act independently and there is no evidence of tissue organization. Most live attached to rocks, plants, or other animals in marine environments.

Members of the phylum Cnidaria include hydras, jellyfish, corals, and sea anemones. Cnidarians show simple tissue organization and have a body plan displaying radial symmetry. That is, they are circular with structures that radiate outward. The ends of these structures have tentacles with stinging devices called cnidoblasts that help in defense and trapping food. Digestion occurs within a central cavity, called the gastrovascular cavity. Cnidarians also have a loose network of nerve cells that coordinate the animals' activities.

Members of the phylum Platyhelminthes are flatworms, such as planaria and tapeworms. These animals display bilateral symmetry, meaning the left and right halves of their body are mirror images of each other. Platyhelminthes are also characterized by cephalization, which means that one end of the animal functions as a "head." The "head" contains a mass of nerve cells that act as a brain and specialized regions for sensing light, chemicals, and pressure. Platyhelminthes have three distinct layers of tissue and true organs that function in digestion, movement, excretion, and reproduction. The digestive system consists of a muscular tube with one opening at the mouth. The excretory system consists of a network of water-collecting tubules that empty into sacs leading to the exterior. Movement occurs by contraction of muscle cells that lie below the epidermis.

The phylum Aschelminthes is also known as Nematoda. Its members are nematodes, or roundworms, and many are microscopic. Nematodes share many of the same characteristics as flatworms. Some are free-living organisms that help consume dead plant and animal matter; however, others are parasitic and cause human diseases, including trichinosis and hookworm.

Members of the phylum Annelida are segmented worms, such as earthworms and leeches. The segmented worms display bilateral symmetry, cephalization, an open digestive system, and a true body cavity, called a coelom. The coelom is a fluid-filled space lined with cells in which internal organs are suspended. Within this cavity, the digestive and reproductive organs have evolved into complex structures. The circulatory system is closed, and blood is circulated by contraction of muscular vessels called hearts. Each segment on the animals' body has longitudinal and circular muscles that contract, compressing fluid to form a water-based skeleton called a hydrostatic skeleton.

Members of the phylum Mollusca are soft-bodied animals, such as the snail, clam, squid, oyster, and octopus. Some members secrete a hard shell. All mollusks have a muscular organ called a foot that is used for gripping or creeping over surfaces. These animals each have a head with a mouth; a brain or sense organ; and groups of internal organs for circulation, excretion, respiration, and reproduction.

The largest number of species in the animal kingdom belongs to the phylum Arthropoda. Members of this phylum, called arthropods, include spiders, ticks, centipedes, lobsters, and insects. Arthropods are characterized by having an external skeleton, a segmented body, and jointed appendages. The external skeleton, called an exoskeleton, surrounds the animal and provides support. The bodies of arthropods are usually divided into distinct regions called the head, thorax, and abdomen. Respiration occurs through microscopic holes in the exoskeleton and body wall. The largest group of arthropods is the insects. Insects have well-developed organs for various senses including smell, touch, taste, and hearing. Insects have three pairs of jointed legs and most have one or two pairs of wings.

The phylum Echinodermata includes members having an internal skeleton and a water-based pressure system for locomotion. The structure of echinoderm embryos suggests an ancestry to the phylum Chordata. Echinoderms have spiny skin that helps protect them from predators. Members of this phylum include sea stars, brittle stars, sea urchins, and sea cucumbers. All echinoderms have an internal support system called an endoskeleton and a large body cavity containing a set of canals called a water vascular system.

The phylum Chordata includes both invertebrate members and members that have a backbone (vertebrates). All chordates have bilateral symmetry, a head, a body cavity, a digestive system, and body segmentation. In addition, chordates share several structures that distinguish them from members of the other phyla. One such structure is the notochord; a stiff-yet-flexible rod of tissue extending the length of the animal to provide support. A second unique structure is a hollow nerve chord (also called a spinal cord) that extends the length of the animal just above the notochord. Another unique characteristic of chordates is the presence of gill slits—paired openings from the back of the organisms mouth to the outside of the body. Not all characteristics exist in the adult form of chordates; some exist only in the embryonic stages. The most primitive chordates are invertebrates, including tunicates and lancelets, animals that resemble tadpoles and are typically found clinging to rocks in marine environments.

## Vertebrates

Members of the phylum Chordata that have backbones are classified in the subphylum Vertebrata. There are more than 40,000 living species of vertebrates, divided into several classes encompassing the fishes, amphibians, reptiles, birds, and mammals.

Fishes are aquatic animals with a streamlined shape and a functional tail that allows them to move rapidly through water. Fishes exchange gases with their environment through gills, although a few species have lungs that supplement gas exchange.

The amphibians are animals that live both on land and in the water. They are represented by frogs, toads, and salamanders. Amphibians live on land and breathe air to meet their oxygen demands, however, they also are able to exchange gases through their skin and the inner lining of their mouth. Amphibians remain in moist environments to avoid dehydration, and lay their eggs in water because the sperm and egg use water to allow them to come in contact. Young amphibians (for example tadpoles) lead an aquatic life before emerging onto land as adults.

Reptiles dominated the earth for a period of more than 150 million years. The modern survivors include lizards, snakes, crocodiles, alligators, and turtles. Reptiles display a number of adaptations that support their life on land. They have a dry, scaly skin that retards water loss, and the structure of their limbs provides better support for moving quickly on land. Their lungs have a greater surface area than those of amphibians, allowing greater quantities of air to be inhaled. The circulatory system in reptiles includes a three-chambered heart that separates oxygen-rich blood from oxygen-poor blood. Reproduction in reptiles occurs exclusively on land.

Birds have many structural adaptations for flight. For example, the body is streamlined to minimize air resistance, and the endoskeleton bones are light and hollow. To enable flight, birds also have feathers, which are lightweight adaptations of reptilian scales. Feathers also serve to insulate against loss of body heat and water. Birds are homeothermic, meaning they are able to maintain a constant body temperature. The rapid pumping of their four-chambered heart and a high blood flow rate contribute to this characteristic.

Mammals are animals that have hair and nourish their young with milk produced by mammary glands. The presence of body hair or fur helps maintain a constant body temperature in these homeothermic animals. Several types of mammals exist: the monotremes, marsupials, and placentals. The Monotremes are egg-laying mammals that produce milk. The duck-billed platypus and the spiny anteater are monotremes. Marsupials are mammals whose embryos develop within the mother's uterus for a short period of time before birth. After birth, the immature babies crawl into the mother's abdominal pouch where they complete their development. Kangaroos, opossums, and koala bears are marsupials. The placental mammals include rabbits, deer, dogs, cats, whales, monkeys, and humans. These mammals have a placenta—a nutritive connection between the embryo and the mother's uterine wall. Embryos are attached to the placenta and complete their development within their mother's uterus. Mammals have a highly developed nervous system, and many have developed acute senses of smell, hearing, sight, taste, or touch. Mammals rely on memory and learning to guide their activities. They are considered the most successful group of animals on earth today.

# Human Anatomy and Physiology

## Nutrition and Digestion

Nutrition refers to the activities by which living organisms obtain raw materials from their environment and transport them into their cells. The cells metabolize these raw materials and synthesize structural components, enzymes, energy-rich compounds, and other biologically important substances. All the elements and compounds taken into a living organism are nutrients. Animals, including humans, are heterotrophic organisms, and their nutrients consist of preformed organic molecules. These organic molecules are rarely in forms that can be directly absorbed. Therefore, they must be processed into usable forms by digestion.

The nutrients used by animals include carbohydrates, lipids, nucleic acids, proteins, minerals and vitamins. Carbohydrates are the basic source of energy for all animals. Glucose is the carbohydrate most often used as an energy source; it is metabolized during cellular respiration to provide energy in the form of adenosine triphosphate (ATP). Other useful carbohydrates include maltose, lactose, sucrose, and starch.

Lipids are used to form cellular and organelle membranes, the sheaths surrounding nerve fibers, and certain hormones. One type of lipid, fat, is an extremely useful energy source.

Nucleic acids are used for the construction of deoxyribonucleic acid (DNA) and ribonucleic acid (RNA). They are obtained from plant and animals tissues. During digestion, the nucleic acids are broken down into their component nucleotides, which are absorbed into the cells.

Proteins form the framework of the animal body. They are essential components of the cytoplasm, membranes, and organelles. They are also the major constituents of muscles, ligaments, and tendons, as well as enzymes. Proteins are composed of 20 different amino acids. While some amino acids can be synthesized, others must be supplied to the diet. During digestion, proteins are broken down into their constituent amino acids, which are then absorbed into the body.

Among the minerals required by animals are phosphorous, sulfur, potassium, magnesium, and zinc. Animals usually obtain these minerals when they consume plants. Vitamins are organic compounds essential in trace amounts for animal health. Some vitamins are water-soluble, while others are fat-soluble.

# The Human Digestive System

The human digestive system is a complex process that consists of breaking down large organic masses into smaller particles that the body can use as fuel. The major organs or structures that coordinate digestion in humans include the mouth, esophagus, stomach, small intestine, and large intestine.

In the human body, the mouth is a specialized organ for receiving food and breaking up large organic masses into smaller particles. This is accomplished through a combination of biting and chewing by the teeth and moistening by saliva. Also, saliva contains an enzyme, called amylase, which digests starch molecules into smaller sugar molecules. During chewing, the tongue moves food around and manipulates it into a mass called a bolus. The bolus is pushed back into the pharynx (throat) and is forced through the opening to the esophagus.

The esophagus is a thick-walled muscular tube located behind the windpipe that extends through the neck and chest to the stomach. The bolus of food moves through the esophagus by a series rhythmic muscular contractions (peristalsis). The esophagus joins the stomach at a point just below the diaphragm. A valve-like ring of muscle called the cardiac sphincter surrounds the opening to the stomach. The sphincter relaxes as the bolus passes through and then quickly closes.

The stomach is an expandable pouch located high in the abdominal cavity. Layers of stomach muscle contract and churn the bolus of food with gastric juices to form a soupy liquid called chyme. The stomach stores food and prepares it for further digestion. The chyme spurts from the stomach through a sphincter into the small intestine.

An adult's small intestine is about 23 feet long and is divided into three sections: the first 10–12 inches form the duodenum; the next 10 feet form the jejunum; and the final 12 feet form the ileum. Most chemical digestion takes place in the duodenum. In this region, enzymes digest nutrients into simpler forms that can be absorbed by the body. Intestinal enzymes are supplemented by enzymes from the pancreas, a large glandular organ lying near the stomach. In addition, bile enters the small intestine from the gall bladder to assist in fat digestion. Most absorption in the small intestine occurs in the jejunum, and is completed in the ileum. Substances that have not been digested or absorbed then pass into the large intestine.

The large intestine, also known as the colon, is about three feet in length. The colon's chief functions are to absorb water and to store, process, and eliminate the residue following digestion and absorption. The intestinal matter remaining after water has been reclaimed is known as feces. Feces consist of nondigested food particles, billions of mostly harmless bacteria, bile pigments, and other materials. The feces are stored in the rectum and passed out through the anus to complete the digestion process.

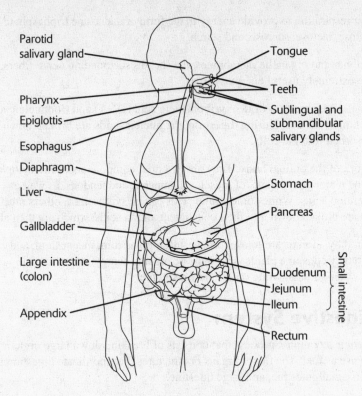

Parotid salivary gland

Pharynx

Epiglottis

Esophagus

Diaphragm

Liver

Gallbladder

Large intestine (colon)

Appendix

Tongue

Teeth

Sublingual and submandibular salivary glands

Stomach

Pancreas

Duodenum
Jejunum
Ileum

Small intestine

Rectum

The human digestive system.

# Human Respiratory System

The human respiratory system consists of a complex set of organs and tissues that capture oxygen from the environment and transport the oxygen to the lungs. The organs and tissues that comprise the human respiratory system include the nose, pharynx, trachea, and lungs. The human respiratory system begins with the nose, where air is conditioned by warming and moistening. Hairs and hair-like cilia trap dust particles and purify the air. The nasal chambers open into a cavity at the rear of the mouth called the pharynx (throat). From the pharynx, two tubes called Eustachian tubes open to the middle ear to equalize pressure. The pharynx also contains tonsils and adenoids, which are pockets of lymphatic tissue used to trap and filter microorganisms.

After passing through the pharynx, air passes into the windpipe, or trachea. The opening to the trachea is a slit-like structure called the glottis. A thin flap of tissue called the epiglottis folds over the opening during swallowing and prevents food from entering the trachea. At the upper end of the trachea, several folds of cartilage form the larynx, or voicebox. In the larynx, flap-like tissues called vocal cords vibrate when a person exhales and produce sounds. At its lower end, the trachea branches into two large bronchi. These tubes branch into smaller bronchioles, which terminate into sacs called alveoli.

Human lungs are composed of approximately 300 million alveoli, which are cup-shaped sacs surrounded by a capillary network. Red blood cells pass through the capillaries, and oxygen from each alveolus enters and binds to the hemoglobin. In addition, carbon dioxide contained in the red blood cells and blood plasma leaves the capillaries and enters the alveoli when a breath is taken.

# Human Circulatory System

The human circulatory system functions to transport blood and oxygen from the lungs to the various tissues of the body. The heart pumps the blood throughout the body. The lymphatic system is an extension of the circulatory system that includes cell-mediated and antibody-mediated immune systems. The components of the human circulatory system include the heart, blood, red and white blood cells, platelets, and the lymphatic system.

The human heart is about the size of a clenched fist. It contains four chambers: two atria and two ventricles. Oxygen-poor blood enters the right atrium through a major vein called the vena cava. The blood passes into the right ventricle and is pumped through the pulmonary artery to the lungs for gas exchange. Oxygen-rich blood returns to the left atrium via the pulmonary vein. The oxygen-rich blood flows into the left ventricle, from which it is pumped through a major artery, the aorta. Coronary arteries supply the heart muscle with blood. The heart is controlled by nerves that originate on the right side in the upper region of the atrium at a node called the pacemaker.

Blood is the medium of transport in the human body. The fluid portion of the blood, the plasma, is a straw-colored liquid composed primarily of water. All the important nutrients, the hormones, the clotting proteins, and waste products are transported in the plasma. Red blood cells and white blood cells are also suspended in the plasma.

Red blood cells are called erythrocytes. These are disk-shaped cells produced in the bone marrow. They do not have a nucleus and are filled with hemoglobin. Hemoglobin is a red-pigmented protein that binds loosely to oxygen and carbon dioxide. It is the mechanism of transport for these substances. Red blood cells commonly have immune-stimulating antigens on their surfaces.

White blood cells are called leukocytes. They are generally larger than red blood cells and have clearly defined nuclei. They are also produced in the bone marrow and have various functions in the body. Certain white blood cells, called lymphocytes, are essential components of the immune system. Other cells, called neutrophils and monocytes, function primarily as phagocytes; they attack and engulf invading microorganisms.

Platelets are small disk-shaped blood fragments produced in the bone marrow. They lack nuclei and are much smaller than erythrocytes. They serve as the starting material for blood clotting.

The lymphatic system is an extension of the circulatory system consisting of a fluid known as lymph, capillaries called lymphatic vessels, and small structures called lymph nodes. Lymph is a watery fluid derived from plasma that has seeped out of the blood system capillaries. It enters a series of lymphatic vessels that return the fluid to the circulatory system. Along the way, it passes through hundreds of tiny, capsule-like bodies called lymph nodes. Located in the neck, armpits, and groin, the lymph nodes contain cells that filter the lymph and phagocytize foreign particles. The spleen is composed primarily of lymph node tissue, and is the site where red blood cells are destroyed.

# Human Excretory System

The human excretory system functions to remove waste from the body. This system includes the kidney and its functional unit, the nephron. The human kidneys are the major organs of bodily excretion. They are bean-shaped organs located on either side of the backbone at about the level of the stomach and liver. Blood enters the kidneys through renal arteries and leaves through renal veins. Tubes called ureters carry waste products from the kidneys to the urinary bladder for storage or release. The product of the kidneys is urine, a watery solution of waste products, salts, organic compounds, uric acid, and urea. Uric acid results from nucleic acid decomposition and urea results from amino acid breakdown in the liver. Both of these nitrogenous compounds can be poisonous to the body and must be removed in the urine. The functional and structural unit of the kidney is the nephron; it produces urine and is the primary unit of homeostasis in the human body.

# Human Endocrine System

The human body has two levels of coordination: nervous coordination and chemical coordination. Chemical coordination is centered on a system of glands known as endocrine glands. These glands are situated throughout the body and include such glands and organs as the pancreas, thyroid, pituitary gland, and adrenal gland. These glands secrete hormones, which bring about changes that help coordinate body systems.

The pituitary gland is located at the base of the human brain. One of the hormones secreted by the pituitary gland, human growth hormone (HGH), promotes body growth by accelerating protein synthesis. Another pituitary hormone, lactogenic hormone (LH), promotes breast development and milk secretion in females. A third pituitary hormone, thyroid-stimulating hormone (TSH), control secretion of hormones from the thyroid gland, while a fourth hormone, adrenocorticotropic hormone (ACTH) controls secretion of hormones from the adrenal gland. Additional hormones produced by the pituitary gland include follicle-stimulating hormone (FSH), which stimulates the development of follicles (that contain eggs) in females and the production of sperm in males; luteinizing hormone (LH), which stimulates the secretion of female hormones in the corpus luteum; and interstitial cell-stimulating hormone (ICSH), which stimulates production of male hormones in the testes. Melanocyte-stimulating hormone (MSH), which stimulates production of the pigment melanin, also is secreted by the pituitary gland. In addition, the pituitary gland stores and then releases two hormones that are produced in the hypothalamus of the brain. One is antidiuretic hormone (ADH), which stimulates water re-absorption in the kidneys. The other is oxytocin, which stimulates uterine muscle contractions during childbirth.

The thyroid gland lies against the pharynx at the base of the neck. It produces thyroxine, a hormone that regulates the rate of metabolism in the body, and calcitonin, which regulates the level of calcium in the blood. Thyroxine production depends on the availability of iodine. A deficiency of iodine causes thyroid gland enlargement (a condition called goiter). An undersecretion of thyroxine in babies results in a condition known as cretinsism (dwarfism with abnormal body proportions and possible mental retardation). In adults, an under-secretion results in myxedema, characterized by physical and mental sluggishness. Thyroxine over-secretion results in an unusually high metabolic rate and Grave's disease.

The adrenal glands are two pyramid-shaped glands lying atop the kidneys. These glands secrete a family of steroids called corticosteroids, including cortisol and cortisone, which control glucose metabolism and protein synthesis in the body. They also serve as anti-inflammatory agents. Another hormone produced by the adrenal glands, epinephrine (adrenaline), increases heart rate, blood pressure, and blood supply to skeletal muscles, and is therefore useful in stressful situations to promote the fight-or-flight response.

The pancreas is located just behind the stomach. It produces two hormones: insulin and glucagon. Insulin is a protein that promotes passage of glucose molecules into the body's cells and regulates glucose metabolism. In the absence of insulin, glucose is removed from the blood and excreted in the kidneys; a condition known as diabetes mellitus, which is characterized by heavy urination, excessive thirst, and a sluggish metabolism. Glucagon stimulates the breakdown of glycogen to glucose in the liver and releases fat from adipose tissue so the fat can be used for the production of carbohydrates.

The ovaries in females and testes in males also function as endocrine glands. The ovaries secrete estrogens, which encourage the development of secondary female characteristics. The testes secrete androgens (including testosterone), which promote secondary male characteristics. The hormones in the endocrine system function to regulate homeostasis.

# Human Nervous System

Nervous coordination enables the body to rapidly respond to external or internal stimuli. The human nervous system is divided into the central nervous system (the brain and spinal cord) and the peripheral nervous system (the nerves extending to and from the central nervous system). The spinal cord of the central nervous system is a cord of tissue passing through the bony tunnel made by the vertebrae of the spine. It extends from the base of the brain to the bottom of the backbone. Three membranes called meninges surround the spinal cord and protect it. The neurons of the spinal cord serve as a coordinating center for the reflex arc and a connecting system between the peripheral nervous system and the brain.

The brain is the organizing and processing center of the central nervous system. It is the site of consciousness, sensation, memory, and intelligence. The brain receives impulses from the spinal cord and from 12 pairs of cranial nerves coming from and extending to the other senses and organs. The brain can also initiate activities without external stimuli. Three majors regions of the brain are recognized: the hindbrain, the midbrain, and the forebrain.

The hindbrain consists of the medulla, cerebellum, and pons. The medulla is a mass located at the tip of the brain and serves as a passageway for nerves extending to and from the brain. The cerebellum lies adjacent to the medulla and serves as a coordinating center for motor activity, coordinating muscle contractions. The pons is the mass located between the medulla and the midbrain. It acts as a bridge between various regions of the brain.

The midbrain lies between the hindbrain and forebrain. It consists of a collection of crossing nerve tracts and is the site of reticular formation, a group of fibers that arouse the forebrain when something unusual happens.

The forebrain consists of the cerebrum, thalamus, hypothalamus, and limbic system. The cerebrum is the site of such activities as speech, vision, movement, hearing, and smell. Higher mental activities such as learning, memory, logic, creativity, and emotion also occur in the cerebrum. The thalamus serves as an integration point for sensory impulses, while the hypothalamus synthesizes hormones for storage in the pituitary gland. The hypothalamus also serves as the control center for such visceral functions as hunger, thirst, body temperature, and blood pressure.

The limbic system is a collection of structures that ring the edge of the brain and function as centers of emotion.

The peripheral nervous system is a collection of nerves that connect the brain and spinal cord to other parts of the body and the external environment. The sensory somatic system carries impulses from the external environment and the senses. It permits humans to be aware of the outside environment and react to it voluntarily. The autonomic nervous system works on an involuntary basis. One subdivision of the autonomic nervous system, the sympathetic nervous system, prepares the body for emergencies. Impulses propagated by the sympathetic nervous system cause the heartbeat to increase, the arteries to constrict, and the pupils to dilate. The other subdivision, the parasympathetic nervous system allow the body to return to its normal state following an emergency.

## Human Reproductive System

Reproduction is an essential process for the survival of a species. Human reproduction takes place by the coordination of the male and female reproductive systems. In humans, both males and females have evolved specialized organs and tissues that produce haploid cells by meiosis, the sperm and the egg. These cells fuse to form a zygote that eventually develops into a growing fetus. A network of hormones is secreted that controls both the make and female reproductive systems and assists in the growth and development of the fetus, as well as the birthing process.

The male reproductive organs are the testes (or testicles). The testes are two egg-shaped organs located in a pouch outside the body called the scrotum. Sperm production in the testes takes place within coiled passageways called seminiferous tubules. Within the tubules, primitive cells called spematogonia undergo meiosis to yield sperm cells. The organ responsible for carrying the sperm cells to the female reproductive tract is the penis. Within the penis, the sperm are carried in a tube called the urethra. The sperm are mixed with secretions from the prostate gland, seminal vesicles and Cowper's glands. These secretions and the sperm cells together constitute the semen.

The organs of the female reproductive system include the ovaries, two oval organs lying within the pelvic cavity, and adjacent to them, two Fallopian tubes. The Fallopian tubes are the passageways that eggs enter after they are released from the ovaries following meiosis. The Fallopian tubes lead to the uterus, a muscular organ in the pelvic cavity. The inner lining of the uterus, called the endometrium, thickens with blood and tissue in anticipation of a fertilized egg cell. If fertilization fails to occur, the endometrium degenerates and is shed in the process of menstruation.

The opening at the lower end of the uterus is a constricted area called the cervix. The tube leading from the cervix to the exterior is a muscular organ called the vagina. The vagina receives the penis and the semen. The sperm cells in the semen pass through the cervix and uterus into the Fallopian tubes, where fertilization takes place. Fertilization brings together 23 chromosomes from the male (sperm) and 23 chromosomes from the female (egg), resulting in the formation of a fertilized egg cell (called a zygote) with 46 chromosomes—the number present in normal human cells.

## Practice Questions

*The following questions are based on some of the material you have read in this chapter and your own knowledge of Life Science. For each question, select the choice that best answers the question. When you're finished, check your answers against those that follow this test.*

1. In the human reproductive system, fertilization of the egg by the sperm takes place in the

   A. vagina
   B. uterus
   C. Fallopian tube
   D. ovary

2. In a food chain, autotrophic organisms that produce their own food are called _____, while heterotrophic organisms that feed on autotrophs are called _____.

   A. decomposers, producers
   B. producers, consumers
   C. primary consumers, secondary consumers
   D. prey, predators

3. Interactions between the organisms in communities and their physical environment form _____.

   A. food chains
   B. food webs
   C. populations
   D. ecosystems

4. A reproductive cell containing 30 chromosomes will produce _____ cells with _____ chromosomes during meiosis.

   A. 2, 30
   B. 2, 15
   C. 4, 30
   D. 4, 15

5. The _____ is the genetic make-up of an individual, while the _____ is the physical appearance of the individual.

   A. gene, allele
   B. genotype, phenotype
   C. phenotype, genotype
   D. chromosome, protein

6. Which of the following series of events represents the Central Dogma of Molecular Biology?

   A. protein → DNA → mRNA
   B. protein → mRNA → DNA
   C. DNA → mRNA → protein
   D. DNA → protein → mRNA

7. Which of the following lines of evidence in support of evolution is based in part on the fact that the genetic code is virtually identical in all living organisms?

   A. embryology
   B. paleontology
   C. comparative biochemistry
   D. comparative anatomy

8. Which of the following mechanisms of evolution is most likely to result in a decrease in genetic variation within a population?

   A. mutation
   B. migration
   C. natural selection
   D. genetic drift

9. Between 3 and 3.5 billion years ago, simple prokaryotic organisms evolved that were able to capture energy from the sun and create their own food, releasing oxygen into the atmosphere as a by-product. These organisms are known as

   A. plants
   B. green algae
   C. cyanobacteria
   D. eukaryotes

10. *Homo sapiens* is believed to have descended from

    A. Homo erectus
    B. Homo habilis
    C. Homo africanus
    D. Australopithecus africanus

11. Which of the following is an identifying cellular feature for bacteria?

    A. bacterial cells are eukaryotic
    B. bacterial cells are prokaryotic
    C. bacterial cells contain mitochondria
    D. bacterial cells have a nucleus

12. Which of the following groups of organisms is NOT classified in the kindgom Protista?

    A. protozoans
    B. algae
    C. fungi
    D. slime molds

13. Lichens are an example of a mutualistic relationship between which of the following pairs of organisms?

    A. algae and cyanobacteria
    B. algae and protozoa
    C. cyanobacteria and slime molds
    D. cyanobacteria and fungi

14. Bryophytes (mosses, liverworts, and hornworts) are members of which of the following groups of plants?

    A. vascular, fruit-producing
    B. vascular, seed-producing
    C. vascular, spore-producing
    D. non-vascular

**15.** Following fertilization in flowering plants, the _____ becomes the fruit and the _____ becomes the seed.

    **A.**  ovule, ovary

    **B.**  ovary, ovule

    **C.**  ovule, egg

    **D.**  egg, ovary

**16.** The tissue responsible for conducting water and minerals through the plants from the roots upward is known as

    **A.**  meristem

    **B.**  xylem

    **C.**  phloem

    **D.**  epidermis

**17.** Which of the following phyla includes both members that have backbones and members without backbones?

    **A.**  Porifera

    **B.**  Cnidaria

    **C.**  Echinodermata

    **D.**  Chordata

**18.** _____ spend part of their life on land and part of their life in water.

    **A.**  sponges

    **B.**  fishes

    **C.**  amphibians

    **D.**  reptiles

**19.** Which of the following represents the correct order of structures through which food travels in the human digestive system?

    **A.**  mouth → duodenum → esophagus → stomach → large intestine

    **B.**  mouth → pancreas → stomach → small intestine → large intestine

    **C.**  mouth → esophagus → stomach → large intestine → small intestine

    **D.**  mouth → esophagus → stomach → small intestine → large intestine

**20.** Oxygen-poor blood enters the human heart through the _____, is pumped to the lungs where it receives oxygen, and returns to the heart through the _____.

    **A.**  right atrium, left atrium

    **B.**  left atrium, right atrium

    **C.**  left ventricle, right ventricle

    **D.**  pulmonary artery, vena cava

**21.** Which of the following hormones is NOT produced by the pituitary gland?

    **A.**  epinephrine

    **B.**  human growth hormone

    **C.**  lactogenic hormone

    **D.**  follicle-stimulating hormone

**22.** The human nervous system is subdivided into

    **A.**  the spinal cord and the brain.

    **B.**  the sympathetic nervous system and the parasympathetic nervous system.

    **C.**  the central nervous system and the peripheral nervous system.

    **D.**  the autonomic nervous system and the sympathetic nervous system.

**23.** Which of the following structure-function pairs is mismatched?

    **A.**  ribosome—protein synthesis

    **B.**  mitochondrion—cellular respiration

    **C.**  chloroplast—photosynthesis

    **D.**  nucleus—ATP production

**24.** The process by which green plants manufacture food in the form of glucose is

    **A.**  photosynthesis

    **B.**  photorespiration

    **C.**  cellular respiration

    **D.**  fermentation

**25.** Which of the following events takes place during the S portion of interphase?

    **A.**  spindle fibers are formed

    **B.**  DNA molecules are replicated

    **C.**  DNA molecules are copied onto mRNA

    **D.**  sister chromatids separate from each other

# Answers and Explanations

1. **C.** In human females, eggs are produced by the ovaries (D) and move into the Fallopian tubes. Semen containing sperm is deposited in the vagina (A) by the penis of a male. The sperm move through the vagina and through the uterus (B) into the Fallopian tubes where fertilization of the egg takes place.

2. **B.** In any food chain, the autotrophic organisms are called producers; they are capable of synthesizing their own food through photosynthesis. Heterotrophic organisms that must obtain their food by eating other organisms are called consumers. Primary consumers feed directly on the producers, while secondary consumers eat the primary consumers. Decomposers can be found at each level of the food chain and are responsible for breaking down organic matter.

3. **D.** An ecosystem is formed through the interaction of the living organisms in communities and their physical environment (rocks, soil, light, air, water). Food chains (A) and food webs (B) describe the transfer of energy among organisms in an ecosystem. A population (C) is a group of individuals of the same species occupying a defined area.

4. **D.** Meiosis leads to the production of four haploid daughter cells from one diploid parent cell.

5. **B.** The genetic make-up of an individual constitutes that individual's genotype, while the appearance of the individual (the expression of the genes in the genotype) constitutes that individual's phenotype. An allele is one version of a gene (A); for example, the red allele at the gene for flower color. The chromosome (D) is the physical structure that contains the DNA of an organism, but does not itself confer the genotype.

6. **C.** The order of events in the conversion of the genetic code on the DNA molecule to the amino acid code of a polypeptide begins with the copying of the DNA message onto a mRNA molecule during transcription, followed by the conversion of the message encoded on the mRNA molecule to a polypeptide during translation. This series of events is known as the Central Dogma of Molecular Biology.

7. **C.** Comparative biochemistry includes the study of the components of DNA, RNA, and proteins. Embryology (A) is concerned with the study of embryo development; paleontology (B) is the study of fossils; and comparative anatomy (D) is concerned with the similarities and differences in anatomical features of different organisms.

8. **D.** Genetic drift occurs when a population is reduced to a very small number of individuals, and the likelihood that genes will be lost from the gene pool is quite high, leading to a decrease in genetic variation in the gene pool. Both mutation (A) and migration (B) promote genetic variation by introducing new alleles or genes into a population. Natural selection (C) is a force that operates in conjunction with mutation to ensure the most reproductively fit individuals survive and pass on their genes to the next generation. Depending on the selection pressures present, natural selection may lead to an increase, a decrease, or have no affect on genetic variation in a population; however, it is typically associated with an increase in genetic variation, and is the driving force behind the evolution of new species.

9. **C.** Cyanobacteria are thought to be the first photosynthetic, autotrophic organisms to inhabit the earth. Other organisms including plants (A), green algae (B), and other eukaryotes (D) could not exist on earth without the oxygen produced as a byproduct of photosynthesis in the relatively simple (prokaryotic) cyanobacteria.

10. **A.** *Homo sapiens* (the species to which modern humans belong) descended from *Homo erectus*. *Homo habilis*, (B) pre-dated *Homo erectus*, while *Australopithecus aficanus* (D) pre-dated *Homo habilis*. There was no such species as *Homo africanus* (C).

11. **B.** Only bacteria have prokaryotic cells. All other groups of living organisms have eukaryotic cells.

12. **C.** Fungi are classified in their own kingdom (kingdom Fungi). The other organisms listed are all classified in the kingdom Protista.

13. **D.** The mutualistic relationship found in lichens is typically between a fungal species and a species of cyanobacteria, although some lichens are composed of a fungal species and a green alga.

14. **D.** Bryophytes are non-vascular plants; they do possess vascular conducting tissues (xylem and phloem).

**15. B.** Following fertilization in flowering plants, the ovary develops into a fruit, while the ovule develops into a seed. The egg is fertilized by a sperm cell in the pollen grain and becomes the zygote, which develops into an embryo, and eventually a young plant.

**16. B.** Xylem is responsible for conducting water and minerals upward in the plant from the roots. Phloem (C) is responsible for conducting dissolved sugars made during photosynthesis throughout the plant. A meristem (A) is a region of actively dividing cells. Epidermis (D) is the outer cell layer of the plant, generally covering all plant surfaces where it serves as a protective barrier.

**17. D.** Phylum Chordata includes both members that lack backbones (e.g., tunicates and lancelets) and members that have backbones (e.g., fishes, amphibians, reptiles, birds, and mammals). The other phyla listed only contain invertebrate members.

**18. C.** Amphibians spend the early part of their life cycle (from the egg stage through the tadpole stage) in water before moving onto land, where they spend their adult stages. Sponges (A) and fishes (B) spend their entire life cycle in the water, whereas, reptiles (D) spend their entire life cycle on land.

**19. D.** Movement of food in the human digestive system begins in the mouth where it is chewed and moisturized to form a bolus. It then moves down the esophagus to the stomach where it is combined with gastric juices and churned into a soupy liquid called chyme. From the stomach, it moves into the small intestine where much of the digestion and absorption occurs. Any substances that have not been digested or absorbed move into the large intestine, which processes the residue into feces for elimination from the body.

**20. A.** The pathway for blood through the human heart starts when oxygen-poor blood enters the right atrium through a major vein called the vena cava. The blood passes through the tricuspid valve into the right ventricle, and is then pumped through the pulmonary artery to the lungs for gas exchange. Oxygen-rich blood returns to the left atrium of the heart through the pulmonary vein. It then flows through the bicuspid (mitral) valve into the left ventricle, from which it is pumped through a major artery called the aorta.

**21. A.** Epinephrine is made by the adrenal glands.

**22. C.** The two major subdivisions of the human nervous system are the central nervous system (the brain and spinal cord) and the peripheral nervous system (the network of nerves that connect the brain and spinal cord to other parts of the body and to the external environment). Thus, the spinal cord and the brain (A) are both components of the same nervous system (the central nervous system). The peripheral nervous system is further subdivided into the sensory somatic system (which carries impulses from the external environment) and the autonomic nervous system (an involuntary system). The autonomic nervous system is subdivided into the sympathetic nervous system (which prepares the body for emergencies) and the parasympathetic nervous system (which allows the body to return to its normal state following an emergency).

**23. D.** The nucleus contains the genetic information for an organism in the form of DNA. ATP is produced by cellular respiration, which takes place in the mitochondria and the cytoplasm.

**24. A.** Answers B, C, and D are all forms of cellular respiration, which is the process by which organisms break down glucose to obtain energy.

**25. B.** DNA is replicated during the S (synthesis) portion of interphase. The spindle fibers (A) are formed during prophase. The copying of a DNA molecule into mRNA (C) occurs during transcription and is not part of the cell cycle. Sister chromatids separate from each other (D) during anaphase.

# Physical Science Review

This section of the book is designed to evaluate your understanding of the basic concepts studied in the Physical Sciences including: The Laws of Force and Motion; The Principles of Energy; The Properties of Fluids and Gases; Atomic Structure; and the Principles of Chemistry. You will undoubtedly find much of this material on whatever Nursing exam you plan to take, as well as in the classroom.

Read through the material, answer the questions at the end of the chapter, and check the answers carefully to ensure your complete understanding of the material.

# Chemistry

Chemistry is called the central science because all branches of the physical and life sciences are intricately related to matter. Since matter is made of atoms, a study of the types of atoms, their properties alone and in combination with other atoms, and the transformation from one material to another is very important. In this section, a brief review of chemical principles is included along with an overview of some important elements and their uses.

## Matter and Atomic Structure

**Matter** is defined as anything with a definite mass that takes up volume. There are three common states of matter with which you are familiar: solids, liquids, and gases. Matter can be made of simple things like diamond, water, or neon, or it can be made of very complex things like heat-resistant shields on the Space Shuttle, blood plasma, or anesthesiology gases. There are several considerations when looking at the differences between solids, liquids, and gases, but they can be summarized as follows: **solids** have a defined mass, volume, and shape; **liquids** have a defined mass and volume, but not a defined shape; **gases** have a defined mass, but not a defined volume or shape (they will expand to fill any container).

All of the matter you see and use is made of a few fundamental particles called protons, neutrons, and electrons. These **subatomic particles** make up atoms. **Atoms** are specific collections of protons and neutrons surrounded by electrons. Each of these subatomic particles is different by mass and charge, as seen in the following table.

| Comparison of Subatomic Particles Making up Atoms | | | |
|---|---|---|---|
| **Subatomic particle** | **Symbol** | **Actual mass (grams)** | **Relative Charge** |
| Proton | p or p$^+$ | $1.672 \cdot 10^{-24}$ | +1 |
| Neutron | n | $1.674 \cdot 10^{-24}$ | 0 |
| Electron | e or e$^-$ | $9.109 \cdot 10^{-28}$ | −1 |

Protons and neutrons are located at the center of the atom and make up a region called the **nucleus**. Outside of the nucleus are the electrons that make up the electron cloud. The current model of an atom is fairly complex, but the following figure shows a simplified but useful model. The electrons are not randomly arranged in the electron cloud, but occupy locations called orbitals. These orbitals can be arranged in shells. The illustration shows how electrons can be arranged in shells around the nucleus of an atom, although the actual picture is much more complex than this "solar system model" of the atom would suggest.

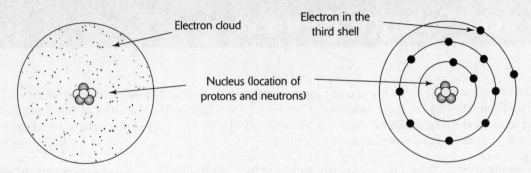

With these three particles, atoms can be made, and from these atoms, every solid, liquid, and gas in the universe is formed. Conceivably, there could be an infinite number of combinations of subatomic particles, but not all combinations are stable. In fact only 112 elements have been found or created. An **element** is a material that cannot be chemically broken down into something simpler. Elements are made of atoms, and as noted, atoms are made of electrons, protons, and neutrons.

## The Periodic Table

| 1A | | | | | | | | | | | | | | | | | 8A |
|---|---|---|---|---|---|---|---|---|---|---|---|---|---|---|---|---|---|
| 1<br>**H**<br>1.00794 | 2A | | | | | | | | | | | 3A | 4A | 5A | 6A | 7A | 2<br>**He**<br>4.00260 |
| 3<br>**Li**<br>6.941 | 4<br>**Be**<br>9.01218 | | | | | | | | | | | 5<br>**B**<br>10.811 | 6<br>**C**<br>12.011 | 7<br>**N**<br>14.0067 | 8<br>**O**<br>15.9994 | 9<br>**F**<br>18.99840 | 10<br>**Ne**<br>20.1797 |
| 11<br>**Na**<br>22.98977 | 12<br>**Mg**<br>24.305 | 3B | 4B | 5B | 6B | 7B | ←— | 8B | —→ | 1B | 2B | 13<br>**Al**<br>26.9815 | 14<br>**Si**<br>28.0855 | 15<br>**P**<br>30.97376 | 16<br>**S**<br>32.066 | 17<br>**Cl**<br>35.4527 | 18<br>**Ar**<br>39.948 |
| 19<br>**K**<br>39.0983 | 20<br>**Ca**<br>40.07838 | 21<br>**Sc**<br>44.9556 | 22<br>**Ti**<br>47.88 | 23<br>**V**<br>50.9415 | 24<br>**Cr**<br>51.994 | 25<br>**Mn**<br>54.938 | 26<br>**Fe**<br>55.847 | 27<br>**Co**<br>58.9332 | 28<br>**Ni**<br>58.6934 | 29<br>**Cu**<br>63.546 | 30<br>**Zn**<br>65.39 | 31<br>**Ga**<br>69.723 | 32<br>**Ge**<br>72.61 | 33<br>**As**<br>74.9216 | 34<br>**Se**<br>78.96 | 35<br>**Br**<br>79.904 | 36<br>**Kr**<br>93.80 |
| 37<br>**Rb**<br>85.4678 | 38<br>**Sr**<br>87.62 | 39<br>**Y**<br>88.9059 | 40<br>**Zr**<br>91.224 | 41<br>**Nb**<br>92.9064 | 42<br>**Mo**<br>95.94 | 43<br>**Tc**<br>(98) | 44<br>**Ru**<br>101.07 | 45<br>**Rh**<br>102.9055 | 46<br>**Pd**<br>105.42 | 47<br>**Ag**<br>107.868 | 48<br>**Cd**<br>112.41 | 49<br>**In**<br>114.82 | 50<br>**Sn**<br>118.710 | 51<br>**Sb**<br>121.757 | 52<br>**Te**<br>127.60 | 53<br>**I**<br>126.9045 | 54<br>**Xe**<br>131.29 |
| 55<br>**Cs**<br>132.9045 | 56<br>**Ba**<br>137.33 | 57<br>**La**<br>138.9055 | 72<br>**Hf**<br>178.49 | 73<br>**Ta**<br>180.9479 | 74<br>**W**<br>183.85 | 75<br>**Re**<br>186.207 | 76<br>**Os**<br>190.2 | 77<br>**Ir**<br>192.22 | 78<br>**Pt**<br>195.08 | 79<br>**Au**<br>196.966 | 80<br>**Hg**<br>200.59 | 81<br>**Ti**<br>204.383 | 82<br>**Pb**<br>207.2 | 83<br>**Bi**<br>208.98 | 84<br>**Po**<br>(209) | 85<br>**At**<br>(210) | 86<br>**Rn**<br>(222) |
| 87<br>**Fr**<br>(223) | 88<br>**Ra**<br>226.0254 | 89<br>**Ac**<br>(227) | 104<br>**Rf**<br>(261) | 105<br>**Ha**<br>(263) | 106<br>**Sg**<br>(263) | 107<br>**Ns**<br>(265) | 108<br>**Hs**<br>(265) | 109<br>**Mt**<br>(266) | 110<br>**–**<br>(269) | 111<br>**–**<br>(272) | 112<br>**–**<br>(277) | | | | | | |

| 58<br>**Ce**<br>140.12 | 59<br>**Pr**<br>140.9077 | 60<br>**Nd**<br>144.24 | 61<br>**Pm**<br>(145) | 62<br>**Sm**<br>150.36 | 63<br>**Eu**<br>151.965 | 64<br>**Gd**<br>157.25 | 65<br>**Tb**<br>158.9253 | 66<br>**Dy**<br>162.50 | 67<br>**Ho**<br>164.9303 | 68<br>**Er**<br>167.26 | 69<br>**Tm**<br>168.9342 | 70<br>**Yb**<br>173.04 | 71<br>**Lu**<br>174.967 |
|---|---|---|---|---|---|---|---|---|---|---|---|---|---|
| 90<br>**Th**<br>232.0381 | 91<br>**Pa**<br>231.0359 | 92<br>**U**<br>238.029 | 93<br>**Np**<br>237.0482 | 94<br>**Pu**<br>(244) | 95<br>**Am**<br>(243) | 96<br>**Cm**<br>(247) | 97<br>**Bk**<br>(247) | 98<br>**Cf**<br>(251) | 99<br>**Es**<br>(252) | 100<br>**Fm**<br>(257) | 101<br>**Md**<br>(258) | 102<br>**No**<br>(259) | 103<br>**Lr**<br>(260) |

The Periodic Table

To save time and space, elements have been assigned a one or two-letter designation called an **atomic** or **elemental symbol**. For some elements, the symbol is readily determined from the name of the element; the elemental symbol for hydrogen is H, for helium it is He, for calcium it is Ca. Some elements have elemental symbols based on the Latin name of the element; the symbol for silver is Ag, for sodium it is Na, for iron it is Fe, and for mercury it is Hg. Whether the symbol is based on the Latin name or the English name, one rule remains constant: always capitalize the first letter and, if there is a second letter, always write that in lowercase. Without this rule, some chemical formulas might be misinterpreted. (Co is the symbol for cobalt, but CO is the symbol for a compound containing one carbon atom and one oxygen atom). A list of all atomic symbols is given by the periodic table.

Though it may appear to have an unusual shape, the periodic table is an incredibly useful document. Reading left to right across the periodic table, the elements are arranged in order of the number of protons in their nucleus (the number of protons in a nucleus is called an element's **atomic number**). Thus, the element hydrogen is listed first since atoms of hydrogen have only one proton in the nucleus. The element helium has two protons in the nucleus, so it is listed second.

The atomic number of iron (Fe) is 26 so it has 26 protons in its nucleus and is listed just after manganese (Mn, atomic number 25) and just before cobalt (Co, atomic number 27). The atomic number is a very important concept in chemistry. Not only does every iron atom have 26 protons in its nucleus, but any atom that has 26 protons in its nucleus *must be* an iron atom. The atomic number is the defining characteristic of an atom. All atoms of the same element must have the same number of protons but can have differing numbers of neutrons and electrons.

If the number of electrons is the same as the atomic number (number of protons), then the atom is neutral since there are the same number of equal negative and positive charges from the electrons and protons, respectively. If there are fewer electrons than protons, a **cation** (pronounced CAT-ion) will result which will have a positive charge. Metals usually form cations (*for example*, Ag forms $Ag^+$). If there is an excess of electrons compared to the number of protons, a negative charge will arise on the atom resulting in an **anion** (pronounced AN-ion). Non-metals usually form anions (*for example*, N forms $N^{3-}$). An atom, or group of atoms, with a charge is called an **ion**.

Elements that have the same number of protons, but different numbers of neutrons, are called **isotopes**. An example of an element with two isotopes is copper. All copper atoms contain 29 protons, however 69% of copper atoms contain 34 neutrons and 31% contain 36 neutrons. The two types of copper atoms will have different masses because they have a different number of neutrons; however, they are both copper atoms. Magnesium is an element with three isotopes; all magnesium atoms have 12 protons, but 79% have 12 neutrons, 10% have 13 neutrons, and 11% have 14 neutrons. To differentiate between these isotopes, a value called the mass number is used. The **mass number** of an element is the number of protons and neutrons in an atom. Thus, 79% of magnesium atoms have a mass number of 24, 10% have a mass number of 25, and 11% have a mass number of 26.

This difference in atomic composition is reflected by the atomic mass (or atomic weight) of an element. In the periodic table, it is the number found underneath each atomic symbol. By definition the **atomic mass** is the average mass of all the naturally occurring isotopes of an element. The atomic mass of magnesium is listed as 24.305 amu (atomic mass units), although no atom of Mg actually has this mass; it is obtained by averaging the masses of the three Mg isotopes. The atomic mass also includes the mass of the electrons, and there is even a third subtle reason why the atomic numbers do not come out even, but that reason is beyond the scope of this book.

Another piece of useful information found within the periodic table is the number of electrons found in the outer shell of an atom. These electrons are known as the **valence electrons** and are responsible for holding atoms together when making a compound. Each column in the periodic table is called a **group** or **family**, and each group of atoms has a similar configuration of electrons. Taking a look at the first column of the periodic table (1A), you will find H, Li, Na, K, Rb, Cs, and Fr. Each of these elements has only one electron in its outer shell; group 2A elements have two electrons in their outer shell; group 8A elements have 8 electrons in their outer shell.

The periodic table gets its name from the repetitive trends occurring for the elements when the elements are arranged by atomic number (*not* the atomic mass). This allows distinctions between the different elements and a major distinction is that of metals and non-metals. Notice that in the periodic table there is a dark "stair step" line found on the right-hand side of the periodic table. Elements to the left of the line are **metals**, elements to the right of the line are called **non-metals**, and elements that straddle the line are called **metalloids** (or **semimetals**). Two exceptions to this rule are hydrogen (H) and aluminum (Al). Clearly, hydrogen is a non-metal, though it is often written to the left of the bold line and aluminum is a metal, despite the fact that it is next to the bold line.

## Atoms, Molecules, and Compounds

From the periodic table, you can see that there are several dozen different elements. Think for a moment about the matter around you. The number of different materials, colors, odors, tastes, and tactile sensations is almost limitless. How can 112 different elements make up the billions of different materials that we perceive everyday? Most of the materials you see are not made of just one type of element. Most of the materials are made of compounds. **Compounds** are substances with two or more *different* atoms of an element bound together. Examples of compounds are water ($H_2O$), sulfuric acid (battery acid, $H_2SO_4$), sodium hydrogen carbonate (baking soda, $NaHCO_3$), sucrose (table sugar, $C_{12}H_{22}O_{11}$), and sodium chloride (table salt, NaCl). Each of these substances is made of more than one kind of element. If those elements are nonmetals (*that is*, $H_2O$, $H_2SO_4$, and $C_{12}H_{22}O_{11}$), they are classified as molecules. **Molecules** are collections of non-metalic atoms that are tightly bound together. In the case where atoms of a metal and a non-metal are bound together (*that is*, NaCl or $Na_2CO_3$), they are classified as **formula units**.

Some elements also occur in molecular form, and examples include oxygen ($O_2$), hydrogen ($H_2$), nitrogen ($N_2$), and fluorine ($F_2$). Thus, when chemists speak of elemental hydrogen, they actually refer to two hydrogen atoms bound together in a diatomic molecule, which is different than just two atoms of hydrogen.

A compound will have different properties than the elements that make it up. Thus, hydrogen is a gas at room temperature and is quite flammable, oxygen is a gas at room temperature that supports combustion, but water (made from hydrogen and oxygen) is a *liquid* at room temperature and *doesn't* burn or support combustion. Because water has different properties than the elements that comprise it, water is a compound of hydrogen and oxygen, not simply a mixture.

# Chemical Equations and Reactions

In order to describe the chemical changes that are occurring around and inside of you, chemists have developed a short-hand notation in which the symbols for elements and compounds are written showing the chemical change. An example of a chemical equation is the combustion of propane ($C_3H_8$) with elemental oxygen ($O_2$) to form carbon dioxide ($CO_2$) and water ($H_2O$).

$$C_3H_8 + O_2 \rightarrow CO_2 + H_2O$$

The equation is written with **reactants** on the left and the **products** of the reaction on the right. The arrow shows that a reaction is taking place. While this shows the transformation of propane and oxygen into two different compounds, the equation is not quite complete. Because of the **Law of Mass Conservation**, matter cannot be created or destroyed, and the same kind and number of atoms must be on each side of the reaction arrow. Thus, to correctly write the equation above, coefficients in front of each chemical species must be added to express the balanced equation.

$$C_3H_8 + 5O_2 \rightarrow 3CO_2 + 4H_2O$$

Thus, one molecule of propane will react with five molecules of oxygen to form three molecules of carbon dioxide and 4 molecules of water. Information about the state of the reactant or product is written after each chemical formula to indicate if that substance is a gas (g or ()), liquid (l), solid (s or ()), or dissolved in water (aq).

$$C_3H_8(g) + 5O_2(g) \rightarrow 3CO_2(g) + 4H_2O(l)$$

There are many different types of chemical reactions, however, some of these can be classified according to one of the four basic reaction types:

1. **Synthesis (or combination) reaction**: When two or more different substances react to form one compound.
   Examples: $Mg(s) + F_2(g) \rightarrow MgF_2(s)$
   $2Mg(s) + O_2(g) \rightarrow 2MgO(s)$
2. **Decomposition reaction**: When one substance breaks down into two or more different materials.
   Examples: $2NaHCO_3(s) \rightarrow Na_2CO_3(s) + CO_2(g) + H_2O(l)$
   $Cu(OH)_2(s) \rightarrow CuO(s) + H_2O(l)$
3. **Single replacement (or single displacement) reaction**: When an element reacts with a compound and an exchange takes place.
   Examples: $Zn(s) + CuBr_2(aq) \rightarrow Cu(s) + ZnBr_2(aq)$
   $3Ag(NO_3)(aq) + Al(s) \rightarrow Al(NO_3)_3(aq) + 3Ag(s)$
   In the first reaction, zinc (Zn) replaces copper (Cu) in the compound; in the second reaction, silver (Ag) replaces aluminum (Al).
4. **Double replacement (or double displacement or metathesis) reactions**: When two compounds react and an exchange occurs.
   Examples: $Ag(NO_3)(aq) + NaCl(aq) \rightarrow Na(NO_3)(aq) + AgCl(s)$
   $FeCl_3(aq) + 3Na(OH)(aq) \rightarrow 3NaCl(aq) + Fe(OH)_3(s)$
   In the first reaction, silver (Ag) and sodium (Na) exchange; in the second reaction iron (Fe) and sodium (Na) exchange.

# Acids, Bases, and Solutions

Although acids can be defined in alternative ways, an **acid** is commonly defined as a compound that increases the quantity of hydrogen ions ($H^+$) in an aqueous solution. A **base** is commonly defined as a compound that decreases the $H^+$ concentration by increasing hydroxide ($OH^-$) concentration. The **pH scale** is a measure of the degree to which a solution is acidic or basic. Solutions with low pH's (0–7) are considered acidic, solutions with a pH of exactly 7 are neutral (neither acidic nor basic), and solutions with a high pH (7-14) are considered basic. The farther the pH is from 7, the stronger is the acid or base. For example, pH 2 is a strong acid, pH 6 is a weak acid, and pH 8 is a weak base.

Because acids and bases are ubiquitous, it is a good idea to know some of the more common compounds that constitute acids and bases. Examples of common acids are

- acetic acid ($HC_2H_3O_2$) vinegar is a 5% solution of acetic acid
- carbonic acid ($H_2CO_3$) found in carbonated beverages, resulting from $CO_2$ dissolving in water
- citric acid ($H_3C_6H_5O_7$) found in citrus fruits and is responsible for their tangy flavor
- hydrochloric acid (HCl) found in gastric juices of humans
- nitric acid ($HNO_3$) used in fertilizer production
- phosphoric acid ($H_3PO_4$) used in colas to prevent bacterial growth and in fertilizer production
- sulfuric acid ($H_2SO_4$) the most industrially produced compound in the world, also used in car batteries

Examples of common bases:

- ammonia ($NH_3$) used as a general cleanser and in fertilizers
- lime (CaO) used to raise the pH of soil for farming
- lye (NaOH) used in the manufacture of soap
- milk of magnesia ($Mg(OH)_2$) used as an antacid
- sodium carbonate ($Na_2CO_3$) used in paper manufacturing and water softening

Pure water is neutral and is neither acidic nor basic. When acids and bases react, they form water and salt as the products.

$$\text{Example: } NaOH(aq) + HCl(aq) \rightarrow H_2O(l) + NaCl(aq)$$

The sodium hydroxide (base) reacts with hydrochloric acid to form water and sodium chloride (salt).

A **solution** is a homogeneous mixture that is composed of a **solvent** (the material in greater proportion) and a **solute** (the material dissolved in the solvent). Salt water is an example in which water is the solvent and sodium chloride (NaCl) is the solute.

# Important Elements of the Periodic Table

The first 20 elements of the periodic table are among the most abundant on earth and in the universe. These elements are important in the materials we use and especially in our own metabolic function.

**Hydrogen (H):** Atomic number: 1. A clear, colorless, odorless, low-density gas that is the most abundant element in the universe (although not on earth). It occurs as a diatomic molecule in its elemental form ($H_2$) and was used in balloons and dirigibles until the *Hindenburg* disaster. When hydrogen ions ($H^+$) are dissolved in water, they cause the solution to be acidic. Water is made of two parts hydrogen to one part oxygen ($H_2O$).

**Helium (He):** Atomic number: 2. This clear, colorless, odorless, low-density gas is the second most abundant element in the universe, although it is only present as a very small fraction of the Earth. Because it is not flammable, it is used as a substitute for hydrogen in balloons and blimps. It is very unreactive and occurs as single atoms in its elemental form.

**Lithium (Li):** Atomic number: 3. This low-density metal is very reactive in the elemental state, and easily forms a +1 ion ($Li^+$). A major use of lithium is to treat bipolar disorders like schizophrenia.

**Beryllium (Be):** Atomic number: 4. This low density metal is used in high-tech alloys for its strength, but machinists must be careful since the dust is very toxic.

**Boron (B):** Atomic number: 5. Boron is a metalloid, but its oxide finds use in heat resistant glass and in borax, a cleaning agent.

**Carbon (C):** Atomic number: 6. Carbon is a solid at room temperature, but it is a very versatile element. Diamond, one of the hardest substances known, and graphite, a material used as a lubricant and in pencil "lead," are both made of pure carbon. Obviously, these two materials are remarkably different, and their properties have to do with how the carbon atoms are bonded together. Carbon always forms four bonds and is one of the few elements that can form stable, long chains with itself. Carbon is the basis of organic chemistry. A major environmental concern is the production of carbon dioxide ($CO_2$) from the burning of fossil fuels. Although $CO_2$ only constitutes a small percentage of the overall atmosphere (less than 0.1%), it is one of the major contributors to the greenhouse effect.

**Nitrogen (N):** Atomic number: 7. This clear, colorless, odorless gas makes up more than 75 percent of the earth's atmosphere. In its elemental form, it occurs as a diatomic molecule ($N_2$) and is very stable. It is not flammable and reacts with very few other elements. SCUBA divers have to be careful about not rising to the water's surface too quickly or nitrogen bubbles can form in their blood vessels and cause the bends. A major use of nitrogen is in ammonia ($NH_3$) and in nitrates ($NO_3.$), both of which are used in fertilizers. Nitrogen isn't toxic, and it isn't metabolized by plants or animals, either. Certain bacteria (nitrogen-fixing bacteria) can metabolize nitrogen.

**Oxygen (O):** Atomic number: 8. Oxygen is a clear, colorless, odorless gas that supports combustion. It reacts with almost all elements to form stable oxides. In its elemental state, it is a diatomic molecule ($O_2$) and makes up ≈20% of the atmosphere. The ozone layer in the stratosphere is made of a triatomic oxygen molecule ($O_3$). Hydrogen peroxide ($H_2O_2$) is, common disinfectant for minor cuts, decomposes into water and molecular oxygen.

**Fluorine (F):** Atomic number: 9. Fluorine is a pale yellow gas that is very reactive. Elemental fluorine occurs as a diatomic molecule ($F_2$) and can etch glass. Compounds containing fluoride (F⁻, the anion of fluorine) are used in toothpaste to make tooth enamel more resistant to decay.

**Neon (Ne):** Atomic number: 10. Neon is a clear, colorless, odorless gas that is not flammable, nor does it support combustion. Neon is quite unreactive. It is used in "neon signs," but not exclusively, other gases may be used, too.

**Sodium (Na):** Atomic number: 11. Sodium is a shiny, soft, solid, reactive metal in its elemental state. It reacts vigorously with water to liberate elemental hydrogen and sometimes this reaction is violent enough to ignite the evolving $H_2$. It readily forms +1 cations ($Na^+$) and is only found in the cationic state in nature. It makes up a major constituent of ocean brine; table salt is made of one part sodium with one part chlorine (NaCl).

**Magnesium (Mg):** Atomic number: 12. Magnesium is a shiny, solid metal that reacts only slowly with water at room temperature. Elemental magnesium burns very brightly when ignited. Chlorophyll, a chemical responsible for the green color of plants and used by plants to capture the sun's energy, contains a magnesium atom in the center of the molecule.

**Aluminum (Al):** Atomic number: 13. Aluminum is a light, shiny, solid metal that is used in applications from soft drink cans to airplane wings. It is a durable metal that forms a thin oxide coating ($Al_2O_3$) that prevents further reaction. As a result, you often find aluminum in applications where iron would rust (*for example*, railings at a beach).

**Silicon (Si):** Atomic number: 14. Silicon is a solid, shiny semimetal whose oxide ($SiO_2$) is a major constituent in glass, sand, and quartz. Computer technology is a large user of elemental silicon on computer chips. Many caulking materials use silicone, a silicon-based polymer.

**Phosphorous (P):** Atomic number: 15. Phosphorous is a solid at room temperature, but can occur as white, red, or even black forms. White and red are the most common and can be symbolized as $P_4$. White phosphorous is so reactive it must be stored in water so it will not ignite spontaneously with oxygen in the air. Phosphate salts ($PO_{43}.$) are mined for use in fertilizers, matches, and even soft drinks.

**Sulfur (S):** Atomic number: 16. Sulfur is a yellow, brittle solid that is mined in its elemental form ($S_8$). The major use of sulfur is as sulfuric acid ($H_2SO_4$) which finds many industrial uses, but the common consumer is familiar with its use in car batteries. Sulfur emissions from coal burning power plants results in the formation of sulfur oxides ($SO_2$ and $SO_3$), which ultimately are converted to $H_2SO_4$, the principal acid in acid rain.

**Chlorine (Cl):** Atomic number: 17. Chlorine is a greenish-yellow gas with a choking odor. In its elemental form it is diatomic ($Cl_2$), toxic, and quite reactive. This element readily forms anions with a –1 charge ($Cl^-$). This ion is a major constituent of ocean brine and when reacted with sodium will form table salt. Bleach consists of a solution of hypochlorite ($ClO^-$), a chlorine-oxygen anion. Swimming pools are kept relatively free of mold and bacteria by chemicals that contain chlorine. Ozone destruction in the stratosphere is thought to occur when chlorofluorocarbons (CFCs) are subjected to high-intensity ultraviolet radiation causing chlorine atoms to be torn off CFC molecules and react with $O_3$.

**Argon (Ar):** Atomic number: 18. Argon is a clear, colorless, odorless, non-reactive gas that makes up ≈1% of the atmosphere. Its major uses are in light bulbs to blanket tungsten filaments, "neon" signs, and in welding to avoid more reactive gases (*for example*, oxygen) from reacting with hot materials.

**Potassium (K):** Atomic number: 19. Potassium is a shiny, soft, solid, reactive metal in its elemental state. It reacts with water even more vigorously than sodium to liberate hydrogen. In nature, only the +1 cation ($K^+$) is found, not the elemental state. Potassium is an important nutrient in muscle contraction and is used in fertilizers.

**Calcium (Ca):** Atomic number: 20. Calcium is a shiny metal that reacts with water more vigorously than magnesium, but not enough to ignite the liberated hydrogen like sodium and potassium metals. Calcium readily forms a +2 cation ($Ca^{2+}$) and is a major constituent of tooth enamel ($Ca_5(PO_4)_3(OH)$) and bones. Marble is the mineral calcium carbonate ($CaCO_3$) and lime, used to reduce soil acidity, is $CaO$.

By looking at the various descriptions of the elements, note that there is a reoccurrence of properties. This periodic nature of the elements is why the periodic table is so useful. Some of the groups of the periodic table are particularly important.

**Group 1A, The Alkali Metals.** This group consists of Li, Na, K, Rb, Cs, and Fr and all react to form +1 ions. These elements form salts that are soluble in water.

**Group 2A, The Alkaline Earth Metals.** This group consists of Be, Mg, Ca, Sr, Ba, and Ra and all react to form +2 ions.

**Group 5A, The Pnictogens.** This group consists of N, P, As, Sb, and Bi and all react to form –3 ions.

**Group 6A, The Chalcogens.** This group consists of O, S, Se, Te, and Po and all react to form –2 ions.

**Group 7A, The Halogens.** This group consists of F, Cl, Br, I, and At and all react to form –1 ions.

**Group 8A, The Noble Gases.** This group consists of He, Ne, Ar, Kr, Xe, and Rn, none of which are very reactive. These elements do not readily form ions, or even compounds.

# Measurements

Knowing the chemical properties of various elements and compounds is obviously essential to understanding chemistry, but of nearly equal importance is being able to measure quantities of chemicals. In order to systematically quantify such properties as mass, length, temperature, and the quantity of material, the *Systeme Internationale d'Unites* (SI units) was developed. The following table lists common SI units.

| Common SI Units of Measurement in Chemistry | | |
|---|---|---|
| *Property* | *Unit* | *Abbreviation* |
| Mass | kilogram | Kg |
| Length | meter | M |
| Temperature | kelvin | K |
| Amount of material | mole | Mol |

To express very large or very small numbers, another concept is used, metric system prefixes. The following table lists common prefixes encountered in chemistry.

| Common Metric Prefixes | | |
|---|---|---|
| **Prefix name** | **Prefix abbreviation** | **Meaning** |
| giga- | G | 1 billion, 1,000,000,000 |
| mega- | M | 1 million, 1,000,000 |
| kilo- | k | 1 thousand, 1,000 |
| hecta- | h | 100 |
| deka- | da | 10 |
| - | - | - |
| deci- | d | 0.1 |
| centi- | c | 0.01 |
| milli- | m | 1 thousandth, 0.001 |
| micro- | μ | 1 millionth, 0.000 001 |
| nano- | n | 1 billionth, 0.000 000 001 |

With these two concepts, it is possible to express very large or very small quantities in a uniform way that other scientists can understand. Thus, if you have 1,000,000 grams, it can be reported as 1 megagram or 1 Mg. If the length of a piece of material is 0.00005 meters, it can be reported as 0.05 mm or 50 μm.

There is no SI unit for volume. Since volume will have units of length cubed, officially, scientists would use cubic meters ($m^3$) to express volume. In practice, this is rarely done, and a unit called the liter was established. See the following table for common conversions for mass, length, and volume.

| Common Conversions for Mass, Length, and Volume | | |
|---|---|---|
| **Mass conversions** | **Length conversions** | **Volume** |
| 1 pound = 453.59 g | 1 inch = 2.54 cm | $1\ m^3$ = 264.17 gallons |
| 1 kg = 1000 g | 1 km = 0.6214 miles | $1\ dm^3$ = 1 liter (1 L) |
| 1 g = 1000 mg | 1 m = 100 cm | $1\ cm^3$ = 1 mL |
| | 1 m = 1000 mm | 1 L = 1000 mL |
| | 1 km = 1000 m | |

Though the SI unit of temperature is the kelvin, it is also common to measure temperature in the Celsius scale (this used to be called the centigrade scale) or in Fahrenheit. The formulas to convert from one scale to another are as follow:

To convert from Celsius (°C) to kelvin (K), K = 273 + °C

To convert from Celsius (°C) to Fahrenheit (°F), °F = [1.8 × (°C)]+ 32

To convert from Fahrenheit (°F) to Celsius (°C), °C = [(°F)-32]/1.8

The unit most useful to chemists is the mole, since this describes how much material is present. By definition, one **mole** of anything is $6.022 \cdot 10^{23}$ of those things. This is an unfathomable number because it is so large. (For example, a mole of pennies would stretch to the sun and back 38 billion times stacked side-by-side!) The reason this is useful for chemists is because dealing with individual atoms means dealing with masses so small, no balance in the world would be able to measure it. Due to the way mass and moles are defined, the atomic weight of any atom is equivalent to one mole of that element. Thus, 55.847 grams of element 26 (iron, Fe) is $6.022 \cdot 10^{23}$ Fe atoms. For oxygen (atomic number 8), only 15.9994 grams contains 1 mole ($6.022 \cdot 10^{23}$) of oxygen atoms. This concept can be further extended to compounds so that one mole of water ($H_2O$) has a mass of 18.01528 grams (this was obtained by adding the atomic mass of two hydrogens and one oxygen). The value 18.01528 g/mol is called the **molar mass** (the mass of one mole of a compound or element).

This is directly applicable to chemical reactions since chemical reactions are written in terms of molar ratios. Look at this balanced chemical reaction:

$$C(s) + O_2(g) \rightarrow CO_2(g)$$

Previously this was interpreted as one atom of carbon reacted with one molecule of oxygen to form one molecule of carbon dioxide. This can also be interpreted as one mole of carbon reacted with one mole of oxygen molecules to form one mole of carbon dioxide. Furthermore, we can now associate masses with this reaction since one *mole* of carbon is 12 grams, one *mole* of $O_2$ is 32 grams, and one *mole* of $CO_2$ is 44 grams. In all reactions, the combined masses of the reactants should equal the combined masses of all of the products. This is a result of the **Law of Mass Conservation** that was stated previously.

Let's apply this concept to another chemical reaction, $2C(s) + O_2(g) \rightarrow 2CO(g)$.

In this reaction, two moles of carbon reacted with one mole of molecular oxygen to yield two moles of carbon monoxide. In such a case, 24 grams of carbon (2 moles of C × 12 g/mole) and 32 grams of $O_2$ will form 56 grams of CO (2 moles of CO × 28 g/mole).

# Energy

In addition to mass conservation, energy is conserved, too. Energy can be either released or absorbed in a chemical reaction. There are two main types of energy, kinetic and potential. **Kinetic energy** is the energy of motion. The faster something is moving, the higher the kinetic energy. This will often express itself in terms of temperature; materials that are hot generally have atoms that are moving more quickly than materials that are cold. **Potential energy** is associated with forces and is energy that is stored. This type of energy might depend on the distance an object is to the ground or, more importantly for chemists, the types of chemical bonds that are present. When bonds are formed, energy is released; when bonds are broken, energy is absorbed.

# Radioactivity

Although most chemical behavior is caused by the number, pattern, and energy of electrons, the energy stored inside the nucleus of an atom is also a type of potential energy. This energy is used in nuclear power plants, radiation therapy medical treatments, and even to build powerful bombs. This energy is released when an unstable nucleus decomposes into a more stable nucleus. Oftentimes, this nuclear change results in the emission of a **gamma ray** (a high energy light particle) or it may even emit a neutron, **beta particle** (an electron), or an **alpha particle** (two neutrons and two protons).

Because the timing of the decay of a nucleus is based on probability, it is impossible to determine exactly when an individual atom will emit radiation, but scientists can measure an average decay time. The most useful measurement for this purpose is the half-life. The **half-life** of a material is the time it takes for 50% of it to decay into another species. The half-life of the uranium isotope with a mass number of 235 (U-235, the isotope used in building the first nuclear bomb) is 700 million years; if you had 100 grams of U-235, in 700 million years (one half-life), there would only be 50 grams left. After 1.4 billion years (two half-lives), only 25 grams of U-235 would be left. After 2.1 billion years (three half-lives), only 12.5 grams of U-235 would remain. After each half-life period, 50% of the remaining material is converted to a new material.

# Metals

A quick look at the periodic table indicates that the vast majority of elements are metals. Because of this, many elements share common properties. The metals: (1) are solids at room temperature (mercury (Hg) is an exception since it is a liquid); (2) are **malleable**, which means they can be hammered into thin sheets; (3) are **ductile**, which means they can be drawn into thin wires; (4) are **sectile**, which means they can be cut into thin sheets; (5) are good conductors of heat and electricity; (6) are shiny; (7) have a silvery color (except for copper and gold).

Most metals are found combined with oxygen or sulfur in nature, however the **coinage metals** (copper, silver, and gold) can occur in their native (*that is*, elemental) state.

Metals can also form **alloys**, which are solid mixtures of two or more metals. An **amalgam** is a mixture of mercury with some other metal and will be a solid or liquid, depending on the amount of mercury.

# Organic Chemistry

Organic chemistry is the study of carbon-based molecules. (There are a few exceptions, materials that contain pure carbon [diamond, graphite, charcoal, anthracite, etc.] and carbon oxides like $CO$, $CO_2$, or carbonates [$CO_{32-}$] are not considered organic molecules.) Because carbon can attach to other carbon atoms and form long chains, the number and variety of organic compounds is vast. Proteins, DNA, cell walls, oils, hair, pharmaceuticals, gasoline, ethanol, herbicides, and plastics are all examples of organic (carbon-based) materials.

As an example of the differences between organic compounds, look at the properties of these various alcohols:

1. Methanol (wood alcohol), $CH_4O$, is used as a solvent in chemistry, but can cause blindness if consumed orally by humans.
2. Ethanol (grain alcohol), $C_2H_6O$, is the main ingredient in alcoholic beverages for consumption.
3. Propanol (rubbing alcohol), $C_3H_8O$, is used topically to disinfect open cuts.

Simple organic compounds are named by the number of carbon atoms in a continuous chain, so that the prefix *meth-* indicates one carbon atom, *eth-* indicates two carbon atoms, *prop-* indicates three carbon atoms. The following table shows common prefixes.

| Organic Prefixes | | | |
|---|---|---|---|
| *Number of C atoms in a chain* | *Prefix* | *Number of C atoms in a chain* | *Prefix* |
| 1 | Meth- | 6 | hex- |
| 2 | Eth- | 7 | hept- |
| 3 | Prop- | 8 | oct- |
| 4 | But- | 9 | non- |
| 5 | Pent- | 10 | dec- |

# Physics

## Motion

*Motion* occurs when an object or body is moved from one place to the next. There are three types of motion: *translational*, *rotational*, and *vibrational*. Translational or linear motion involves motion in a straight line, rotational motion happens when motion occurs about an axis, and vibrational motion entails motion about a fixed point.

# Translational Motion

Two factors characterize the motion of an object in a straight line: a change in position or *displacement* of the object over a period of time and movement with respect to a reference point. The motion of an object can be described quantitatively by making references to its *speed*, *velocity*, and *acceleration*.

## Speed and Velocity

The *speed* of an object is a measure of how fast it is moving and can be calculated using the following equation:

$$\text{Speed} = \frac{\text{Distance traveled}}{\text{Time taken}}$$

Like speed, *velocity* describes how fast an object is moving but unlike speed, specifies the direction of motion as well. In this respect, speed is said to be a *scalar quantity* while velocity is described as a *vector quantity, that is a quantity with both magnitude and direction*. The mathematical representation of the velocity of an object is given by the following equation:

$$\text{Velocity} = \frac{\text{Displacement}}{\text{Time}}$$

## Acceleration

When the velocity of an object changes with time the object is said to be *accelerating*. In general, an increase in velocity is called *acceleration*, and a decrease in velocity can be called a negative acceleration or a *deceleration*. Both can be calculated using the following equation:

$$\text{Acceleration} = \frac{\text{Change in velocity}}{\text{Time}}$$

Acceleration, like velocity, is a vector quantity. Acceleration is considered positive when acceleration occurs in the same direction in which the object is moving *(acceleration)*, and negative when acceleration occurs in a direction opposite to that in which the object is moving *(deceleration)*.

# Graphical Analysis of Motion

The motion of an object can be analyzed using two types of graph: *position-time graph* and *velocity-time graph*.

- A position-time graph shows how the displacement or position of a moving object changes with time. As a result the velocity of such an object is equal to the slope of the graph.
- A velocity-time graph illustrates how the velocity of an object changes over time. Hence, the acceleration of an object can be determined from the slope of a velocity-time graph. In addition, the area under a velocity time graph can be used to determine the distance covered by a moving object.

# Motion in One Dimension

Motion occurs in one dimension when an object or body moves along either the *x* or *y*-coordinate. Motion along the *x*-coordinate is often referred to as *"linear motion,"* while motion along the *y*-coordinate often depicts *"motion in a vertical plane"* or *"free fall."* In many instances the acceleration of an object along either coordinate is constant or nearly so. When this situation occurs, motion can be quantified using a series of equations called the *equation of kinematics*.

## Equation of Kinematics

The equations of kinematics consist of five main equations that are the result of the mathematical manipulation of the equations used to calculate velocity and acceleration. These equations involve five variables:

| | Equations of Kinematics for *Constant Acceleration* | |
|---|---|---|
| 1. | $x$ = displacement | |
| 2. | $a$ = acceleration | |
| 3. | $v$ = final velocity | |
| 4. | $v_0$ = initial velocity | |
| 5. | $t$ = time | |

The equations are

$$v = v_0 + at$$
$$x = \frac{1}{2}(v_0 + v)t$$
$$x = v_0 t + \frac{1}{2}at^2$$
$$v^2 = v_0^2 + 2ax$$

Each of the equation of kinematics contains four of these five variables. Therefore, if three of them are known, the fourth variable can be calculated by transposing the relevant equation. (The equations look simpler if one of the potential variables happens to be zero.)

## Motion in Vertical Plane

All objects above but near the earth undergo vertical motion with an acceleration of about $9.81 m/s^2$. This *vertical motion* is called *free fall* and is the result of the force of gravity. Because all objects above the earth have the same acceleration, the motion of an object undergoing vertical motion can be quantified using the equations of kinematics.

When using the equations of kinematics to describe the motion of an object in free fall, the acceleration due to gravity, $g$, is substituted for $a$, and $x$ is substituted for $y$. In addition, the vector quantities $v$ and $y$ are usually considered positive if they are directed downward and negative when directed upward, but the assignment of + and – directions is really an arbitrary choice that can change from one situation or problem to the next.

When an object is thrown upward it will undergo uniform deceleration, as a result of gravity, until it comes to rest. The object will then begin to fall, during which time it is uniformly accelerated by the force of gravity. If air resistance is neglected, then the time required for the object to rise is the same as the time required for the object to fall.

## Newton's Laws of Motion

A force is defined as a "*push*" or "*pull*" and can result in the motion of an object initially at rest, or a change in the velocity of an object already in motion. At any particular time multiple forces may act on an object. How these multiple forces affect the motion of the object is governed by a collection of laws called *Newton's laws of motion*. The laws of motion are as follows:

1. *First Law of Motion*: An object that has no *net* or unbalanced force acting on it will remain at rest or, it will move with a constant velocity in a straight line.
2. *Second Law of Motion*: The acceleration of an object is directly proportional to the net force acting on it and inversely proportional to its mass.
3. *Third Law of Motion*: When one object exerts a force on a second object, the second object will exert a force on the first that is equal in magnitude but opposite in direction.

The first law of motion emphasizes the concept of *inertia*, which is defined as the tendency of an object to resist changes in its motion. Thus, the first law is often called the *law of inertia*. On the other hand, the second law enables us to calculate the net force acting on an object and is often stated in the form of the following equation:

$$F = ma$$

where $F$ is the net force in Newtons, $m$ is the mass of the object in kilograms, and $a$ is acceleration in meters per second squared ($\text{m/s}^2$).

Like velocity, force is a vector quantity, having both magnitude and direction. Force is considered positive when it is applied in the same direction as the motion it generates and negative when applied in a direction that is opposite to the motion.

## Weight and Mass

The *weight* ($W$) of an object is the force exerted on it by the force of gravity and like all forces is measured in Newtons. The force of gravity acts on an object whether or not it is falling, resting on the ground, or is being lifted and results in a downward acceleration of $9.81\ \text{m/s}^2$. The weight of an object can be calculated using this equation that is just a special case of Newton's Second Law:

$$W = mg$$

where $W$ is the weight of the object, $m$ is the mass of the object and $g$ is the acceleration due to gravity.

From the weight equation, it is obvious that the *mass* of an object is not the same as its *weight*. The weight of an object depends on the acceleration due to gravity, and thus varies from place to place. On the other hand, *mass* is a measure of the amount of matter contained within an object and is independent of gravity. Hence, an astronaut weighs less on the moon, where the acceleration due to gravity is about $1.6\ \text{m/s}^2$, but his mass is the same as it is on earth.

## Frictional Force

*Friction* is the force that opposes the motion between two surfaces that are in contact. There are two types of friction, static and kinetic friction. *Static friction* is the force that opposes motion of an object at rest, while *kinetic friction* is the opposing force between surfaces in relative motion, and it is always less than static friction.

## Energy and Work

The mass of an object not only measures the amount of matter it contains, but also the amount of energy. The energy of an object can be divided into two main types: *potential* and *kinetic energy*. Potential energy is the energy possessed by an object due to its position or condition and is often called *stored energy*. Kinetic energy is the energy possessed by an object because of its motion.

Both the kinetic and potential energy of an object may change when *work* is done by or on the object. Therefore, *work* is defined as the transfer of energy to an object when the object moves due to the application of a force. The work done on an object can be calculated using the formula:

$$W = F \times d$$

where $W$ is work measured in Joules, $F$ is force in the direction of the motion measured in Newtons and $d$ is distance measured in meters.

## Gravitational Potential Energy

*Energy* is defined as the capacity to do work. When an object, such as a hammer, is raised above the earth, work is done against gravity. The work done against gravity causes the object to have gravitational potential energy and can be calculated using the equation:

$$PE = mgh$$

where $PE$ is the potential energy in Joules, $m$ is mass of the object in kilograms, $g$ is the acceleration due to gravity, and $h$ is the height above the ground or other reference altitude such as a table top.

As the object falls it is accelerated by the force of gravity and the object loses gravitational potential energy. According to the *law of conservation of energy*, energy can neither be created nor destroyed but can be converted from one form to another. Thus, any decrease in the gravitational potential energy of the object is accompanied by a corresponding increase in the object's kinetic energy. The kinetic energy of a moving body can be calculated from the following equation:

$$KE = \frac{1}{2} mv^2$$

where *KE* is the kinetic energy of the object, *m* is its mass and *v* is its velocity.

# Power

The conversion of energy from one form to another is generally carried out by a number of practical devices. Such devices include

1. *Generators*: convert mechanical energy into electrical energy.
2. *Motors*: convert electrical energy into mechanical energy.
3. *Batteries*: convert chemical, thermal, nuclear, or solar energy into electrical energy.
4. *Photocell or Photovoltaic cell*: converts light energy into electrical energy.

The rate at which any device converts energy from one form to another is called the **power** and is mathematically defined as:

$$P = \frac{W}{t} = E/t$$

where *P* is power in watts, *W* is work in Joules, E is energy in Joules, and *t* is time in seconds.

# Fluids

A *fluid* is any substance that offers little resistance to changes in its shape when pressure is applied to it and is therefore a material that will flow. Of the three common states of matter, only *gases* and *liquids* are considered fluids. Of all the properties that characterize fluids, one of the most important is their ability to exert *pressure*.

# Pressure

*Pressure* is defined as the force exerted per unit area and is mathematically represented by the following equation:

$$P = \frac{F}{A}$$

where *P* is pressure in Pascal, $(N/m^2)$, *F* is force in Newtons, and *A* is area in meter squared.

The ability of fluids to exert pressure can be explained by the *kinetic molecular theory*, which states that the particles that make up fluids are in continuous, random motion, as illustrated. These particles will undergo collisions with the walls of their container or any surface with which they make contact. Each time a particle makes contact, a force is exerted, and it is this force that causes pressure.

When dealing with fluids in motion or at rest, there are three governing principles that are essential: *Archimedes', Pascal's,* and *Bernoulli's principles.*

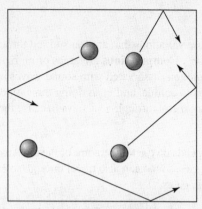

Molecular motion and collisions
of particles in a fluid

# Archimedes' Principle

According to *Archimedes' principle*, an object immersed in a fluid is buoyed up by a force equal to the weight of the fluid displaced by the object. The magnitude of the buoyant force is given by the equation:

$$F = \rho V g$$

where $F$ is the buoyant force in Newtons, $\rho$ is density of the fluid, $V$ is volume of the fluid displaced, and $g$ is acceleration due to gravity. It can be proven that the volume of an object, immersed in a fluid, is the same as the volume of the fluid that it displaces.

An object immersed in a fluid will sink or float depending on the relative value of its weight and the buoyant force exerted on it by the fluid. An object will sink if the buoyant force is less than the weight of the object. If the buoyant equals the weight of the object, the object will float at any depth in the liquid; and if the buoyant force is greater than the weight of the object, the object floats with part of its volume above the surface.

# Pascal's Principle

*Pascal's principle* states that any pressure applied to a confined fluid, at any point, is transmitted undiminished throughout the fluid. Pascal's principle led to the development of hydrostatics in which machines, such as the hydraulic lift, use pistons to multiply forces applied to fluids at rest. Pascal's Principle can be represented by the following equation:

$$\frac{F_1}{A_1} = \frac{F_2}{A_2}$$

where $F1$ and $F2$ are the forces on pistons 1 and 2, respectively, and $A1$ and $A2$ are their respective areas.

# Bernoulli's Principle

According to this principle as the velocity of a fluid increases, the pressure exerted by that fluid decreases. This principle underlies the study of hydrodynamics, which is a study of the effects of fluids in motion. Most aircrafts get most of their lift by taking advantage of this principle.

# Sound Waves

**Sound waves** consist of a series of pressure variations that are transmitted through matter. These pressure variations are of two types: *compressions* and *rarefactions*. **Compressions** are areas of high pressure and **rarefactions** are areas of low pressure. The compressions and rarefactions associated with sound waves are produced when a vibrating source, such as a tuning fork, causes air molecules to collide, and in so doing transmit the pressure variations away from the source of the sound. As such, sound cannot travel through a vacuum because there are no particles present for motion and collision to occur.

The speed at which sound travels in air depends on the temperature of the air. At sea level and room temperature, the speed of sound is about 343 m/s. In addition to gases, sound can also travel through solids and liquids. In general, the speed of sound is greater in solids and liquids than in gases.

When sound waves encounter hard surfaces, they undergo reflections called *echoes*. The time required for an echo to return to its source can be used to determine the distance between the source and the reflecting surface. The use of echoes to determine distance is used by bats to navigate their flight at nights, as well as by ships equipped with sonar.

The number of compressions or rarefactions generated in one second by sound waves is called the frequency of the sound and determines our perception of pitch. However, if the source of the sound is in motion, an observer detecting the sound will perceive sound of higher or lower pitch than would be perceived by the source if it were standing still. If the source of the sound is moving away from the observer, the observer will detect sound waves of decreased pitch. Conversely, if the source is moving toward the observer, the observer will detect sound waves of increased pitch. This apparent change in the frequency of sound, due to movement on the part of the sound source or an observer, is called the *Doppler effect*. The Doppler effect has many practical applications such as its use in radar detectors and ultrasound.

# Electricity

*Electricity* involves the flow of electrical energy from a source, such as a battery or generator, to *load* such as a lamp or motor. A load is any device that transforms electrical energy into other forms of energy. For example, a lamp transforms electrical energy into light and heat energy, while a motor transforms electrical energy into mechanical energy.

Electrical energy is transported in the form of an *electric current*, usually consisting of the flow of negatively charged *electrons*. This flow of electrons occurs in a closed conducting path, called an *electrical circuit*, in which conducting metal wires provide the pathway for the flow of electrons from the source of the electrical energy to the various loads within the circuit. A substance that allows for the flow of an electric current is called a *conductor,* and a substance that does not is called an *insulator*.

In order for an electric current to flow in a conductor, a *potential difference* or *voltage* must exist between its ends. The greater the voltage, the greater the current, and vice versa. All substances, insulators, or conductors offer some form of **resistance** to the flow of an electric current. The amount of resistance depends on the length of the material, the cross sectional area of the material, an intrinsic property called resistivity, as well the temperature. The magnitude of the current flowing in a conductor can be calculated using the following equation called Ohms's Law:

$$I = \frac{V}{R}$$

where $I$ is current in amperes, $V$ is voltage in Volts, and $R$ is resistance in ohms.

# Practice Questions

*The following questions are based on some of the material you have read in this chapter and your own knowledge of Chemistry and Physics. For each question, select the choice that best answers the question. When you're finished, check your answers against those that follow this test.*

1. Which of the following compounds would form a basic solution?

   A. battery acid
   B. water
   C. lye
   D. vinegar

2. The elements in the periodic table are listed in order of increasing _____

   A. atomic number.
   B. atomic weight.
   C. mass number.
   D. valence electrons.

3. Which substance makes up the majority of the Earth's atmosphere?

   A. $CO_2$
   B. Ar
   C. $N_2$
   D. $O_2$

4. Which group of the periodic table has eight valence electrons?

   A. Alkali Metals
   B. Alkaline Earth Metals
   C. Halogens
   D. Noble Gases

5. The nucleus of an atom is made of

   A. protons only.
   B. protons and neutrons.
   C. protons and electrons.
   D. none of the above.

6. Classify the reaction as to the reaction type.
   $Mg(OH)_2 + 2HCl \rightarrow MgCl_2 + 2H_2O$

   A. Synthesis
   B. Decomposition
   C. Single replacement
   D. Double replacement

7. What mass of product would you expect given that you started with 17 g of $NH_3$ and 36.5 g of HCl?
   $NH_3 + HCl \rightarrow NH_4Cl$

   A. 17 g
   B. 36.5 g
   C. 53.5 g
   D. 19.5 g

8. Which of the following elements is found in bones?

   A. iron
   B. calcium
   C. fluorine
   D. helium

9. A metal has the following properties *except*

   A. shininess.
   B. brittleness.
   C. malleability.
   D. ductility.

10. If two atoms are isotopes, they will

    A. have the same number of protons and neutrons.
    B. have the same number of neutrons, but different numbers of protons.
    C. have the same number of protons, but different numbers of neutrons.
    D. have the same number of neutrons and electrons.

11. This element is used as a disinfectant in swimming pools.

    A. chlorine
    B. fluorine
    C. sulfur
    D. nitrogen

12. If the temperature is 25 °C, what is the temperature in °F?

    A. 25 °F
    B. 298 °F
    C. 0 °F
    D. 77 °F

13. Toothpaste contains _____ in order to prevent tooth decay.

    A. calcium
    B. phosphorous
    C. iron
    D. fluoride

14. A major constituent of sea water is _____

    A. sodium chloride.
    B. nitrogen.
    C. iron.
    D. aluminum.

**15.** What element is found in matches, soft drinks, DNA, and fertilizers?

    **A.** phosphorous

    **B.** fluorine

    **C.** iron

    **D.** silicon

**16.** What is the velocity of a car if it travels 300 km in 4 hours?

    **A.** 0.014 km/hr

    **B.** 304 km/hr

    **C.** 296 km/hr

    **D.** 75 km/hr

**17.** What force is required to give a 2.0 kg mass an acceleration of 5 m/s$^2$?

    **A.** 0.4 N

    **B.** 2.5 N

    **C.** 10 N

    **D.** 20 N

**18.** An object is in free-fall near the surface of the earth. What is the velocity before impact if it takes 5 seconds to fall from rest until it hit the ground? Assume $g$ to be 10m/s$^2$, a common approximation

    **A.** 5 m/s

    **B.** 2 m/s

    **C.** 50 m/s

    **D.** 125 m/s

**19.** What is the acceleration of a car whose velocity changes from 60 m/s to 45 m/s in 5 seconds?

    **A.** 3.0 m/s$^2$

    **B.** 53 m/s$^2$

    **C.** 15 m/s$^2$

    **D.** 9.8 m/s$^2$

**20.** What is the approximate weight of an object having a mass of 5 kg?

    **A.** 5.0 kg

    **B.** 25 N

    **C.** 49 kg

    **D.** 49 N

**21.** What is the kinetic energy of body that has a mass of 2 kg and a velocity of 4 m/s?

    **A.** 16 Joules

    **B.** 32 Joules

    **C.** 4 Joules

    **D.** 8 Joules

**22.** As an object slides across a horizontal surface, its gravitational potential energy

    **A.** decreases.

    **B.** increases.

    **C.** remains the same.

    **D.** increases and then decreases.

**23.** How much work is done by force of 8 N acting parallel to a displacement of 6 meters?

    **A.** 0 J

    **B.** 12 J

    **C.** 192 J

    **D.** 48 J

**24.** How much power is developed by a machine that does 300 Joules of work in 10 seconds?

    **A.** 30 W

    **B.** 2500 W

    **C.** 240 W

    **D.** 260 W

**25.** What is the magnitude of the current flowing through a lamp with resistance of 30 Ω and a potential difference of 10.0 volts?

    **A.** 0.25 A

    **B.** 0.33 A

    **C.** 3.0 A

    **D.** 0.5 A

# Answers and Explanations

1. **C.** Lye is sodium hydroxide, and any compound that increases the hydroxide concentration is considered a base. Battery acid (sulfuric acid) and vinegar (acetic acid) are acidic. Water is neutral (neither acidic nor basic).

2. **A.** Atomic number is the number of protons in the nucleus. Although most elements are listed in terms of atomic weight, too, there are a few cases where this is not true, so atomic weight is not a good indicator of trends for the periodic table. Mass number is the number of protons and neutrons, but the periodic table is listed only in order of increasing protons.

3. **C.** Diatomic nitrogen makes up $\approx 75\%$ of the atmosphere; $\approx 20\%$ is $O_2$, $\approx 1\%$ is Ar, and other gases are found in trace amounts.

4. **D.** The Noble Gases have an octet of electrons; all other groups have less than 8.

5. **B.** The nucleus contains the positively charged protons and the neutral neutrons. Electrons are outside of the nucleus.

6. **D.** Because Mg and H exchange partners, this is a double displacement reaction. Synthesis reactions have only one product; decomposition reactions have only one reactant; single replacement reactions will have an elemental species as a reactant.

7. **C.** The Law of Mass Conservation must be obeyed, so the mass of products must equal the mass of reactants ($17 + 36.5 = 53.5$).

8. **B.** Bones are made mostly of a calcium phosphate mineral. Iron is an important component in red blood cells; fluorine is not biologically important, although it can be used to reduce dental caries; and helium has no known human biological activity.

9. **B.** As a rule, metals are shiny, malleable (able to be hammered into thin sheets), and ductile (able to be drawn into thin wires). Metals are not brittle, or they would shatter when hit with a hammer, instead of being pounded into a thin sheet.

10. **C.** Isotopes of the same element *must* have the same number of protons, but will have different numbers of neutrons. Electrons will make atoms into ions, but has no effect on whether atoms are isotopes.

11. **A.** Chlorine is used as a disinfectant for pools and many of the water treatment plants in the USA. Fluorine is added to municipal water supplies (as fluoride) to reduce tooth decay. Neither phosphorous nor nitrogen are added to disinfect water.

12. **D.** Using the formula, $°F = [1.8 \times (°C)] + 32$, you can see that the answer will be 77 °F. For answer **B**, 273 was added to 25, which would give the temperature in kelvin.

13. **D.** Calcium and phosphorous are important nutrients to maintain teeth and bones, but fluoride is added to react with the surface of the tooth enamel so that it becomes less soluble to the acids secreted by bacteria.

14. **A.** Sodium chloride (NaCl) is table salt and causes sea water to be salty.

15. **A.** Phosphorous is found in all of these applications.

16. **D.** The velocity is calculated by dividing the distance traveled by the time taken.

17. **C.** This is a strict application of Newton's second law and as such the force is simply the product of the object's mass and acceleration.

18. **C.** The answer is obtained by direct substitution into one of the equations of kinematics: $v = v_0 + gt$. Since the object falls from rest, $v_0$ is equal to 0 m/s and the equation is reduced to $v = gt$.

19. **A.** The first step in solving the problem is to determine the change in velocity, which is simply the difference between the final and initial velocity. Dividing the difference by the time gives us the acceleration of the car. In this case the difference in velocity is negative and is an indication that the car is decelerating.

20. **D.** The weight of an object is a force and as such is simply the product of its mass and the acceleration due to gravity. It should be noted that the unit of force is expressed in Newtons and not kilograms.

**21. A.** The solution requires direct substitution into the equation: KE = ½ mv² = ½(2kg)(4m/s)² =16J.

**22. C.** A change in the gravitational energy of a body requires movement in the vertical plane; in other words it requires a change in height.

**23. D.** The answer is obtained by direct substitution into the equation: W = Fd

**24. A.** The solution requires direct substitution into the equation: P = W/t

**25. B.** The result is obtained by substituting the known values into the equation: I = V/R

PART III

# PRACTICE TESTS

# Practice Test 1

## Verbal

### Synonyms

**Directions:** Select the word or phrase that best completes the sentence.

1. Repeal most nearly means

   A. abolish
   B. build
   C. support
   D. change

2. A poignant story is

   A. absurd
   B. touching
   C. poisonous
   D. hilarious

3. An archaic expression is

   A. religious
   B. arched
   C. unattractive
   D. old-fashioned

4. Culmination most nearly means

   A. combination
   B. beginning
   C. climax
   D. continuation

5. Undermines most nearly means

   A. asserts
   B. tunnels
   C. weakens
   D. suggests

6. A frivolous answer is

   A. relaxed
   B. silly
   C. serious
   D. frilly

7. Exacerbate most nearly means

   A. worsen
   B. scratch
   C. improve
   D. trap

8. Depicted most nearly means

   A. told
   B. duplicated
   C. showed
   D. resemble

9. Something that is indeterminable is

   A. unknowable
   B. partial
   C. definite
   D. transparent

10. Morphology most nearly means

    A. size
    B. color
    C. structure
    D. material

11. A lucid explanation is

    A. light
    B. confusing
    C. clear
    D. dull

12. Revere most nearly means

    A. esteem
    B. pray
    C. consider
    D. age

GO ON TO THE NEXT PAGE

**13.** An audacious act is

    **A.** loud
    **B.** cowardly
    **C.** unimportant
    **D.** bold

**14.** An austere room is

    **A.** crowded
    **B.** tuneful
    **C.** frightening
    **D.** bare

**15.** Nadir most nearly means

    **A.** pinnacle
    **B.** outstanding
    **C.** bottom
    **D.** average

**16.** Incisive most nearly means

    **A.** stimulating
    **B.** accidental
    **C.** brief
    **D.** penetrating

**17.** Something that is derelict is

    **A.** abandoned
    **B.** widowed
    **C.** faithful
    **D.** insincere

**18.** To be pungent is to be

    **A.** biting
    **B.** smooth
    **C.** wrong
    **D.** quarrelsome

**19.** Benevolence most nearly means

    **A.** good fortune
    **B.** well-being
    **C.** violence
    **D.** charitableness

**20.** Corroborate means to

    **A.** deny
    **B.** elaborate
    **C.** confirm
    **D.** state

# Antonyms

**Directions:** Select the word or phrase that best completes the sentence.

1. Contradict is the *opposite* of
   A. dislike
   B. agree
   C. pronounce
   D. meet

2. Static is the *opposite* of
   A. dynamic
   B. quiet
   C. funny
   D. laborious

3. Ancient is the *opposite* of
   A. faint
   B. useful
   C. antique
   D. modern

4. Dispose is the *opposite* of
   A. throw
   B. acquire
   C. consolidate
   D. oppose

5. Temporary is the *opposite* of
   A. permanent
   B. late
   C. fragile
   D. written

6. Familiar is the *opposite* of
   A. akin
   B. lost
   C. strange
   D. maternal

7. Destroy is the *opposite* of
   A. decimate
   B. restore
   C. history
   D. change

8. Important is the *opposite* of
   A. useful
   B. settled
   C. imaginary
   D. trivial

9. Completely is the *opposite* of
   A. totally
   B. sadly
   C. partially
   D. thoughtlessly

10. Bungle is the *opposite* of
    A. complain
    B. handle badly
    C. fix
    D. live in

11. Jilt is the *opposite* of
    A. cast aside
    B. move about
    C. join
    D. bargain

12. Justice is the *opposite* of
    A. eventually
    B. in time
    C. fair
    D. lawless

GO ON TO THE NEXT PAGE

**13.** Reject is the *opposite* of

    A.  fool
    B.  accept
    C.  cast away
    D.  stall

**14.** Opposed is the *opposite* of

    A.  allied
    B.  released
    C.  forward
    D.  enmity

**15.** Pastoral is the *opposite* of

    A.  pacific
    B.  normal
    C.  urban
    D.  harmonious

# Analogies

**Directions:** Select the word or phrase that best completes the sentence.

1. Dentist is to teeth as plumber is to

   A. bones
   B. shovel
   C. drill
   D. pipes

2. Professor is to lecture as actor is to

   A. performs
   B. script
   C. tests
   D. stage

3. Duet is to solo as quart is to

   A. single
   B. trio
   C. pint
   D. gallon

4. Freeze is to cold as boil is to

   A. steam
   B. ice
   C. smoke
   D. heat

5. Deny is to contradict as obtain is to

   A. acquire
   B. lose
   C. disagree
   D. stubborn

6. Food is to nutrition as soap is to

   A. dirt
   B. suds
   C. cleanliness
   D. health

7. Infant is to toddler as kid is to

   A. goat
   B. baby
   C. joke
   D. calf

8. Tight is to loose as gritty is to

   A. coarse
   B. relaxed
   C. pavement
   D. smooth

9. Rotor is to helicopter as tuner is to

   A. radio
   B. piano
   C. airplane
   D. dial

10. Slow is to snail as thin is to

    A. skinny
    B. kitten
    C. heavy
    D. twig

11. HAMBURGER : COW :: PORK CHOP :

    A. cat
    B. fish
    C. pig
    D. bird

12. TELEVISION : RADIO :: NEWSPAPER :

    A. telephone
    B. town crier
    C. bell
    D. movie projector

13. EGG : CHICKEN :: ROSEBUD :

    A. flower
    B. tree
    C. petal
    D. leaf

14. EAGLE : ROBIN :: SHARK :

    A. small fish
    B. snake
    C. swan
    D. whale

## GO ON TO THE NEXT PAGE

**15.** WRENCH : MECHANIC :: HOSE :

- **A.** firefighter
- **B.** axe
- **C.** mail deliverer
- **D.** judge

**16.** APPLE : PEAR :: CORN :

- **A.** sandwich : cookie
- **B.** roll : frankfurter
- **C.** corn : carrot
- **D.** vine : grapes

**17.** HAT : CAP

- **A.** glove : ring
- **B.** pearl : necklace
- **C.** cotton : socks
- **D.** pants : shirt

**18.** CIRCUS TENT : TRAPEZE ARTIST

- **A.** fishing : rod
- **B.** lion tamer : lion
- **C.** hospital : doctor
- **D.** secretary : computer

**19.** COOKIE : BOX OF COOKIES

- **A.** tree : hedge
- **B.** biscuit : cake
- **C.** rain cloud : white cloud
- **D.** flower : bouquet

**20.** JACK O'LANTERN : SKELETON

- **A.** Christmas Tree : Santa Claus
- **B.** rabbit : Easter Bunny
- **C.** broom : witch
- **D.** bank : firecracker

# Spelling

**Directions:** In Questions 1–10, look for mistakes in spelling only. If you find no mistake, mark **D** on your answer sheet.

1. **A.** Professor Gray teaches history.
   **B.** Kate wants to develope her public speaking skills.
   **C.** The novel was written in 1995.
   **D.** No mistakes.

2. **A.** Lee is an amature golfer.
   **B.** Every afternoon he practices at the driving range.
   **C.** He tries to improve his performance.
   **D.** No mistakes.

3. **A.** The state experienced a severe drought.
   **B.** Zoology is the study of animals.
   **C.** Electricity can be generated by nucular power plants.
   **D.** No mistakes.

4. **A.** The circus tent was set up in the field.
   **B.** Clowns crowded into tiny cars.
   **C.** I probly will go to the show on Friday.
   **D.** No mistakes.

5. **A.** Most libraries use computer catalogs.
   **B.** Ted kept his shirts and socks in separate drawers.
   **C.** Are you familiar with the new system?
   **D.** No mistakes.

6. **A.** The colonists celebrated their independance.
   **B.** It's likely that rain will fall on Monday.
   **C.** The mayor's speech was applauded by the crowd.
   **D.** No mistakes.

7. **A.** Do you plan to attend colledge?
   **B.** A laboratory science is a required course for graduation.
   **C.** The officer relieved the guard from her post.
   **D.** No mistakes.

8. **A.** In February, Alice moved to Florida.
   **B.** Did you go skiing last winter?
   **C.** This dress and that one are very similar.
   **D.** No mistakes.

9. **A.** Nancy enjoyed her mathmatics class.
   **B.** Take advantage of this wonderful opportunity.
   **C.** Multiply the length by the width.
   **D.** No mistakes.

10. **A.** Nina planned her project carefully.
    **B.** Do not start untill you hear the instructions
    **C.** Using a dictionary can make you a better speller.
    **D.** No mistakes.

*In Questions 11–20, one of the words is misspelled. Select the word that is incorrect.*

11. **A.** weightless
    **B.** reddened
    **C.** obstacle
    **D.** aweful

12. **A.** invigorate
    **B.** massacre
    **C.** negitive
    **D.** courtesy

13. **A.** backround
    **B.** combustible
    **C.** accustomed
    **D.** slurred

14. **A.** sacrafice
    **B.** executive
    **C.** mortgage
    **D.** restaurant

15. **A.** idolize
    **B.** donor
    **C.** fuedal
    **D.** inflammatory

16. **A.** television
    **B.** perdicament
    **C.** hindrance
    **D.** officious

GO ON TO THE NEXT PAGE

**17.** A. excessive
    B. appraise
    C. government
    D. cemetary

**18.** A. management
    B. supposedly
    C. adolesent
    D. abutment

**19.** A. performance
    B. advertisement
    C. triumphant
    D. appologize

**20.** A. similarity
    B. profiteer
    C. dissapear
    D. beggarly

# Answers and Explanations

## Synonyms

1. **A.** To repeal is to take back something previously established, like a law or a rule, making *abolish* the best choice.

2. **B.** Something *poignant* creates deep emotions. They may be positive or negative emotions. Therefore, choices **A** and **D** are incorrect. **C** doesn't make sense.

3. **D.** *Archaic* means out of date, something used in the past but not the present.

4. **C.** The culmination is what a series of events or statements lead up to, a *climax*.

5. **C.** When you undermine something, you take away that which is supporting it, so you *weaken* it.

6. **B.** *Frivolous* means not serious or unimportant. *Silly* is a good synonym for the word.

7. **A.** This is a tricky word. It means to make more intense is a negative way, which is why *improve*, **C**, is not a correct choice.

8. **C.** To *depict* something is to draw a picture of it or portray it.

9. **A.** The prefix *–in* is your clue that the correct choice is a word meaning something is *not*.

10. **C.** The prefix *morph* refers to form or shape.

11. **C.** Choice **A** is confusing. Does *light* mean the opposite of heavy? Or, does it mean the same as bright? Even if the latter is the case, **C** is a better answer.

12. **A.** Although **B**, pray, is a way of revering something, prayer is not the only means of reverence. Therefore, **A** is the best choice.

13. **D.** To act audaciously is to act in a daring manner.

14. **D.** When something is *austere*, it lacks decorations or adornments.

15. **C.** The *nadir* refers to the utmost depths.

16. **D.** To be incisive is to be penetrating.

17. **A.** Something that is derelict is abandoned.

18. **A.** Pungent means sharp or biting.

19. **D.** Benevolence means charitableness. The recipient of benevolence may have a sense of good fortune **A** and well-being **B**, but that is not the meaning of the word. Choice **C** is incorrect.

20. **C.** Corroborate means to confirm. Choice **A** is the opposite, and **B** and **D** may be part of the corroboration, but these are not the appropriate definitions.

# Antonyms

1. **B.** To contradict is to say the opposite of what has been said; the opposite is *agree*.

2. **A.** *Static* means motionless or inert; *dynamic*, meaning *lively* or *energetic,* is the best choice.

3. **D.** Choice C, *antique*, is a synonym. *Modern* is the opposite.

4. **B.** To *dispose* is to throw away or get rid of something; to *acquire* is to get or obtain something.

5. **A.** Something temporary only lasts for a period of time; something *permanent* lasts forever.

6. **B.** Don't be confused by **A.** *Familiar* does not mean of the family.

7. **B.** Choice **A** is a synonym. To *restore*, to bring back to the original condition, is the opposite of *destroy*.

8. **D.** *Trivial,* meaning small or unimportant, is the best choice.

9. **C.** A is a synonym for *completely.*

10. **C.** To *bungle* is to handle badly. The opposite is to *fix.*

11. **C.** To *jilt* means to cast off or get rid of. To join would be the opposite.

12. **D.** The opposite of *justice* is *lawless.* Justice has to do with the law.

13. **B.** The word *reject* means to *cast away*. The antonym would be accept.

14. **A.** To be *opposed* to something is to be *against*. The word allied is the opposite.

15. **C.** *Pastoral* means countrified and serene, while urban is the opposite—city, noisy, bustling.

# Analogies

1. **D.** A dentist works on teeth and a plumber works on pipes.

2. **B.** A professor reads lectures and an actor reads scripts. **A**, although it sounds likely, is not a good choice because performing is what the actor does, not what the actor reads.

3. **C.** The relationship is from more to less or greater to smaller.

4. **D.** The relationship is effect to cause. Choices **A** and **C** would be cause to effect.

5. **A.** The words are synonyms.

6. **C.** The relationship is purpose. Food is eaten for nutrition; soap is used to maintain cleanliness.

7. **A.** You may not know that a kid is a baby goat. But the relationship of the first two words is from younger to older. None of the other choices would fit that sequence.

8. **D.** The relationship is opposites.

9. **A.** The relationship is part to whole.

10. **D.** The relationship is characteristic. A snail is slow, and a twig is a thin branch of a tree.

11. **C.** Hamburger is made of beef, which comes from cattle, and pork chops come from pigs.

12. **B.** The relationship is of opposites: new and old. Just as television is a newer way to communicate information than radio is, a newspaper is a newer way to communicate information than a town crier.

13. **A.** An egg becomes a chicken as a bud becomes a flower.

14. **A.** The relationship is one of degree, large to small.

15. **A.** The relationship is one of function. A wrench is used by a mechanic; a hose is used by a firefighter.

16. **C.** Apples and pears are parts of the whole category fruit: corn and carrots are part of the whole category vegetables.

17. **A.** Both hats and caps are worn on the head; both gloves and rings are worn on the hand.

18. **C.** The relationship is characteristic place of work of a specific job.

19. **D.** The relationship is part to whole.

20. **A.** Jack O'Lanterns and skeletons are associated with Halloween; a decorated tree and Santa Claus are associated with Christmas.

GO ON TO THE NEXT PAGE

# Spelling

1. **B.** develop

2. **A.** amateur

3. **C.** nuclear

4. **C.** probably

5. **D.** No mistakes

6. **A.** independence

7. **A.** college

8. **D.** No mistakes

9. **A.** mathematics.

10. **B.** until

11. **D.** awful

12. **C.** negative

13. **A.** background

14. **A.** sacrifice

15. **C.** feudal

16. **B.** predicament

17. **D.** cemetery

18. **C.** adolescent

19. **D.** apologize

20. **C.** disappear

# Reading Comprehension

**Directions:** This section measures your ability to read and understand written English similar to that which one may expect in a college or university setting. Read each passage and answer the questions based on what is stated or implied in the passage.

## Passage 1

Tube worms live anchored to the sea floor, 1,700 feet below the ocean surface, near natural spring vents that spew forth water from the earth. They live off geothermal energy instead of sunlight. There are two species of the tube worm family, with very different lengths of life and growth rates, but similarities as well.

The slow-growing tube worms are known to live as long as 250 years, making them the longest-living sea invertebrates known. This species lives near cold sea-floor seeps and may not grow at all from one year to the next. Even when they do grow, it is generally from a half an inch to four inches per year. In spite of their slow growth, due to their long lives, they can reach nine feet before they die, although they are thinner than the hot-water worms.

The seeps under the slow-growing tube worms are rich with oily materials. The environment in which they live is slow and peaceful, stable and low-energy. The cold water seeps and the tube worms that reside there may live hundreds or thousands of years.

In stark contrast, the fast-growing tube worms live a quick and short life, growing rapidly. They attach themselves near hot steaming vents that force water into the sea, growing about two and a half feet a year, and up to eight feet overall. They live by absorbing sulfur compounds metabolized by bacteria in a symbiotic relationship.

The hot water vents spew forth scalding water filled with hydrogen sulfide, which the tiny bacteria living in the worms' tissues consume. These tube worms live a rapid life, with none of the relaxing characteristics of the cold-water tube worms.

1. The word anchored in the first sentence is closest in meaning to

   A. affixed
   B. contentedly
   C. feeding
   D. above

2. The expression spew forth in the first sentence is closest in meaning to

   A. inhale
   B. discharge
   C. control
   D. eliminate

3. The author implies that a vent and a seep are

   A. the same
   B. different in that a vent involves rapid discharge while a seep involves slow discharge
   C. different in that a vent involves discharge while a seep involves intake
   D. different in that a vent involves slow discharge while a seep involves rapid discharge

4. The passage indicates that the two types of tube worms discussed are

   A. from totally different families
   B. different in that one is not a true tube worm at all
   C. from the same family but different species
   D. from the same species and only differ because of habitat

5. The author states that the cold-water tube worm

   A. grows slower than the hot-water tube worm
   B. grows faster than the hot-water tube worm
   C. does not grow as high as the hot-water tube worm
   D. does not live as long as the hot-water tube worm

6. The word stark in the fourth paragraph is closest in meaning to

   A. complete
   B. somewhat
   C. comparative
   D. interesting

GO ON TO THE NEXT PAGE

**7.** The word overall in the fourth paragraph is closest in meaning to

    **A.** lifetime
    **B.** annually
    **C.** generally
    **D.** rapidly

**8.** The word scalding in the last paragraph is closest in meaning to

    **A.** hydrogen-filled
    **B.** bacteria-filled
    **C.** boiling
    **D.** rapidly spewing

## Passage 2

A new procedure has been developed to treat aneurysms, particularly those that occur near the brain stem, where surgery is dangerous.

Aneurysms are blood sacs formed by enlargement of the weakened wall of arteries or veins. They are dangerous and thus must generally be removed before they cause considerable damage. If one ruptures, it can cause strokes or fatal hemorrhaging, the latter of which occurs in 50 percent of all patients. Before rupturing, an aneurysm frequently shows no sign or symptom that it exists. Brain aneurysms occur in approximately 5 percent of the population. Most patients are between 40 and 65 years old, with hemorrhages most prevalent in those between 50 and 54.

The new procedure involves inserting a soft, flexible micro-catheter through the femoral artery in the groin area and snaking it up through blood vessels to the brain. Inside the catheter is a small, coiled wire, which can be extruded after it reaches its destination. After the coil is outside the catheter, a low voltage electrical current is applied, and the coil detaches at a preset solder point. Additional coils are snaked through the catheter and also detached at the site, creating a basket, or metal framework, which causes the blood to clot around it. The micro-catheter is withdrawn, the clot remains, and the healed aneurysm no longer is exposed to the stress that can cause another rupture.

The procedure lasts two hours, which is half as long as invasive surgery, and recovery time is generally limited to a few days instead of a few weeks. The procedure was discovered in the 1990s, was approved by the U.S. Food and Drug Administration in 1995, and is available in various hospitals where there are advanced neurology departments and specialists trained in the procedure. Many lives have been saved by use of the procedure, because the alternative would have been to watch and wait rather than risk the hazards of surgery.

**9.** The author indicates that the ingredients in the water that comes from the two types of vents are

    **A.** different only because the heat of the hot vents destroys the oil as it spews forth
    **B.** different in that one contains bacteria and the other contains oily materials
    **C.** the same
    **D.** different in that one contains oily materials and the other contains hydrogen sulfide

**10.** The author implies that the procedure described is useful for

    **A.** all aneurysms
    **B.** aneurysms that occur anywhere in the brain
    **C.** aneurysms that occur near the brain stem only
    **D.** aneurysms that occur near large blood vessels

**11.** The word They in the first paragraph refers to

    **A.** aneurysms
    **B.** brain stems
    **C.** surgeries
    **D.** procedures

**12.** The word considerable in the first paragraph is closest in meaning to

    **A.** slight
    **B.** kind
    **C.** significant
    **D.** recurring

**13.** The word one in the first paragraph refers to

    **A.** brain stem
    **B.** aneurysm
    **C.** procedure
    **D.** surgery

**14.** The word snaking in the second paragraph is closest in meaning to

    **A.** meandering
    **B.** extruding
    **C.** living
    **D.** damaging

15. The word withdrawn in the second paragraph is closest in meaning to

   A.  removed
   B.  too large
   C.  charged
   D.  inserted

16. An aneurysm is most similar to

   A.  an ulcer
   B.  a hernia
   C.  a heart attack
   D.  cancer

17. The author indicates that half of the patients who have a brain aneurysm could also have

   A.  a stroke
   B.  a seizure
   C.  a heart attack
   D.  hemorrhaging that results in death

18. The author indicates that the point of creating a basket near the aneurysm is to

   A.  catch the aneurysm when it breaks off
   B.  serve as a base for a blood clot to form
   C.  dissolve the aneurysm
   D.  provide a means of studying the aneurysm

19. The author indicates that the femoral artery is

   A.  small
   B.  in the upper thigh
   C.  in the brain
   D.  connected to the brain

20. The author states that the electrical charge is applied in order to

   A.  stimulate the brain
   B.  stimulate the aneurysm
   C.  dissolve the aneurysm
   D.  separate the coil from the wire

21. The author implies that the wire breaks off

   A.  randomly
   B.  by being cut with an additional tool
   C.  at a predetermined and prepared location on the wire
   D.  inside the micro-catheter

22. According to the passage, traditional surgical techniques take

   A.  longer and require more recuperation time than the new procedure
   B.  longer but require less recuperation time than the new procedure
   C.  less time and require less recuperation time than the new procedure
   D.  less time but require longer recuperation time than the new procedure

23. The author implies that the new procedure

   A.  can be performed at any hospital
   B.  is performed only at hospitals containing the required equipment and certified doctors
   C.  is performed by certified doctors but requires no special equipment
   D.  is performed by any surgeon using special equipment

GO ON TO THE NEXT PAGE

## Passage 3

Scientists have discovered the bones of what may be the largest meat-eating dinosaur ever to walk the earth. The discovery was made by a team of researchers from Argentina and North America in Patagonia, a desert on the eastern slopes of the Andes in South America. Besides the interesting fact that the dinosaur was huge and horrifying, it is even more astounding that the bones of a number of the dinosaurs were found together. This discovery challenges the prior theory that the biggest meat-eaters lived as loners and instead indicates that they may have lived and hunted in packs. The Tyrannosaurus Rex lived in North America and was believed to hunt and live alone.

The newly discovered meat-eater appears to be related to the Giganotosaurus family, being as closely related to it as a fox would be to a dog. It is actually not of the same family at all as the Tyrannosaurus Rex, being as different from it as a cat is from a dog.

The fossilized remains indicate that the animals lived about 100 million years ago. With needle-shaped noses and razor sharp teeth, they were larger than the Tyrannosaurus Rex, although their legs were slightly shorter, and their jaws were designed to be better able to dissect their prey quickly and precisely.

24. The author states that the newly discovered dinosaur remains are evidence that it was the largest

    A. dinosaur ever
    B. carnivorous dinosaur
    C. herbivorous dinosaur
    D. South American dinosaur

25. The word besides in the first paragraph is closest in meaning to

    A. in spite of
    B. in addition to
    C. although
    D. mostly

26. The word horrifying in the first paragraph is closest in meaning to

    A. frightening
    B. large
    C. fast
    D. interesting

27. The word astounding in the first paragraph is closest in meaning to

    A. terrifying
    B. pleasing
    C. displeasing
    D. surprising

28. The author implies that the most interesting fact about the find is that this dinosaur

    A. lived and hunted with others
    B. had a powerful jaw and sharp teeth
    C. was found in the Andes
    D. was larger than Tyrannosaurus Rex

29. The passage indicates that prior to this discovery scientists believed that

    A. meat-eating dinosaurs lived alone
    B. there were no meat-eating dinosaurs in the Andes
    C. Tyrannosaurus Rex lived in the Andes
    D. meat-eating dinosaurs were small in stature

30. The word it in the second paragraph refers to

    A. newly discovered meat-eater
    B. relationship
    C. Giganotosaurus
    D. dog

31. The author states that the newly discovered meat-eating dinosaur is

    A. closely related to Tyrannosaurus Rex
    B. not closely related to Tyrannosaurus Rex
    C. not closely related to Giganotosaurus
    D. closely related to the large cat family

32. The word dissect in the last sentence is closest in meaning to

    A. dismember
    B. swallow
    C. chew
    D. escape

33. The word prey in the last sentence of the passage is closest in meaning to

    A. victim
    B. enemy
    C. dinosaurs
    D. attacker

## Passage 4

Scientists have developed a new bionic computer chip that can be mated with human cells to combat disease. The tiny device, smaller and thinner than a strand of hair, combines a healthy human cell with an electronic circuitry chip. Doctors can control the activity of the cell by controlling the chip with a computer.

It has long been established that cell membranes become permeable when exposed to electrical impulses. Researchers have conducted genetic research for years with a trial-and-error process of bombarding cells with electricity in an attempt to introduce foreign substances such as new drug treatments or genetic material. They were unable to apply a particular level of voltage for a particular purpose. With the new invention, the computer sends electrical impulses to the chip, which triggers the cell's membrane pores to open and activate the cell in order to correct diseased tissues. It permits physicians to open a cell's pores with control.

Researchers hope that eventually they will be able to develop more advanced chips whereby they can choose a particular voltage to activate particular tissues, whether they be muscle, bone, brain, or others. They believe that they will be able to implant multiple chips into a person to deal with one problem or more than one problem.

34. The word mated in the first sentence is closest in meaning to

    A. avoided
    B. combined
    C. introduced
    D. developed

35. The word strand in the second sentence is closest in meaning to

    A. type
    B. thread
    C. chip
    D. color

36. The author implies that scientists are excited about the new technology because

    A. it is less expensive than current techniques
    B. it allows them to be able to shock cells for the first time
    C. it is more precise than previous techniques
    D. it is possible to kill cancer with a single jolt

37. The author states that scientists previously were aware that

    A. they could control cells with a separate computer
    B. electronic impulses could affect cells
    C. electric charges could harm a person
    D. cells interact with each other through electrical charges

38. The word bombarding in the second paragraph is closest in meaning to

    A. barraging
    B. influencing
    C. receiving
    D. testing

39. The author implies that up to now, the point of applying electric impulse to cells was to

    A. kill them
    B. open their walls to introduce medication
    C. stop growth
    D. combine cells

40. The word triggers in the second paragraph is closest in meaning to

    A. damages
    B. causes
    C. shoots
    D. assists

41. The word eventually in the third paragraph is closest in meaning to

    A. finally
    B. in the future
    C. possibly
    D. especially

42. The word they in the first sentence of the third paragraph refers to

    A. researchers
    B. chips
    C. voltages
    D. tissues

GO ON TO THE NEXT PAGE

**43.** The word particular in the third paragraph is closest in meaning to

    **A.** huge

    **B.** slight

    **C.** specific

    **D.** controlled

**44.** The word others in the third paragraph refers to other

    **A.** researchers

    **B.** chips

    **C.** voltages

    **D.** tissues

**45.** The author indicates that it is expected doctors will be able to

    **A.** place one large chip in a person to control multiple problems

    **B.** place more than one chip in a single person

    **C.** place a chip directly inside a cell

    **D.** place a chip inside a strand of hair

# Answers and Explanations

**1. A.** affixed

**2. B.** discharge

**3. B.** different in that a vent involves rapid discharge while a seep involves slow discharge. The author uses the two words in different contexts.

**4. C.** from the same family but different species

**5. A.** grows slower than the hot-water tube worm. See paragraphs two and five, which distinguish between the growth rates of the two worms.

**6. A.** complete

**7. A.** lifetime

**8. C.** boiling

**9. D.** different in that one contains oily materials and the other contains hydrogen sulfide

**10. C.** aneurysms that occur near the brain stem only. The first paragraph explains that these aneurysms are dangerous to repair with surgery.

**11. A.** aneurysms. The noun is found in the previous sentence, and no other noun in the sentence could make sense.

**12. C.** significant

**13. B.** aneurysm. The noun to which one refers actually appears two sentences before the reference.

**14. A.** meandering. The idea is that it moves slowly and deliberately towards its destination.

**15. A.** removed

**16. B.** a hernia

**17. D.** hemorrhaging that results in death. The first paragraph states that this can occur in 50 percent of patients.

**18. B.** serve as a base for a blood clot to form. This is explained in the second paragraph.

**19. B.** in the upper thigh. In the reading, it states that the femoral artery is in the groin area. The word "femoral" is related to femur, which is the thigh bone, and the groin area is where the thigh meets the hip area.

**20. D.** separate the coil from the wire. This is explained in the second paragraph. After the coil is outside the catheter, a low voltage electrical current is applied, and the coil detaches at a preset solder point.

**21. C.** at a predetermined and prepared location on the wire. The same sentence that answers question 20 says it is a preset location.

**22. A.** longer and require more recuperation time than the new procedure. This is explained in the last paragraph where it says: The procedure lasts two hours, which is half as long as invasive surgery, and recovery time is generally limited to a few days instead of a few weeks.

**23. B.** is performed only at hospitals containing the required equipment and certified doctors. This is also explained in the last paragraph where it says, . . . is available in various hospitals where there are advanced neurology departments and specialists trained in the procedure.

**24. B.** carnivorous dinosaur. Carnivorous means the same as meat-eating, which is stated in the first sentence.

**25. B.** in addition to

**26. A.** frightening

**27. D.** surprising

GO ON TO THE NEXT PAGE

**28. A.** lived and hunted with others. The first paragraph states that it is more astounding that the bones were found with other bones, because that indicates they were not loners.

**29. A.** meat-eating dinosaurs lived alone. The same sentences say that this discovery challenges the prior theory that they were loners.

**30. C.** Giganotosaurus

**31. B.** not closely related to Tyrannosaurus Rex. The passage states that it is as close to T. Rex as a cat to a dog, which is not close.

**32. A.** dismember

**33. A.** victim

**34. B.** combined

**35. B.** thread

**36. C.** it is more precise than previous techniques. The passage indicates that they will have control, whereas they previously did not.

**37. B.** electronic impulses could affect cells. The first paragraph indicates that they have known this for a while.

**38. A.** barraging

**39. B.** open their walls to introduce medication. The passage states that they have used electrical charges in an attempt to introduce foreign substances such as new drug treatments or genetic material.

**40. B.** causes

**41. B.** in the future

**42. A.** researchers. The noun to which they refers is in the previous sentence.

**43. C.** specific

**44. D.** tissues. The passage indicates that others is a pronoun for other tissues, because it says: . . . to activate particular tissues, whether they be muscle, bone, brain, or others.

**45. B.** place more than one chip in a single person. The last sentence of the passage answers this question: They believe that they will be able to implant multiple chips into a person to deal with one problem or more than one problem.

# Arithmetic Reasoning

**Directions:** For each of the following questions, select the choice that best answers the question or completes the statement.

1. Emily earns $9.50 an hour plus 3% commission on all sales made. If her total sales during a 30-hour work week were $500, how much did she earn?

   A. $15
   B. $250
   C. $285
   D. $300

2. The area of one circle is 4 times as large as a smaller circle with a radius of 3 inches. The radius of the larger circle is

   A. 12 inches
   B. 9 inches
   C. 8 inches
   D. 6 inches

3. Two runners finished a race in 80 seconds, another runner finished the race in 72 seconds, and the final runner finished in 68 seconds. What is the average time for all of the runners?

   A. 73 seconds
   B. 74 seconds
   C. 75 seconds
   D. 76 seconds

4. If 400 people can be seated in 8 subway cars, how many people can be seated in 5 subway cars?

   A. 200
   B. 250
   C. 300
   D. 350

5. An employee earns $8.25 an hour. In 30 hours, what earnings are made?

   A. $240.00
   B. $247.50
   C. $250.00
   D. $255.75

6. There are 72 freshmen in the band. If freshmen make up $\frac{1}{3}$ of the entire band, the total number of students in the band is

   A. 24
   B. 72
   C. 144
   D. 216

7. Dana receives $30 for her birthday and $15 for cleaning the garage. If she spends $16 on a CD, how much money does she have left?

   A. $29
   B. $27
   C. $14
   D. $1

8. A television is on sale for 20% off. If the sale price is $800, what was the original price?

   A. $160
   B. $640
   C. $960
   D. $1,000

9. A bread recipe calls for $3\frac{1}{4}$ cups of flour. If you only have $2\frac{1}{8}$ cups, how much more flour is needed?

   A. $1\frac{1}{8}$
   B. $1\frac{1}{4}$
   C. $1\frac{3}{8}$
   D. $1\frac{3}{4}$

10. How many omelets can be made from 2 dozen eggs if an omelet contains 3 eggs?

   A. 1
   B. 3
   C. 6
   D. 8

GO ON TO THE NEXT PAGE

11. You use a $20 bill to buy a magazine for $3.95. What change do you get back?

    A. $16.05
    B. $16.95
    C. $17.05
    D. $17.95

12. Standing by a pole, a boy $3\frac{1}{2}$ feet tall casts a 6 foot shadow. The pole casts a 24 foot shadow. How tall is the pole?

    A. 14 feet
    B. 18 feet
    C. 28 feet
    D. 41 feet

13. Rae earns $8.40 an hour plus an overtime rate equal to $1\frac{1}{2}$ times her regular pay for each hour worked beyond 40 hours. What are her total earnings for a 45 hour work week?

    A. $336
    B. $370
    C. $399
    D. $567

14. A sweater originally priced at $40 is on sale for $30. What percent has the sweater been discounted?

    A. 25%
    B. 33%
    C. 70%
    D. 75%

15. A cardboard box has a length of 3 feet, height of $2\frac{1}{2}$ feet, and a depth of 2 feet. If the length and depth are doubled, the increase in volume is what percentage of the original volume?

    A. 200%
    B. 300%
    C. 400%
    D. 600%

16. Mr. Triber earns a weekly salary of $300 plus 10% commission on all sales. If he sold $8,350 last week, what were his total earnings?

    A. $835
    B. $865
    C. $1,135
    D. $1,835

17. Jamie collects 300 stamps one week, 420 stamps the next week, and 180 stamps the last week. He can trade the stamps for collector coins. If 25 stamps earns him one coin, how many coins can Jamie collect?

    A. 36
    B. 50
    C. 900
    D. 925

18. On a map, 1 centimeter represents 4 miles. A distance of 10 miles would be how far apart on the map?

    A. $1\frac{3}{4}$ cm
    B. 2 cm
    C. $2\frac{1}{2}$ cm
    D. 4 cm

19. Davis donates $\frac{4}{13}$ of his paycheck to his favorite charity. If he donates $26.80, what is the amount of his paycheck?

    A. $8.25
    B. $82.50
    C. $87.10
    D. $348.40

20. Rachel ran $\frac{1}{2}$ mile in 4 minutes. At this rate, how many miles can she run in 15 minutes?

    A. $1\frac{7}{8}$
    B. 4
    C. 30
    D. 60

21. Tiling costs $2.89 per square foot. What is the cost to tile a kitchen whose dimensions are 4 yards by 5 yards?

    A. $57.80
    B. $173.40
    C. $289.00
    D. $520.20

**22.** One-eighth of a bookstore's magazines are sold on a Friday. If $\frac{1}{4}$ of the remaining magazines are sold the next day, what fractional part of the magazines remains at the end of the second day?

　　A. $\frac{1}{32}$

　　B. $\frac{1}{8}$

　　C. $\frac{7}{32}$

　　D. $\frac{21}{32}$

**23.** Roxanne deposited $300 into a savings account earning $5\frac{1}{4}$% annually. What is her balance after one year?

　　A. $15.75

　　B. $315

　　C. $315.25

　　D. $315.75

**24.** One phone plan charges a $20 monthly fee and $0.08 per minute on every phone call made. Another phone plan charges a $12 monthly fee and $0.12 per minute for each call. After how many minutes would the charge be the same for both plans?

　　A. 60 minutes

　　B. 90 minutes

　　C. 120 minutes

　　D. 200 minutes

**25.** The length of a rectangle is three times its width. If the perimeter of the rectangle is 48, what is its area?

　　A. 108

　　B. 96

　　C. 54

　　D. 48

**26.** A machine can produce 8,000 widgets in 3 hours. How many widgets are produced in one day?

　　A. 96,000

　　B. 64,000

　　C. 32,000

　　D. 8,000

**27.** Sam buys 3 candy bars for 45 cents each and two packs of gum for 79 cents each. What is the total cost of this purchase?

　　A. $1.24

　　B. $2.93

　　C. $6.20

　　D. $6.24

**28.** Devin throws a football $7\frac{1}{3}$ yards. Carl throws it $2\frac{1}{2}$ times farther. How much farther did Carl's throw travel than Devin's?

　　A. $2\frac{1}{2}$ yards

　　B. $7\frac{1}{3}$ yards

　　C. 11 yards

　　D. $18\frac{1}{3}$ yards

**29.** This morning, Taryn drove 13 miles to the library and then returned home. In the afternoon, she drove 9 miles to the movies and returned home. How much farther did Taryn travel in the morning?

　　A. 4 miles

　　B. 6 miles

　　C. 8 miles

　　D. 9 miles

**30.** Heidi tallied the different car colors in the parking lot and summarized her results in a pie chart. There are 260 cars in the lot. How many cars are either red or black?

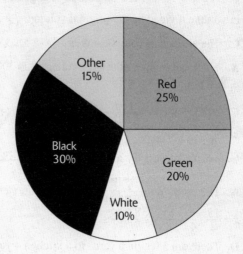

　　A. 65

　　B. 78

　　C. 130

　　D. 143

# Answers and Explanations

1. **D.** For a 30 hour week with $500 in sales, total earnings are $(30 \times \$9.50) + (3\% \times \$500) = \$285 + \$15 = \$300$.

2. **D.** The area of the circle with a radius of 3 is $\pi r^2 = \pi \cdot 3^2 = 9\pi$. The area of the larger circle is $4 \times 9\pi = 36\pi$. Therefore, $r^2 = 36$ so $r = \sqrt{36} = 6$. The radius of the larger circle is 6.

3. **C.** Since two runners finished in 80 seconds, the average of 80, 80, 72, and 68 must be found. This average is $\frac{80 + 80 + 72 + 68}{3} = \frac{300}{4} = 75$ seconds.

4. **B.** If 400 people fit in 8 subway cars, then $400 \div 8$, or 50, people fit in one subway car. Therefore, $50 \times 5$, or 250, people fit in 5 subway cars.

5. **B.** The earnings for 30 hours are $\$8.25 \times 30 = \$247.50$.

6. **D.** Let $n$ represent the number of students in the band. Then $\frac{1}{3}n = 72$, so $n = 72 \times 3 = 216$.

7. **A.** Add the amount of money received and subtract the amount spent. $\$30 + \$15 - \$16 = \$29$.

8. **D.** If an item is discount 20%, the sale price is 80% of the original price. Let $p$ represent the original price. Then $\$800 = 80\% \times p$ and $p = \frac{800}{80\%} = \frac{800}{.80} = \$1,000$.

9. **A.** $3\frac{1}{4} - 2\frac{1}{8} = \frac{13}{4} - \frac{17}{8} = \frac{26}{8} - \frac{17}{8} = \frac{9}{8} = 1\frac{1}{8}$ more cups of flour.

10. **D.** There are 24 eggs in 2 dozen eggs. If 3 eggs are in an omelet, then $24 \div 3$, or 8 omelets can be made.

11. **A.** $\$20 - \$3.95 = \$16.05$.

12. **A.** Using the ratio $\frac{\text{height}}{\text{shadow}}$, the proportion $\frac{3\frac{1}{2}}{6} = \frac{x}{24}$ models this situation, where $x$ represents the height of the pole. Cross multiply. $3\frac{1}{2} \times 24 = 6x$ so $84 = 6x$ and $x = \frac{84}{6} = 14$ feet.

13. **C.** The overtime rate is $\$8.40 \times 1.5 = \$12.60$. Five hours of overtime were completed, so the total earnings are $(\$8.40 \times 40) + (\$12.60 \times 5) = \$336 + \$63 = \$399$.

14. **A.** The amount of discount is $\$40 - \$30 = \$10$. The percent of discount is the amount of discount divided by the original price. $\frac{10}{40} = \frac{1}{4} = 25\%$.

15. **B.** The volume of the original box is $3 \times 2\frac{1}{2} \times 2 = 15$. The volume of the box with the length and depth doubled is $6 \times 2\frac{1}{2} \times 4 = 60$. The amount of change in volume is $60 - 15 = 45$. The percent change is the amount of change in volume divided by the original volume. $\frac{45}{15} = 3 = 300\%$.

16. **C.** The amount of commission is $10\% \times \$8,350 = \$835$. Total earnings are $\$300 + \$835$ commission $= \$1,135$.

17. **A.** The total number of stamps collected is $300 + 420 + 180 = 900$. The number of coins that can be collected is $\frac{900}{25} = 36$.

18. **C.** The proportion $\frac{1\,\text{cm}}{4\,\text{miles}} = \frac{x\,\text{cm}}{10\,\text{miles}}$ models this situation. Cross multiply. $1 \times 10 = 4x$ so $10 = 4x$ and $x = \frac{10}{4} = 2\frac{1}{2}$ cm.

19. **C.** Let $p$ represent the amount of the paycheck. $\frac{4}{13}p = \$26.80$ so $p = \$26.80 \cdot \frac{13}{4} = \$87.10$.

20. **A.** The proportion $\frac{\frac{1}{2}\,\text{mile}}{4\,\text{minutes}} = \frac{x\,\text{cm}}{10\,\text{miles}}$ models this situation. Cross multiply. $\frac{1}{2} \times 15 = 4x$ so $\frac{15}{2} = 4x$ and $x = \frac{15}{2} \cdot \frac{1}{4} = \frac{15}{8} = 1\frac{8}{7}$ miles.

21. **D.** There are 3 feet in a yard, so a kitchen 4 yards by 5 yards is equivalent to $(4 \times 3)$ feet by $(5 \times 3)$ feet, or 12 feet by 15 feet. The area of the kitchen is $12 \times 15 = 180$ square feet. The cost to tile is $\$2.89 \times 180 = \$520.20$.

22. **D.** At the end of the first day, there are $1 - \frac{1}{8} = \frac{7}{8}$ of the magazines remaining. $\frac{7}{8} \times \frac{1}{4} = \frac{7}{32}$ sold the next day. So at the end of the second day, there are $\frac{7}{8} - \frac{7}{32} = \frac{28}{32} - \frac{7}{32} = \frac{21}{31}$ of the magazines remaining.

**23.** **D.** Interest earned in one year is $300 \times 5\frac{1}{4}\% = \$15.75$. The total amount of the account after one year is $300 + \$15.75 = \$315.75$.

**24.** **D.** Let $m$ represent the minutes of the phone calls. The monthly charge for the first plan is $20 + 0.08m$. The monthly charge for the second plan is $12 + 0.12m$. When the monthly charges are the same, $20 + 0.08m = 12 + 0.12m$. Solve for $m$ to find the number of minutes both plans have the same rate.

$20 + 0.08m - 0.08m = 12 + 0.12m - 0.08m$

$20 = 12 + 0.04m$

$20 - 12 = 12 + 0.04m - 12$

$8 = 0.04m$ so $m = \dfrac{8}{0.04} = \dfrac{800}{4} = 200$ minutes

**25.** **A.** Width $\times$ length $= 6 \times 18 = 108$.

**26.** **B.** If a machine produces 8,000 widgets in 3 hours, it produces $\dfrac{8000}{3}$ widgets in one hour. There are 24 hours in a day, so $\dfrac{8000}{3} \times 24$ or 64,000 widgets are produced in one day.

**27.** **B.** The total cost of the purchase is $(3 \times \$0.45) + (2 + \$0.79) = \$1.35 + \$1.58 = \$2.93$.

**28.** **C.** Carl's throw went $7\frac{1}{3} \times 2\frac{1}{2} = \dfrac{22}{3} \times \dfrac{5}{2} = \dfrac{110}{6} = 18\frac{1}{3}$ yards. The difference between the two throws is $18\frac{1}{3} - 7\frac{1}{3} = 11$ yards.

**29.** **C.** The total distance traveled in the morning was $13 \times 2 = 26$ miles. The total distance traveled in the afternoon was $9 \times 2 = 18$ miles. The difference between the two distances is $26 - 18 = 8$ miles.

**30.** **D.** The percent of cars that are either red or black are $25\% + 30\% = 55\%$. The total cars that are either red or black is $260 \times 55\% = 143$.

# Mathematics Knowledge

1. Find the product of $(3 - 4x)$ and $(3 + 4x)$.

   A. 9
   B. $9 + 12x - 16x^2$
   C. $9 - 16x^2$
   D. $9 + 16x^2$

2. Round $(2.5)^4$ to the nearest tenth.

   A. 10.0
   B. 25.4
   C. 39.0
   D. 39.1

3. If $6m - 2$ is divided by 2, the result is $-4$. What is the value of $m$?

   A. $-1$
   B. 0
   C. 1
   D. 2

4. The diagonal of a square is 10 inches. What is the area of the square?

   A. $40 \text{ in}^2$
   B. $50 \text{ in}^2$
   C. $100 \text{ in}^2$
   D. $150 \text{ in}^2$

5. A car travels 20 miles in 30 minutes. At this rate, how far will the car travel in 2 hours?

   A. 40 miles
   B. 60 miles
   C. 80 miles
   D. 100 miles

6. Simplify $\dfrac{15\sqrt{3}}{\sqrt{5}}$.

   A. $3\sqrt{3}$
   B. $3\sqrt{15}$
   C. $15\sqrt{15}$
   D. $75\sqrt{3}$

7. How many blocks with sides 4 inches in length can fit into a crate $3' \times 2' \times 2'$?

   A. 3
   B. 32
   C. 196
   D. 324

8. If $x = -3$ and $y = 2$, evaluate $x^2 y$.

   A. $-64$
   B. $-81$
   C. 64
   D. 81

9. $0.00525 \div 0.01 =$

   A. 5.25
   B. 0.525
   C. 0.0525
   D. 0.000525

10. $\dfrac{3}{4} \div \dfrac{4}{3} =$

    A. 0
    B. 1
    C. $\dfrac{9}{16}$
    D. $\dfrac{16}{9}$

11. If the area of the circle is $121\pi$, find the area of the square.

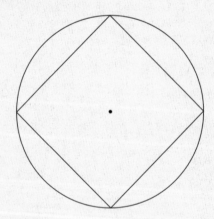

    A. 121
    B. 242
    C. 363
    D. 484

12. Simplify $(3x^2 + 2x - 5) - (2x^2 - 5) + (4x - 7)$.

    A. $x^2 + 6x - 17$
    B. $x^2 + 4x - 7$
    C. $x^2 + 6x - 2$
    D. $x^2 + 6x - 7$

13. One-fourth of the cars purchased at a dealership are luxury models. If 360 luxury models were purchased last year, how many total cars were purchased?

    A.  90
    B.  250
    C.  1440
    D.  3600

14. What is the measure of $\angle A$?

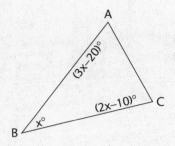

    A.  35°
    B.  60°
    C.  75°
    D.  85°

15. If $w - 3 = 3 - w$, what is the value of $w^2$?

    A.  0
    B.  1
    C.  3
    D.  9

16. $\dfrac{24}{96} - \dfrac{8}{12} =$

    A.  $\dfrac{1}{4}$
    B.  $\dfrac{5}{96}$
    C.  $-\dfrac{5}{12}$
    D.  $\dfrac{4}{21}$

17. The radius of the smaller circle is $\frac{1}{4}$ as long as the larger. What percent of the figure shown is shaded?

    A.  $6\frac{1}{4}\%$
    B.  25%
    C.  75%
    D.  $93\frac{3}{4}\%$

18. The least common multiple of 8, 12, and 20 is

    A.  4
    B.  24
    C.  60
    D.  120

19. Multiply $(5a^3bc^2)(-3a^2c)$.

    A.  $-15a^5bc^3$
    B.  $15a^5bc^3$
    C.  $-15a^6bc^2$
    D.  $2abc$

20. Simplify $\dfrac{x^2 - 25}{5 - x}$.

    A.  $x + 5$
    B.  $x - 5$
    C.  $-(x + 5)$
    D.  $5 - x$

21. Given that the point $(x, 1)$ lies on a line with a slope of $-\frac{3}{2}$ and a $y$-intercept of $-2$, find the value of $x$.

    A.  $-2$
    B.  $-1$
    C.  1
    D.  2

GO ON TO THE NEXT PAGE

**22.** What is the probability of flipping 3 heads in a row using a fair coin?

    **A.** $\frac{1}{2}$

    **B.** $\frac{2}{3}$

    **C.** $\frac{1}{8}$

    **D.** $\frac{3}{8}$

**23.** If $0.08z = 6.4$, then $z =$

    **A.** 0.8

    **B.** 8

    **C.** 80

    **D.** 800

**24.** Find the area of a regular hexagon whose sides measure 6 cm.

    **A.** 36

    **B.** $9\sqrt{2}$

    **C.** $54\sqrt{3}$

    **D.** 108

**25.** The girl's basketball team won 3 times as many games as they lost. How many games were won if they played a total of 24 games?

    **A.** 6

    **B.** 8

    **C.** 12

    **D.** 18

# Answers and Explanations

1. **C.** $(3 - 4x)(3 + 4x) = 9 + 12x - 12x - 16x^2 = 9 - 16x^2$.

2. **D.** $(2.5)^4 = 2.5 \times 2.5 \times 2.5 \times 2.5 = 39.0625$. Rounded to the nearest tenth is 39.1.

3. **A.** $\frac{6m - 2}{2} = -4$ so $3m - 1 = -4$. Solve for $m$ by adding 1 to both sides. $3m - 1 + 1 = -4 + 1$ and $3m = -3$. Dividing both sides by 3 gives $m = -1$.

4. **B.**

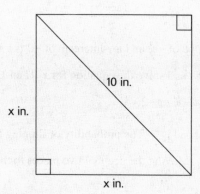

Let $x$ represent a side of the square. The area of the square is $x^2$. To find the value of $x^2$, use the Pythagorean Theorem. $x^2 + x^2 = 10^2$ so $2x^2 = 100$ and $x^2 = \frac{100}{2}$ or 50.

5. **C.** There are 120 minutes in 2 hours. Setting up a proportion yields $\frac{20 \text{ miles}}{30 \text{ minutes}} = \frac{x \text{ miles}}{120 \text{ minutes}}$. Cross multiplying results in $30x = 20 \times 120$ or $30x = 2400$. Dividing both sides by 30 gives $x = \frac{2400}{30} = 80$ miles.

6. **B.** $\frac{15\sqrt{3}}{\sqrt{5}} = \frac{15\sqrt{3}}{\sqrt{5}} \cdot \frac{\sqrt{5}}{\sqrt{5}} = \frac{15\sqrt{15}}{5} = 3\sqrt{15}$.

7. **D.** The volume of each cube is $4 \times 4 \times 4 = 64 \text{ in}^3$. The volume of the crate, in inches, is $(3 \times 12) \times (2 \times 12) \times (2 \times 12) = 20{,}736 \text{ in}^3$. The number of blocks that can fit in the crate is $\frac{20736}{64} = 324$.

8. **D.** If $x = -3$ and $y = 2$, then $x^2 y = (-3)^{2(2)} = (-3)^4 = 81$.

9. **B.** $0.00525 \div 0.01 = \frac{0.00525}{0.01} = 0.525$.

10. **C.** $\frac{3}{4} \div \frac{4}{3} = \frac{3}{4} \times \frac{3}{4} = \frac{9}{16}$.

11. **B.** The area of the circle is $\pi r^2 = 121\pi$. So $r^2 = 121$ and $r = 11$. The radius represents half the diagonal of the square, so the diagonal is 22 units long. If $x$ represents the length of a side of the square, then $x^2$ is the area of the square. Using the Pythagorean Theorem, $x^2 + x^2 = 22^2$ and $2x^2 = 484$. Therefore $x^2 = \frac{484}{2} = 242$.

12. **D.** $(3x^2 + 2x - 5) - (2x^2 - 5) + (4x - 7) = 3x^2 + 2x - 5 - 2x^2 + 5 + 4x - 7 = 3x^2 - 2x^2 + 2x + 4x - 5 + 5 - 7 = x^2 + 6x - 7$.

13. **C.** $\frac{1}{4}$ of the total cars, $t$, sold are luxury. Luxury cars sold = 360, so $\frac{1}{4}t = 360$ and $t = 360 \times 4 = 1{,}440$ total cars sold.

14. **D.** The sum of all angles in a triangle equal 180°. So $(3x - 20)° + x° + (2x - 10)° = 180°$. $3x + x + 2x - 20 - 10 = 180$ and $6x - 30 = 180$. Then $6x = 210$ and $x = \frac{210}{6} = 35$. Therefore, $\angle A$ is $3(35) - 20$ or 85°.

15. **D.** Solve for $w$ by adding $w$ to both sides. $w - 3 + w = 3 - w + w$ so $2w - 3 = 3$. Adding 3 to both sides gives $2w = 6$. So $\frac{2w}{2} = \frac{6}{2}$ and $w = 3$. Therefore $w^2 = 3^2 = 9$.

16. **C.** The least common denominator of 96 and 12 is 96 so $\frac{24}{96} - \frac{8}{12} = \frac{24}{96} - \frac{64}{96} = \frac{-40}{96} = -\frac{5}{12}$.

17. **D.** Let the radius of the smaller circle = 1. Then the radius of the larger circle is 4. The shaded region is found by subtracting the area of the smaller circle from the area of the larger circle. The area of the smaller circle is $\pi(1)^2$ or $\pi$. The area of the larger circle is $\pi(4)^2$ or $16\pi$. The shaded region is $16\pi - \pi$ or $15\pi$. The percent of the whole figure that is shaded is $\frac{15\pi}{16\pi} = 0.9375 = 93\frac{3}{4}\%$.

18. **D.** Factors of 8 are $2 \times 2 \times 2$; factors of 12 are $2 \times 2 \times 3$; factors of 20 are $2 \times 2 \times 5$. The least common multiple of 8, 12, and 20 is $2 \times 2 \times 2 \times 3 \times 5$ or 120.

19. **A.** $(5a^3bc^2)(-3a^2c) = 5 \cdot -3 \cdot a^{3+2}bc^{2+1} = -15a^5bc^3$.

20. **C.** $\frac{x^2 - 25}{5 - x} = \frac{(x+5)(x-5)}{5 - x} = \frac{(x+5)(x-5)}{-(x-5)} = \frac{(x+5)}{-1} = -(x+5)$.

21. **A.** The equation of a line with a slope of $-\frac{3}{2}$ and a $y$-intercept of $-2$ is $y = -\frac{3}{2}x - 2$. To find the value of $x$ in the point $(x, 1)$, substitute 1 for $y$ and solve the equation for $x$. Then $1 = -\frac{3}{2}x - 2$ and $3 = -\frac{3}{2}x$. So $(3)\left(-\frac{2}{3}\right) = \left(-\frac{2}{3}\right)\left(-\frac{3}{2}\right)x$ and $x = -\frac{6}{3}$ or $-2$.

22. **C.** The probability of flipping one head is $\frac{1}{2}$. The probability of flipping three heads in a row is $\frac{1}{2} \times \frac{1}{2} \times \frac{1}{2}$ or $\frac{1}{8}$.

23. **C.** If $0.08z = 6.4$ then $\frac{0.08z}{0.08} = \frac{6.4}{0.08}$. Moving the decimal two places to the right in both the numerator and denominator gives $z = \frac{640}{8} = 80$.

24. **C.**

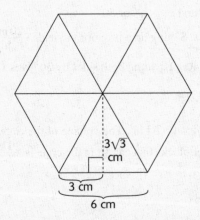

A regular hexagon is made up of six equilateral triangles. Find the area of one equilateral triangle and multiply that by 6 to find the area of the hexagon. The height, or altitude, of a triangle can be found by the Pythagorean Theorem. The right triangle formed by the altitude has a hypotenuse of 6 and a shorter leg of $\frac{6}{2}$ or 3. So $3^2 + h^2 = 6^2$ so $9 + h^2 = 36$ and $h^2 = 27$. Therefore, $h = \sqrt{27} = 3\sqrt{3}$. The area of one equilateral triangle is $\frac{1}{2}bh = \frac{1}{2} \cdot 6 \cdot 3\sqrt{3} = 9\sqrt{3}$ and the area of the hexagon is $6 \cdot 9\sqrt{3} = 54\sqrt{3}$.

25. **D.** Let $w$ represent the games won and $l$ represent the games lost. Then $w = 3 \times l = 3l$. The total number of games played is $w + l = 24$. Substituting $3l$ in for $w$ yields $3l + l = 24$ or $4l = 24$. The number of losses is $\frac{24}{4} = 6$, and the number of wins is $24 - 6 = 18$.

# Quantitative Comparisons

**Directions:** For each of the following questions, two quantities are given, one in each of Column A and Column B. You are to compare the two quantities and mark your answer sheet with the correct choice, based on the following:

Select **A** if the quantity in Column A is the greater;
Select **B** is the quantity in Column B is the greater;
Select **C** if the two quantities are equal
Select **D** if the relationship cannot be determined from the information provided.

| Column A | Column B |
|---|---|
| **1.** $0.03 \times 0.005$ | $0.0015$ |

**2.**
$$5a + 2y = 2y$$

| Column A | Column B |
|---|---|
| $a$ | $-1$ |

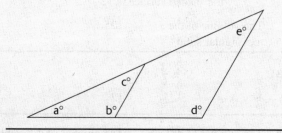

| Column A | Column B |
|---|---|
| **3.** $b + c$ | $d + e$ |

**4.**
$$C > 0$$

| Column A | Column B |
|---|---|
| $\dfrac{C + C + C + C + C}{C}$ | $5C$ |

**5.** Adam scored more points than Chris
Chris scored fewer points than Jody

| Column A | Column B |
|---|---|
| The number of points Jody scored | The number of points Adam scored |

**6.**

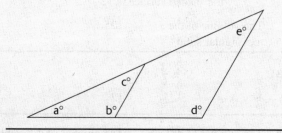

$WXYZ$ is a square
$WX = 8$

| Column A | Column B |
|---|---|
| $WY$ | $12$ |

**7.**
$$\left(\frac{v}{w}\right)\left(\frac{w}{x}\right)\left(\frac{x}{y}\right)\left(\frac{y}{z}\right) = -1$$

| Column A | Column B |
|---|---|
| $0$ | $v + z$ |

**8.** Mr. Wilson invested $2,000 for 5 years
Mr. Torrence invested $1,000 for 10 years

| Column A | Column B |
|---|---|
| The amount of interest Mr. Wilson earned on his investment | The amount of interest Mr. Torrence earned on his investment |

| Column A | Column B |
|---|---|
| **9.** The greatest odd factor of 70 | The greatest odd factor of 120 |

| Column A | Column B |
|---|---|
| **10.** The length of the third side of a triangle whose other two sides are 5 and 11 | The length of the third side of a triangle whose other two sides are 8 and 12 |

**11.**
$$P < -2$$

| Column A | Column B |
|---|---|
| $P - 6$ | $-8$ |

**12.**
$$7 < a < 9$$
$$8 < b < 10$$

| Column A | Column B |
|---|---|
| $a$ | $b$ |

**13.**
$$12^{20} = \frac{12^N}{12^2}$$

| Column A | Column B |
|---|---|
| $N$ | $40$ |

GO ON TO THE NEXT PAGE

| Column A | Column B |
|---|---|

**14.**

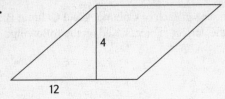

The figure here is a rhombus

| The perimeter of the rhombus | The area of the rhombus |
|---|---|

**15.** $\dfrac{0.624}{0.334}$      $\dfrac{\frac{5}{8}}{\frac{1}{3}}$

**16.** $\dfrac{w}{v} = -7$

$w$      $-7v$

**17.** $a + 3 = 12$
$b - a = 2$

$b$      $9$

**18.**

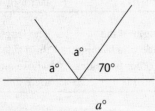

$55°$      $a°$

**19.** The average of a group of 8 numbers is 285

The sum of the numbers in the group      $2{,}285$

| Column A | Column B |
|---|---|

**20.** 7.6% of 6.2      6.2% of 7.6

**21.** $A$, $B$, and $C$ are consecutive odd integers
$$A < B < C$$
$A + B + 6$      $2C$

**22.**

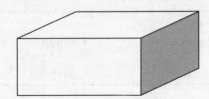

In the rectangular solid, the area of the shaded surface is 12

The volume of the rectangular solid      125

**23.** $35$ is $\dfrac{5}{6}$ of $p$

$\dfrac{p}{3}$      $12$

**24.** The number of different integral divisors of 30      The number of different integral divisors of 40

**25.** $9a^2 + 4b^2 = -12ab$

$a$      $-\dfrac{3}{2}b$

# Answers and Explanations

1. **B.** When multiplying two decimal numbers, the number of digits to the right of the decimal point in the product must equal the sum of the number of digits to the right of the decimal points in the two numbers being multiplied. Since 0.03 has two digits to the right of the decimal point and 0.005 has three digits to the right of the decimal point, the product must have $2 + 3 = 5$ digits to the right of the decimal point. Thus, $0.03 \times 0.005 = 0.00015$. This number is smaller than the number in Column B.

2. **A.** Begin by considering the equation given at the top. Note that if $2y$ is subtracted from both sides, the equation becomes $5a = 0$. This can only be true if $a = 0$. Thus, the value of $a$ is greater than $-1$.

3. **C.** The sum of the measures of the three angles in a triangle is always $180°$. Thus, in the small triangle, we know that $a + b + c = 180$, and, in the large triangle, we know that $a + d + e = 180$. This means that $a + b + c = a + d + e$. Subtracting $a$ from both sides of the equation leaves us with $b + c = d + e$.

4. **D.** Begin by simplifying the algebraic fraction in Column A.

$$\frac{C + C + C + C + C}{C} = \frac{5C}{C} = 5$$

Thus, the value of the fraction in Column A is 5. However, we cannot determine the relative size of $5C$. For example, if $C = 1$, $5C = 5$. But, if $C = \frac{1}{5}$, $5C = 1$.

5. **D.** The common information tells us that both Adam and Jody scored more points than Chris. However, it gives us no information to compare the number of points Adam scored to the number of points Jody scored.

6. **B.** $WY$ is the hypotenuse of a right triangle with legs of length 8. Since the two legs have the same length, the triangle is also a 45–45–90 isosceles triangle, which means the length of the hypotenuse is $8\sqrt{2}$. The value of the $\sqrt{3}$ is about 1.41, which means that $8\sqrt{2}$ is less than 12.

7. **C.** Note that, in the equation given in the common information, the variables $w$, $x$, and $y$ can be cancelled out, leaving us with the equation $\frac{v}{z} = -1$. If both sides of this equation are multiplied by $z$, we obtain $v = -z$. Now, add $z$ to both sides to obtain $v + z = 0$.

8. **D.** We are not told the interest rates that the investments earned, and therefore, we can make no conclusions as to how much interest was earned.

9. **A.** The quickest way to find the greatest odd factor of these numbers is to first prime factor them, and then find the product of all of the odd factors. For example, note that $70 = 2 \times 5 \times 7$, so 70 has the number $5 \times 7 = 35$ as a prime factor. Next, $120 = 2 \times 2 \times 2 \times 3 \times 5$, so the largest prime factor of 120 is only $3 \times 5 = 15$.

10. **D.** The sum of the lengths of any two sides of a triangle must be greater than the length of the third side. Thus, in a triangle with sides 5 and 11, the length of the third side must be less than $5 + 11 = 16$, and greater than $11 - 5 = 6$. In a triangle with sides 8 and 12, the length of the third side must be less than $8 + 12 = 20$, and greater than $12 - 4 = 8$. Clearly, with these possible value ranges, either triangle could potentially have the longer third side.

11. **B.** If $P$ actually was equal to $-2$, then $P - 6$ would equal $-2 - 6 = -8$. Since $P$ is less than $-2$, $P - 6$ is less than $-8$.

12. **D.** Be very careful with this problem. The common error is to conclude that $a$ has to be 8 and $b$ has to be 9. However, you are not told that $a$ and $b$ are integers, so for example, $a$ could be 8.9, and $b$ could be 8.1. There is no way to tell which of the two variables is larger.

13. **B.** Note that $\frac{12^N}{12^2} = 12N^{-2}$. Since this must be equal to $12^{20}$, it follows that $N = 22$.

14. **C.** In a rhombus, all sides have the same length, so the perimeter is $12 + 12 + 12 + 12 = 48$. The area is equal to the length of the base times the height, which is $12 \times 4 = 48$. Thus, the perimeter and the area have the same numerical values.

15. **B.** It is not necessary to perform any computations to solve this problem. Note that the fraction $\frac{5}{8}$ is equal to 0.625, and the fraction $\frac{1}{3}$ is equal to 0.333.... Thus, the numerator of the fraction in Column A, 0.624 is less than

the numerator of the fraction in Column B, $\frac{5}{8}$. Similarly, the denominator of the fraction in Column A, 0.334, is greater than the denominator of the fraction in Column B, $\frac{1}{3}$. Overall, the fraction in Column A must be less than the value of the fraction in Column B.

**16.** **C.** If both sides of the equation are multiplied by $v$, the result is $w = -7v$.

**17.** **A.** If the two equations given in the common information are added together, the result is $3 + b = 14$. This tells us that $b = 11$.

**18.** **C.** Since the three angles, taken together, form a straight line, it follows that $a + a + 70 = 180$, or $2a = 110$. This means that $a = 55$.

**19.** **B.** The formula for the average of a group of numbers can be expressed as $\frac{\text{The sum of the numbers}}{\text{The number of numbers}} = $ The average of the numbers.

Using the numbers given in the problem, we obtain $\frac{\text{The sum of the numbers}}{8} = 285$.

Now, multiply both sides by 8, to obtain:

The sum of the numbers $= 285 \times 8 = 2{,}280$.

**20.** **C.** There is no need to perform a computation here. It is always true that $a\%$ of $b$ is equal to $b\%$ of $a$ for any numbers $a$ and $b$.

**21.** **D.** Note that no information is given about the third dimension of the box; therefore, nothing can be known about the volume of the box. Correct answer is D unless more information is given.

**22.** **B.** The volume of a rectangle solid is equal to the area of the base times the height. Using the shaded surface as the base, the height would be 10, and the area would be $10 \times 12 = 120$.

**23.** **A.** Begin by solving the equation in the common information for $p$.

$$35 = \frac{5}{6} \times p$$

Multiply both sides by $\frac{5}{6}$

$$\left(\frac{6}{5}\right) \times 35 = \left(\frac{6}{5}\right) \times \frac{5}{6} \times p$$

Simplify

$$6 \times 7 = p$$
$$p = 42.$$

Thus, $\frac{p}{3} = \frac{42}{3} = 14$.

**24.** **C.** The divisors of 30 are 1, 2, 3, 5, 6, 10,15, and 30, so there are 8 divisors. The divisors of 40 are 1, 2, 4, 5, 8, 10, 20, and 40. Thus, there are also 8 divisors of 40.

**25.** **C.** Rewrite the equation in the Common Information as $9a^2 + 12ab + 4b^2 = 0$ and factor the left side.

$$(3a + 2b)(3a + 2b) = 0$$

For this to be true, it must be the case that $3a + 2b = 0$. To finish, solve this equation for $a$.

$$3a + 2b = 0$$

Subtract $2b$ from both sides

$$3a = -2b$$

Divide both sides by 3

$$a = -\frac{3}{2}b$$

# Life Science

1. The building blocks of sugars, and the substances used by plants in photosynthesis, are

   A. oxygen and nitrogen
   B. oxygen and carbon dioxide
   C. water and carbon dioxide
   D. water and oxygen

2. Which of the following consists **only** of members of a group that can interbreed and produce fertile offspring?

   A. kingdom
   B. phylum
   C. family
   D. species

3. The normal body temperature of a person is

   A. 37 degrees Fahrenheit
   B. 37 degrees centigrade
   C. 98 degrees Celsius
   D. 98 degrees centigrade

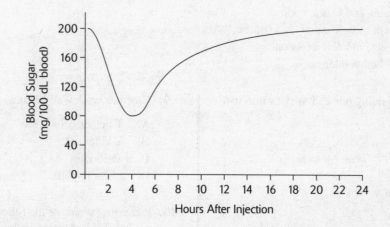

4. Look at the graph of someone's blood sugar after having been injected with a substance. Which of the following statements is true?

   A. The person's blood sugar level fell faster than it rose.
   B. This person had just eaten a big meal.
   C. This person was injected with glucagon, which converts glycogen to glucose.
   D. This person was a diabetic.

GO ON TO THE NEXT PAGE

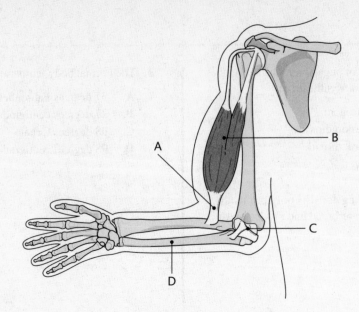

**5.** Using the drawing of the arm, which of the following statements is true?

    **A.** A is a ligament, and C is a tendon.
    **B.** A is the biceps muscle, and C is a tendon.
    **C.** C is a ligament, and A is a tendon.
    **D.** A and C are both tendons.

**6.** The process of dividing one cell nucleus into two nuclei is called

    **A.** mitosis
    **B.** meiosis
    **C.** cytokinesis
    **D.** cell division

**7.** People have 46 chromosomes in each of their cells. How many are in each of their gametes?

    **A.** 46
    **B.** 23
    **C.** 92
    **D.** 2

**8.** In a situation of incomplete dominance, red flowers are crossed with white flowers and all the resulting flowers are pink, what percentage of the offspring of a cross between two pink flowers would be pink?

    **A.** 0 %
    **B.** 25 %
    **C.** 50 %
    **D.** 100 %

**9.** Vaccines work well because they prepare one's

    **A.** T-helper cells
    **B.** T-killer cells
    **C.** antibodies
    **D.** memory cells

**10.** Increasing which of the following factors would not help a plant photosynthesize faster?

    **A.** Oxygen
    **B.** Carbon dioxide
    **C.** Light intensity
    **D.** Water

**11.** A man with O-type blood and a woman with AB-type blood could have which type of children?

    **A.** O
    **B.** AB
    **C.** A or B
    **D.** all of the above

12. When blood leaves the heart and enters the pulmonary artery, it

    A. has just left the right atrium
    B. is heading to the lungs
    C. has just left the left atrium
    D. is heading to the aorta

13. The organ that is most closely associated with the digestion of proteins is the

    A. stomach
    B. liver
    C. small intestine
    D. large intestine

14. Which of the following organisms is NOT an invertebrate?

    A. sponge
    B. jellyfish
    C. snail
    D. fish

15. If you were looking for DNA in a cell, you would find it in the

    A. endoplasmic reticulum
    B. nucleus
    C. vacuole
    D. plasma membrane

16. The male part of a flower is referred to as the

    A. ovary
    B. pistil
    C. sepal
    D. stamen

17. The central nervous system in humans is made up of

    A. the brain and the spinal cord
    B. the brain and the muscles
    C. the brain and the heart
    D. the brain and the lungs

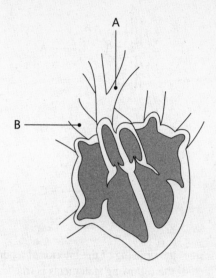

18. When blood is leaving the left ventricle, it is

    A. oxygenated and moving to structure A
    B. not oxygenated and moving to structure A
    C. oxygenated and moving to structure B
    D. not oxygenated and moving to structure B

19. An example of a marine animal with radial symmetry would be

    A. a clam
    B. a jellyfish
    C. a squid
    D. a tuna fish

20. Water moves up a stem because of

    A. the cohesion of water molecules
    B. the adhesion of water molecules
    C. the transpiration of water molecules
    D. all of the above

21. The phase in which the molecules move the fastest is

    A. liquid
    B. solid
    C. gas
    D. plasma

GO ON TO THE NEXT PAGE

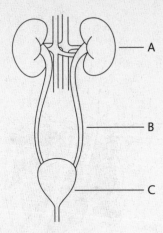

**22.** Consider the drawing of the interior of a human. Which of the following statements is true?

    **A.** A is the kidney, B is the urethra, and C is the bladder.

    **B.** A is the bladder, B is the ureter, and C is the kidney.

    **C.** A is the kidney, B is the ureter, and C is the bladder.

    **D.** A is the bladder, B is the urethra, and C is the kidney.

**23.** Blood is approximately

    **A.** 20 % cells and 80 % plasma

    **B.** 30 % cells and 70 % plasma

    **C.** 45 % cells and 55 % plasma

    **D.** 30 % plasma and 70 % cells

**24.** Organelles that are considered the powerhouse of the cell are

    **A.** mitochondria

    **B.** vacuoles

    **C.** peroxisomes

    **D.** ribosomes

**25.** Red-green color-blindness is a sex-linked trait in humans. If a girl is born color-blind, which of the following statements is true?

    **A.** Her father is color-blind.

    **B.** Her mother is color-blind.

    **C.** Her mother is a carrier for the mutant gene.

    **D.** All of the above could be true.

**26.** The HIV virus infects which type of cells?

    **A.** Cytotoxic T cells

    **B.** Helper T cells

    **C.** Phagocytes

    **D.** Monocytes

**27.** The term "amino acid" is associated with

    **A.** carbohydrates

    **B.** minerals

    **C.** vitamins

    **D.** proteins

**28.** Rod-shaped bacteria are called

    **A.** bacilli

    **B.** cocci

    **C.** spirilla

    **D.** protozoa

**29.** Of the following, which is an infectious disease?

    **A.** tonsillitis

    **B.** asthma

    **C.** mumps

    **D.** rickets

# Answers and Explanations

1. **C.** The water is split, oxygen is given off as a waste product, and the hydrogen is combined with carbon dioxide to form sugars.

2. **D.** The definition of species is artificial, but conveys the idea that only members of the same species meet in the wild and mate to produce fertile offspring.

3. **B.** Celsius and centigrade are the same thing. Water boils at 100 degrees centigrade or 212 degrees Fahrenheit.

4. **A.** The slope of the line is a measure of the rate. Anyone who was injected with insulin would have the same type of response.

5. **C.** Ligaments connect bone to bone and tendons connect bone to muscle.

6. **A.** Mitosis is nuclear division, cytokinesis is cell division, and meiosis is used for sex cell production.

7. **B.** Gametes (eggs and sperm) need to have half the normal chromosome number so that when they combine the correct number appears in the new cell.

8. **C.** In this case of incomplete dominance, each pink flower has one gene for red and one for white. When they combine randomly, one-fourth will be white, one-fourth red, and half pink.

9. **D.** Memory cells help us mount quicker responses to antigens we have previously encountered.

10. **A.** Oxygen slows down the rate because most plants will use it in photorespiration, which is caused by the plant's enzymes picking up oxygen rather than carbon dioxide.

11. **C.** Both A and B are dominant to O and will be expressed.

12. **B.** Arteries carry blood away from the heart.

13. **A.** The only function for the stomach is protein digestion, while the small intestine digests all food types.

14. **D.** Fish are vertebrates (they have backbones). The other organisms listed (sponge, jellyfish, snail) are all invertebrates (they do not have backbones).

15. **B.** DNA never leaves the nucleus.

16. **D.** The stamen is made up of the anther, which makes pollen, and the filament, which holds up the anther. The pistil is the homologous female structure.

17. **A.** The brain and the spinal cord constitute the central nervous system.

18. **C.** The heart pumps blood from its right side to the lungs. The left ventricle pumps blood throughout the rest of the body, initially through the aorta (B).

19. **B.** Radial symmetry is like a wheel with spokes.

20. **D.** Cohesion is the attraction of water molecules to one another. Adhesion is the attraction of water molecules to the walls a vessel. And transpiration is the force that provides the pull of the water molecules up the stem.

21. **D.** Plasma molecules have the highest kinetic energy.

22. **C.** The kidneys produce urine that travels through the ureters to the bladder and then out the urethra.

23. **C.** Blood plasma is about 90% water with dissolved nutrients, waste, hormones, and proteins.

24. **A.** Mitochondria are used in the cell respiration of eukaryotic organisms.

25. **D.** Any sex-linked trait is carried on the X chromosome. Males have one, a copy of which they give to all their daughters. Females have two X chromosomes, and they give a copy of one of them to all their daughters. The mother could have two mutated chromosomes or just one. Women that carry a mutated gene but do not express it are said to be carriers. Any boy born to a carrier has a 50 % chance of inheriting that mutated gene.

26. **B.** The HIV virus infects the T helper cells that are used to initiate many specific immune responses.

27. **D.** Proteins are complex chemicals made of chains of amino acids.

28. **A.** Cocci are spherical or oval-shaped bacterial. Spirilla bacteria are spirally twisted or coiled.

29. **C.** Mumps are caused by a virus, and therefore, infectious. Tonsillitis is an inflammation of the tonsils. Asthma is an allergy, and rickets is caused by the absence of vitamin D and calcium in the diet of infants and young children.

# Physical Science

1. A liter is about the same as

   A. a quart
   B. a gallon
   C. a pint
   D. a half-gallon

2. When heat is added to water, the added energy

   A. raises the electrons to a higher energy level
   B. makes the molecules move faster
   C. splits the molecules apart
   D. increases the number of electrons in the molecules

3. There are 2.54 cm in one inch, 10 millimeters in one centimeter, 12 inches in a foot, and 3 feet in a yard. Approximately how many millimeters are in a yard?

   A. 30
   B. 300
   C. 390
   D. 900

4. The expression 35 parts per million (35 ppm) is the same as

   A. 0.035
   B. 3.5 %
   C. 0.35 %
   D. 0.035 %

5. Two masses fall 3 meters to the ground. If friction is neglected, when they reach the ground

   A. both masses have the same speed
   B. both masses have the same energy
   C. both masses have the same momentum
   D. the heavier mass has a higher speed

6. The electric current in a metal conductor is carried by

   A. positive ions
   B. electrons
   C. both
   D. either, depending on the metal

7. Which of the following statements about diffusion is false?

   A. Diffusion is very effective over very short distances.
   B. Diffusion requires energy to do its work.
   C. The diffusion of water is called osmosis.
   D. Diffusion is the movement of molecules from a greater to a lesser concentration.

8. Sodium ions have a charge of +1. This is because

   A. they have one more proton than electron
   B. they have one more neutron than electron
   C. they have one more electron than neutron
   D. they have one more proton than neutron

9. Which of the following statements is true?

   A. Electrons are negatively charged and are found in the nucleus of an atom.
   B. Electrons are negatively charged and are found outside the nucleus.
   C. Neutrons are positively charged and are found in the nucleus.
   D. Protons are positively charged and are found outside the nucleus.

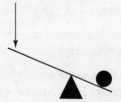

10. In the lever shown here, a force is exerted on the left side to lift the mass on the right. Assuming the lever is ideal, which of following is the same on both sides?

    A. force
    B. momentum
    C. velocity
    D. work

GO ON TO THE NEXT PAGE

11. A gas has a volume of 0.25 liter at a pressure of 1 atmosphere. If the volume increases to 0.50 liter, and the temperature remains constant, the new pressure will be

    A. 1 atmosphere
    B. 0.5 atmosphere
    C. 0.25 atmosphere
    D. 2 atmospheres

12. What are the total number of hydrogen atoms represented in the following formula: $C_6H_{10}(OH)_6$ ?

    A. 6
    B. 16
    C. 22
    D. 60

13. Ammonia can be produced from nitrogen and hydrogen, according to the unbalanced equation

    $$N_2 \text{ (g)} + H_2 \text{ (g)} = NH_3 \text{ (g)}$$

    After balancing the equation, the coefficient before ammonia should be

    A. 1
    B. 2
    C. 3
    D. 4

14. Given the reaction:

    $$2 CO \text{ (g)} + O_2 \text{ (g)} = 2CO_2 \text{ (g)}$$

    When there is an increase in pressure to the system one would expect

    A. an increase in the amount of carbon dioxide
    B. an increase in the amount of carbon monoxide and oxygen
    C. a decrease in the amount of carbon dioxide
    D. no change in the system

15. Given the equation for the production of carbon dioxide above, and the following information:

| element | atomic mass |
| --- | --- |
| carbon | 12 |
| oxygen | 16 |

    What mass of carbon dioxide will be formed from the reaction of 14 grams of carbon monoxide and sufficient oxygen?

    A. 22
    B. 28
    C. 44
    D. 56

16. Jack has 100 ml. of a 12 molar solution of sulfuric acid. How much of it should he put into a graduated cylinder to make 20 ml of a 1.2 molar solution?

    A. 1
    B. 2
    C. 10
    D. 12

17. The transformation of a solid directly into a gas is called

    A. vaporization
    B. ionization
    C. sublimation
    D. polarization

18. A 50-cm long metal rod expands 2mm when heated in an oven. How much would a 75-cm long rod of the same material expand in the same oven?

    A. 2mm
    B. 3mm
    C. 4mm
    D. 6mm

19. Consider the following chemical structure. Which of the following statements is true?

    A. It represents an amino acid, and X points to a disulfide bridge.
    B. It represents two amino acids, and X points to a peptide bond.
    C. It represents three amino acids, and X points to a disulfide bridge.
    D. It represents three amino acids, and X points to a peptide bond.

20. The correct structural formula for ethyne is

    A. $H - C = C - H$
    B. $H - C = C = H$
    C. $H - C \equiv C - H$
    D. $H = C = C = H$

21. A car is driving around a curve on a level road. The force holding the car on the curve is

    A.  friction
    B.  gravity
    C.  tension
    D.  magnetic

22. What is the oxidation number of lead (Pb) in $PbF_2$?

    A.  −1
    B.  −2
    C.  +1
    D.  +2

23. As one moves down a column on the left side of the periodic table, which of the following statements is true?

    A.  The size of the ion becomes smaller.
    B.  The electronegativity decreases.
    C.  The electrons are held more tightly.
    D.  The number of neutrons remain the same.

24. In the Haber process, ammonia is produced according to the following equation:

    $$N_2 (g) + 3H_2 (g) = 2NH_3 (g)$$

    How many moles of hydrogen gas are needed to react with one of nitrogen?

    A.  1
    B.  3
    C.  6
    D.  22.4

25. Given the reaction:

    $$2 CO (g) + O_2 (g) = 2CO_2 (g)$$

    How many liters of oxygen are required to react with the carbon monoxide to make 2 molecules of carbon dioxide at STP?

    A.  1
    B.  2
    C.  22.4
    D.  $6.02 \times 10^{23}$

26. A heavy object is dropped from the top of a tower. If it falls 5 meters after one second, how far from the top will it be three seconds after it was released? Neglect air resistance.

    A.  10 meters
    B.  15 meters
    C.  30 meters
    D.  45 meters

27. Mixing carbon and oxygen together to make carbon dioxide is a:

    A.  chemical reaction
    B.  physical reaction
    C.  liquid reaction
    D.  none of the above

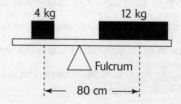

28. Two masses are resting on a beam of negligible mass, as shown above. Where should the fulcrum be positioned so that the masses will be in balance?

    A.  20 cm from the 4 kg mass
    B.  20 cm from the 12 kg mass
    C.  30 cm from the 4 kg mass
    D.  40 cm from the 12 kg mass

29. A liquid sample has a volume of 50 milliliters at 20 degrees Celsius. What will the new volume be at 1192 degrees Celsius if the pressure stays the same?

    A.  1 milliliters
    B.  250 milliliters
    C.  4980 milliliters
    D.  .004 milliliters

30. Which of the following is the best heat conductor?

    A.  metalloid
    B.  plastic
    C.  metal
    D.  wood

# Answers and Explanations

1. **A.** A liter is slightly larger than a quart, about 33 ounces in a liter.

2. **B.** Adding heat to water gives the molecules more kinetic energy, resulting in faster motion. It does not change the energy level of electrons or the number of electrons in the molecules.

3. **D.** A yard is slightly less than a meter. Since there are 1000 millimeters in a meter, there should be slightly less in a yard.

4. **D.** .00035 = .035%.

5. **A.** The acceleration of objects in freefall is independent of mass, resulting in the same speed at the end of a fall. The momentum and energy are proportional to the mass.

6. **B.** Electrons are the only charges free to move in a metal.

7. **B.** Diffusion is the movement of molecules of water from a greater to a lesser concentration. The diffusion of water is osmosis, and no energy is required as these molecules move down a concentration gradient.

8. **A.** Protons have a positive charge and electrons have a negative charge.

9. **B.** Both protons and neutrons exist in the nucleus, while electrons are orbiting the nucleus.

10. **D.** The work done by the force is the same as the work done on the load in an ideal simple machine.

11. **B.** As one decreases the volume, the pressure will increase proportionally, and if one increases the volume, then the pressure will decrease.

12. **B.** The subscript applies to each of the atoms within the parentheses.

13. **B.** The balanced equation is $N_2 (g) + 3H_2 (g) = 2NH_3 (g)$.

14. **A.** To relieve the stress on the system, fewer moles will exist. This is an application of LeChatlier's principle.

15. **A.** Fourteen grams of carbon monoxide are 0.5 mole. Since carbon monoxide and carbon dioxide are in a 1:1 (2:2) ratio, there will be 0.5 mole of carbon dioxide formed. 0.5 of 44 grams (the formula mass for carbon dioxide) is 22 grams.

16. **B.** One should apply the equation $V_1M_1 = V_2M_2$, where V = volume and M = molarity. Solving, $V_1 = V_2M_2/M_1$.

17. **C.** The transformation of a solid directly to a gas is called sublimation.

18. **B.** The amount of thermal expansion of a rod is proportional to its length for a given temperature change. Since the 75cm rod is 50% longer, its expansion is 50% greater.

19. **D.** Amino acids are joined by peptide bonds.

20. **C.** Knowing that carbon has four bonds leaves C as the only choice.

21. **A.** Friction between the tires and the road provide the centripetal force to keep the car in the turn.

22. **D.** Lead (Pb) is a metal and will have a positive oxidation number. Fluorine is the most electronegative, and has an oxidation number of −1.

23. **B.** The most electronegative elements, those that will attract electrons the most readily, are on the top right.

24. **B.** The coefficients are the number of moles.

25. **C.** A mole of any gas occupies 22.4 liters at STP.

26. **D.** The distance a mass travels in freefall is proportional to the square of the time. Since three seconds is three times more than one second, the distance is nine times greater, $9 \times 5 = 45m$.

27. **A.** The two substances come together to form a new compound.

28. **B.** The fulcrum must be placed at the center of gravity of the masses, which is the place where the product of the mass times the distance is the same for all masses. At 20cm from the 12kg mass (60cm from the 4kg mass), the product is the same: $20 \times 12 = 60 \times 4$.

29. **B.** T1 over T2 = V1 over V2.

30. **C.** Metal is the best heat conductor.

# Practice Test 2

## Verbal

### Synonyms

**Directions:** Select the word or phrase that completes the sentence.

1. Contradict most nearly means

    A. discuss
    B. predict
    C. listen to
    D. disagree with

2. An ambiguous answer is

    A. unclear
    B. positive
    C. unkind
    D. deliberate

3. Emit most nearly means

    A. hide
    B. hope for
    C. let out
    D. disturb

4. Evoke most nearly means

    A. hold back
    B. call forth
    C. change
    D. tease

5. Mar most nearly means

    A. sell
    B. spoil
    C. move
    D. upset

6. A punctual student is

    A. late
    B. prompt
    C. missing
    D. quick

7. A vital item is

    A. healthy
    B. useless
    C. necessary
    D. wasted

8. Scurry most nearly means

    A. clean
    B. dash
    C. stroll
    D. fall

9. Divulge most nearly means

    A. care for
    B. leave
    C. reveal
    D. injure

10. Clash most nearly means

    A. conflict
    B. soot
    C. dance
    D. delight

11. Heed most nearly means

    A. avoid
    B. agree with
    C. hear
    D. pay attention to

12. Startle most nearly means

    A. surprise
    B. climb
    C. draw
    D. sparkle

**13.** An irritating remark is

    **A.** annoying

    **B.** itchy

    **C.** funny

    **D.** gloomy

**14.** Seep most nearly means

    **A.** fall

    **B.** rain

    **C.** ooze

    **D.** climb

**15.** Incite most nearly means

    **A.** calm down

    **B.** stir up

    **C.** continue

    **D.** intend

**16.** To fuse is to

    **A.** blend

    **B.** annoy

    **C.** smoke

    **D.** aid

**17.** Incapacitate most nearly means

    **A.** imprison

    **B.** anger

    **C.** embody

    **D.** disable

**18.** A coalition is a(n)

    **A.** addition

    **B.** union

    **C.** failure

    **D.** unexpected event

**19.** Discord most nearly means

    **A.** paid

    **B.** rejection

    **C.** interruption

    **D.** conflict

**20.** Progeny are

    **A.** supporters

    **B.** offspring

    **C.** geniuses

    **D.** forgers

# Antonyms

**Directions:** Select the word or phrase that best completes the sentence.

1. Familiar is the *opposite* of
   - A. lonesome
   - B. well-known
   - C. relative
   - D. strange

2. Cease is the *opposite* of
   - A. stop
   - B. forget
   - C. change
   - D. continue

3. Vacant is the *opposite* of
   - A. full
   - B. empty
   - C. relaxed
   - D. nervous

4. Concur is the *opposite* of
   - A. shout
   - B. argue
   - C. agree
   - D. discuss

5. Sparse is the *opposite* of
   - A. plentiful
   - B. skinny
   - C. ashy
   - D. dry

6. Hostile is the *opposite* of
   - A. sorry
   - B. generous
   - C. homely
   - D. friendly

7. Stingy is the *opposite* of
   - A. calming
   - B. generous
   - C. frugal
   - D. wealthy

8. Interdict is the *opposite* of
   - A. forbid
   - B. accept
   - C. stall
   - D. interfere

9. Grapple is the *opposite* of
   - A. fasten
   - B. welcome
   - C. respond
   - D. release

10. Revile is the *opposite* of
    - A. assail
    - B. love
    - C. fawn
    - D. degrade

11. Feint is the *opposite* of
    - A. stand still
    - B. move aside
    - C. sit down
    - D. speed up

12. To delude is the *opposite* of
    - A. clarify
    - B. obscure
    - C. deceive
    - D. change

GO ON TO THE NEXT PAGE

Practice Test 2

**13.** Spare is the *opposite* of

    **A.** helpful
    **B.** empty
    **C.** lush
    **D.** special

**14.** Passive is the *opposite* of

    **A.** unresponsive
    **B.** energetic
    **C.** dormant
    **D.** sweeping

**15.** Skeptical is the *opposite* of

    **A.** victorious
    **B.** adept
    **C.** distrustful
    **D.** accepting

# Analogies

**Directions:** Select the word or phrase that best completes the sentence.

**1.** Bold is to tame as polite is to

  A.  gentle
  B.  brave
  C.  rude
  D.  dirty

**2.** Green is to plant as creative is to

  A.  imaginative
  B.  monkey
  C.  flower
  D.  inventor

**3.** Clumsy is to trip as late is to

  A.  walk
  B.  early
  C.  forgive
  D.  hurry

**4.** Fall is to winter as bud is to

  A.  leaf
  B.  spring
  C.  root
  D.  curl

**5.** Ruin is to spoil as jump is to

  A.  surprise
  B.  leap
  C.  run
  D.  stand

**6.** Bay is to ocean as pebble is to

  A.  dust
  B.  rock
  C.  lake
  D.  salt

**7.** Mathematics is to algebra as biology is to

  A.  alive
  B.  animals
  C.  botany
  D.  science

**8.** Lead is to heavy as water is to

  A.  wet
  B.  light
  C.  ice
  D.  solid

**9.** Manual is to explain as stapler is to

  A.  staples
  B.  fasten
  C.  define
  D.  paper

**10.** Depth is to trench as height is to

  A.  empty
  B.  size
  C.  hole
  D.  hill

**11.** ANKLE : LEG :: WRIST :

  A.  foot
  B.  finger
  C.  arm
  D.  pair of socks

**12.** APRON : CHEF :: ROBE :

  A.  nurse
  B.  judge
  C.  dress
  D.  oven

**13.** EYES ARE TO NOSE :: ROOF :

  A.  mouth
  B.  carpet
  C.  house
  D.  chair

**14.** LION : CAT :: WOLF :

  A.  tiger
  B.  bird
  C.  fish
  D.  dog

GO ON TO THE NEXT PAGE

**15.** BOUQUET : VASE :: GARBAGE :

   **A.** trash pail

   **B.** sink

   **C.** glass of water

   **D.** carton

**16.** BUTTON : SNAP ::

   **A.** pants : zipper

   **B.** necklace : locket

   **C.** screen : door

   **D.** key : can opener

**17.** DRESS : SEAMSTRESS ::

   **A.** cupcake : pie

   **B.** microwave : toaster

   **C.** cake : baker

   **D.** thread : needle

**18.** CAR : TRUNK ::

   **A.** camera : film

   **B.** automobile : tire

   **C.** gymnasium : locker

   **D.** basketball : team

**19.** LOAF OF BREAD : KNIFE ::

   **A.** hair : scissors

   **B.** teeth : comb

   **C.** shower : hair dryer

   **D.** faucet : garden hose

**20.** VIOLIN : HARP ::

   **A.** piano : keys

   **B.** trumpet : tuba

   **C.** snare : drum

   **D.** strings : guitar

# Spelling

**Directions:** In Questions 1–10, look for mistakes in spelling only. If you find no mistake, mark (D) on your answer sheet.

1. **A.** Mandy usually eats breakfast at 9:00 A.M.
   **B.** Ms. Lee tries to make sure her children have a balanced diet.
   **C.** The cabinet's heigth is 36 inches.
   **D.** No mistakes.

2. **A.** The play *Death of a Salesman* is a modern tradegy.
   **B.** The critic preferred plays written in Shakespeare's time.
   **C.** The hero of the play is named Willy Loman.
   **D.** No mistakes.

3. **A.** In the mayor's absence, the deputy chaired the city council meeting.
   **B.** Cats move gracefully and rarely seem awkward.
   **C.** Edna tried to persuade Tom to vote for the new program.
   **D.** No mistakes.

4. **A.** Human activity is not the only cause of pollution of the envinronment.
   **B.** Eruptions of volcanoes are a possible cause of bad air.
   **C.** Forbidding the use of gasoline engines would not be practical.
   **D.** No mistakes.

5. **A.** The comedian thought she was humorous, but I didn't laugh at her jokes.
   **B.** The earthquake led to disastrous floods because the dam crumbled.
   **C.** Jay wanted to pursue a career in medicine.
   **D.** No mistakes.

6. **A.** I will sacrifice my free time in order to practice playing the violin.
   **B.** Having a driver's license is a privilege, not a right.
   **C.** The house acrost the street from ours is for sale.
   **D.** No mistakes.

7. **A.** The chair appointed Ms. Montez to the Finance Comittee.
   **B.** Pleasant weather created the right atmosphere for the picnic.
   **C.** The American Red Cross offers courses in water safety.
   **D.** No mistakes.

8. **A.** We suggest that you study the manual before taking the test.
   **B.** New construction can often interfere with traffic.
   **C.** A new biznes center opened next to the mall.
   **D.** No mistakes.

9. **A.** The railroad tracks ran paralel to the highway.
   **B.** Saul was grateful for the gift his aunt gave him on his birthday.
   **C.** One benefit of regular exercise is increased muscular strength.
   **D.** No mistakes.

10. **A.** On the eighth day of the festival, closing ceremonies were held.
    **B.** Excellent fireworks displays concluded the activities.
    **C.** The occasion was a complete success.
    **D.** No mistakes.

*In Questions 11–20, one of the words is misspelled. Select the word that is incorrect.*

11. **A.** referendum
    **B.** irregular
    **C.** despised
    **D.** conserning

12. **A.** hypnosis
    **B.** rebellious
    **C.** antibiotic
    **D.** pianoes

**GO ON TO THE NEXT PAGE**

Practice Test 2

13. A. license
    B. piloting
    C. celabration
    D. vulgar

14. A. privilege
    B. sophmore
    C. achieving
    D. accuracy

15. A. lonliness
    B. recognize
    C. forward
    D. diamond

16. A. clothes
    B. surroundings
    C. prominant
    D. democracy

17. A. intermission
    B. compelling
    C. legitamate
    D. executioner

18. A. secretarial
    B. incendiary
    C. dissagreeable
    D. metropolitan

19. A. procedings
    B. integrate
    C. coincidence
    D. dissection

20. A. welfare
    B. fantasy
    C. suspense
    D. concientious

# Answers and Explanations

## Synonyms

1. **D.** To contradict someone is to say that what the person said is wrong—to *disagree*.

2. **A.** Something that is *ambiguous* can be understood in more than one way.

3. **C.** *Emit* means to *give off* or *let out*.

4. **B.** To *evoke* most nearly means to call forth.

5. **B.** When something has been marred, for example, a window that has a crack in it, it is *spoiled*.

6. **B.** To be *punctual* means to be on time. *Prompt* is a good synonym.

7. **C.** Something *vital* is something that cannot be done without.

8. **B.** *Scurry* means to move quickly—to *dash*.

9. **C.** The word usually suggests telling something that had been secret or hidden.

10. **A.** A *clash* is a conflict.

11. **D.** To *heed* advice or an instruction means not only to listen to it, but to follow it.

12. **A.** The word *startle* means to surprise.

13. **A.** Don't be confused by (B). While an itch is irritating, itchy is not what the word means.

14. **C.** Something that seeps slowly trickles out of where it was.

15. **B.** *Incite* most nearly means to stir up, such as to incite a riot.

16. **A.** To fuse is to blend. It is not the same as a fuse that powers electricity.

17. **D.** To incapacitate means to disable. One may be incapacitated if imprisoned (A), but that is not the actual meaning of the word.

18. **B.** A coalition is a union. To coalesce means to bring together.

19. **D.** A discord is a conflict.

20. **B.** The word progeny means offspring, or children.

# Antonyms

1. **D.** Choice B means the same as *familiar*.

2. **D.** Although C may seem like a good choice, when to *cease* is to stop what is already in motion, so *continue* is a better answer.

3. **A.** Although if your mind is *vacant* you may be *relaxed* (choice C), *vacant* means *empty*, so *full* is the best choice.

4. **B.** To *concur* is to agree; to *argue* implies disagreement.

5. **A.** *Sparse* means thin or meager; *plentiful* is its opposite.

6. **D.** To be *hostile* means to dislike or to consider an enemy. *Friendly* is the opposite.

7. **B.** Choice C is a synonym for *stingy*. Do not be confused by choice (D). Not all wealthy people are stingy.

8. **B.** Interdict means prohibit, while accept is the opposite.

9. **D.** To grapple means to struggle and grab on to. The opposite would be release.

10. **B.** A synonym for revile is hate. Thus, the opposite would be love.

11. **A.** The word feint should not be confused with faint. In this case, the word means to move aside, as a boxer might feint to the left and move to the right. The opposite would be to stand still.

12. **A.** The opposite of to delude is to clarify. A synonym for delude is to obscure, to cloud.

13. **C.** Based on the choice of words given, the word spare in this instance means meager or skimpy. Lush is the opposite.

14. **B.** The synonym for passive means unresponsive. It also means uninvolved. The word that is the closest to the opposite would be energetic.

15. **D.** To be skeptical is to be distrustful. Accepting would be the opposite.

# Analogies

1. **C.** The relationship is opposites.

2. **D.** To be green is a characteristic of plants, and to be creative is characteristic of an inventor.

3. **D.** The relationship is cause to effect. To be clumsy can cause one to trip, and to be late can cause one to hurry.

4. **A.** The relationship is sequence. Fall comes before winter, and a bud appears before a leaf opens.

5. **B.** The words are synonyms.

6. **B.** A bay is a small body of salt water, and an ocean is a large body of salt water. A pebble is small, and a rock is large.

7. **C.** Whole to part is the relationship. Algebra is a branch of mathematics; botany is a branch of biology.

8. **A.** What is characteristic is the key to this analogy. Lead is heavy; water is wet.

9. **B.** The function of a manual is to explain something, and the function of a stapler is to fasten things.

10. **D.** Depth is a characteristic of a trench, and height is characteristic of a hill.

11. **C.** The arm is located between the wrist and the hand as the ankle is located between the leg and the foot.

12. **B.** The relationship is what a person in this job usually wears.

13. **C.** The relationship is location. Eyes are above a nose; a roof is above a house.

14. **D.** The relationship is that they are part of the same family of animals. Lions and cats are felines; wolves and dogs are canines.

15. **A.** Locations explains the answer. What is the appropriate place to put the object?

16. **D.** Buttons and snaps close things; keys and can openers open things.

17. **C.** The relationship is object to person who creates the object.

18. **C.** The relationship is function. A trunk is used to store objects in a car; a locker is used to store objects in a gymnasium.

19. **A.** Bread is cut by a knife; hair is cut by scissor.

20. **B.** The relationship is parts of a whole. Both a violin and harp are instruments with strings; a tuba and a trumpet are instruments to blow into.

GO ON TO THE NEXT PAGE

# Spelling

1. **C.** height
2. **A.** tragedy
3. **D.** No mistake
4. **A.** environment
5. **D.** No mistake
6. **C.** across
7. **A.** Committee
8. **C.** business
9. **A.** parallel
10. **D.** No mistake

11. **D.** concerning
12. **D.** pianos
13. **C.** celebration
14. **B.** sophomore
15. **A.** loneliness
16. **C.** prominent
17. **C.** legitimate
18. **C.** disagreeable
19. **A.** proceedings
20. **D.** conscientious

# Reading Comprehension

**Directions:** This section measures your ability to read and understand written English similar to that which one may expect in a college or university setting. Read each passage and answer the questions based on what is stated or implied in the passage.

## Passage 1

Hummingbirds are small, often brightly colored birds of the family Trochilidae that live exclusively in the Americas. About 12 species are found in North America, but only the ruby-throated hummingbird breeds in eastern North America and is found from Nova Scotia to Florida. The greatest variety and number of species are found in South America. Another hummingbird species is found from southeastern Alaska to northern California.

Many hummingbirds are minute. But even the giant hummingbird found in western South America, which is the largest known hummingbird, is only about 8 inches long and weighs about two-thirds of an ounce. The smallest species, the bee hummingbird of Cuba and the Isle of Pines, measures slightly more than 5.5 centimeters and weighs about two grams.

Hummingbirds' bodies are compact, with strong muscles. They have wings shaped like blades. Unlike the wings of other birds, hummingbird wings connect to the body only at the shoulder joint, which allows them to fly not only forward but also straight up and down, sideways, and backward. Because of their unusual wings, hummingbirds can also hover in front of flowers so they can suck nectar and find insects. The hummingbird's bill, adapted for securing nectar from certain types of flowers, is usually rather long and always slender, and it is curved slightly downward in many species.

The hummingbird's body feathers are sparse and more like scales than feathers. The unique character of the feathers produces brilliant and iridescent colors, resulting from the refraction of light by the feathers. Pigmentation of other feathers also contributes to the unique color and look. Male and female hummingbirds look alike in some species but different in most species; males of most species are extremely colorful.

The rate at which a hummingbird beats its wings does not vary, regardless of whether it is flying forward, flying in another direction, or merely hovering. But the rate does vary with the size of the bird—the larger the bird, the lower the rate, ranging from 80 beats per second for the smallest species to 10 times per second for larger species. Researchers have not yet been able to record the speed of the wings of the bee hummingbird but imagine that they beat even faster.

Most hummingbirds, especially the smaller species, emit scratchy, twittering, or squeaky sounds. The wings, and sometimes the tail feathers, often produce humming, hissing, or popping sounds, which apparently function much as do the songs of other birds.

1.  According to the passage, where are hummingbirds found?

    A.  Throughout the world
    B.  In South America only
    C.  In North America only
    D.  In North and South America

2.  The author indicates that the ruby-throated hummingbird is found

    A.  throughout North America
    B.  in California
    C.  in South America
    D.  in the eastern part of North America

3.  The word minute in the second paragraph is closest in meaning to

    A.  extremely tiny
    B.  extremely fast
    C.  unique
    D.  organized

4.  The word which in the second paragraph refers to

    A.  western South America
    B.  the giant hummingbird
    C.  all hummingbirds
    D.  Florida hummingbirds

5.  What does the author imply about the rate hummingbirds' wings beat?

    A.  Although the bee hummingbird is the smallest, its wings don't beat the fastest.
    B.  The hummingbird's wings beat faster when it is sucking nectar than when it is just flying.
    C.  The rate is not much different than that of other birds of its size.
    D.  The speed at which a bee hummingbird's wings beat is not actually known.

GO ON TO THE NEXT PAGE

6.  The author indicates that a hummingbird's wings are different from those of other birds because

    A.  they attach to the body at one point only
    B.  they attach to the body at more points than other birds
    C.  they attach and detach from the body
    D.  they are controlled by a different section of the brain

7.  The author implies that the hummingbird's unique wing structure makes it similar to what type of vehicle?

    A.  A helicopter
    B.  A sea plane
    C.  A jet airplane
    D.  A rocket

8.  The word bill in the third paragraph is closest in meaning to

    A.  beak
    B.  body
    C.  tail
    D.  wing

9.  The word sparse in the fourth paragraph is closest in meaning to

    A.  meager
    B.  thick
    C.  fishlike
    D.  unique

10. According to the passage, what causes the unique color and look of hummingbirds?

    A.  The color of the feathers
    B.  The structure of the feathers as well as pigmentation
    C.  The rapidity of flight
    D.  The pigmentation of the body

11. The author indicates that hummingbirds emit noise from their

    A.  wing and possibly tail movement
    B.  unique vocal chords
    C.  song only
    D.  wing movement only

## Passage 2

The term lichen refers to any of more than 20,000 species of thallophytic plants that consist of a symbiotic association of algae and fungi, plural for alga and fungus. Previously, lichens were classified as single organisms until scientists had the benefit of microscopes, at which time they discovered the association between algae and fungi. Thus, the lichen itself is not an organism, but the morphological and biochemical product of the association. Neither a fungus nor an alga alone can produce a lichen.

The intimate symbiotic relationship between these two living components of a lichen is said to be mutualistic, meaning that both organisms benefit from the relationship. It is not certain when fungi and algae came together to form lichens for the first time, but it certainly occurred after the mature development of the separate components.

It appears that the fungus actually gains more benefit from the relationship than does the alga. Algae form simple carbohydrates that, when excreted, are absorbed by fungi cells and transformed into a different carbohydrate. Algae also produce vitamins that the fungi need. Yet, fungi also contribute to the symbiosis by absorbing water vapor from the air and providing shade for the algae, which are more sensitive to light.

Lichens grow relatively slowly, and it is uncertain how they propagate. Most botanists agree that reproduction is vegetative because portions of an existing lichen break off and fall away to begin a new organism nearby.

Lichens are hardy organisms, being found in hostile environments where few other organisms can survive. Humans have used lichens as food and as sources of medicine and dye. The presence of lichens is a sign that the atmosphere is pure. Lichens help reduce erosion by stabilizing soil. They also are a major source of food for the caribou and reindeer that live in the extreme north.

12. Which of the following is true about the association of the lichen?

    A.  The association is more beneficial to the alga.
    B.  The association is solely of benefit to the fungus.
    C.  The association is merely a joint living arrangement, with neither organism receiving any benefit from the other.
    D.  The association is beneficial to each organism, although it provides more benefit to the fungus.

13. The word previously in the first paragraph is closest in meaning to

   A.  currently
   B.  formerly
   C.  believed
   D.  no longer

14. Prior to the invention of microscopes, what did scientists believe about lichens?

   A.  The entire plant was an alga.
   B.  The entire plant was a fungus.
   C.  A lichen constituted a single plant.
   D.  The fungus was the catalyst of the association.

15. The word intimate in the second paragraph is closest in meaning to

   A.  distant
   B.  parasitic
   C.  close
   D.  unusual

16. The author uses the word mutualistic in paragraph two to describe

   A.  the fungus' benefits from the association
   B.  the harmful effects of the relationship
   C.  the joint benefit each organism receives from the relationship
   D.  the alga's benefits from the association

17. The author implies that

   A.  neither plant requires carbohydrates to survive
   B.  the fungus manufactures carbohydrates on its own
   C.  the alga receives carbohydrates from the fungus
   D.  the fungus uses the carbohydrates manufactured by the alga

18. The author states that the relationship between the words fungus/fungi and alga/algae is

   A.  singular/plural
   B.  compound/complex
   C.  symbiotic/disassociated
   D.  mutual/separate

19. The author implies that vegetative reproduction means

   A.  vegetables combine with other vegetables
   B.  reproduction occurs using vegetative plant growth
   C.  new organisms are grown from pieces of existing organisms
   D.  propagation occurs slowly

20. The author states that

   A.  fungi are more sensitive to light than algae
   B.  neither plant is sensitive to light
   C.  neither plant individually can thrive in sunlight
   D.  algae are more sensitive to light than fungi

21. The word nearby at the end of paragraph four is closest in meaning to

   A.  almost
   B.  completely
   C.  connected
   D.  close

22. The word hardy at the beginning of the last paragraph is closest in meaning to

   A.  tender
   B.  ubiquitous
   C.  scarce
   D.  strong

23. The word hostile in the last paragraph is closest in meaning to

   A.  unusual
   B.  dry
   C.  harsh
   D.  complex

24. The author indicates that lichens are beneficial because they

   A.  purify the air
   B.  reduce fungi
   C.  destroy algae
   D.  reduce soil erosion

GO ON TO THE NEXT PAGE

## Passage 3

Collecting coins can be a good investment, but it requires the study of popularity, availability, and grading techniques. Some coins are more desirable than others, their popularity being affected by the artists' talent, the subject of the design, the material from which the coin is made, and the time period when the coin was created. Availability is just as critical. Providing the coin is otherwise interesting or pleasing to the eye, the number of coins minted and available on the market seems to have a direct relationship to the popularity.

The ability to grade coins is perhaps the most important requirement of a collector. A coin that is popular and scarce, which would normally make it valuable, may be worth much less or nothing at all if it has a low grade. Grading is standardized, and one can buy books and take courses on how to do it.

Grades are given letter designations as well as numbers. The letters represent general levels of the grade, while the numbers are more detailed. For example, there are 11 number grades within the letter grade for a mint state coin. A mint state coin is uncirculated, which means it has never been used in commerce. It is in the condition that it left the mint, the place where a coin is created. The mint state letter designation is MS, and the numbers range from 60 through 70. An absolutely perfect coin is MS-70. It takes much training and a good eye to tell the difference between coins in this range. The things one considers include whether the coin has contact marks, which are marks obtained when coins bounce against each other in a coin bag; hairlines, which are marks appearing on the face of the coin from the minting process; luster, which is the natural coloration; and eye appeal. For example, an MS-70 is said to have no contact marks, no hairlines, very attractive and fully original luster, and outstanding eye appeal, while an MS-60 may have heavy contact marks, noticeable hairlines, impaired luster, and poor eye appeal.

Below the mint state coin, the letter designation and number have the same meaning. That is, there are generally no numbers within the range of letters. But there are categories:

- Coins that are About Uncirculated: Very Choice About Uncirculated, known as AU-58; Choice About Uncirculated, known as AU-55; and About Uncirculated, known as AU-50.

- Coins that are Fine: Choice Extremely Fine, known as EF-45; Extremely Fine, known as EF-40; Choice Very Fine, known as VF-30; Very Fine, known as VF-20; and Fine, known as F-12.

- Coins that are Good: Very Good, known as VG-8; Good, known as G-4; and About Good, known as AG-3.

Thus, a circulated coin can have a number designation between 3 and 58, with only the numbers shown above available. That is, one cannot have a coin with a grade of 6,

for example. It is either G-4 or VG-8. It is possible for a coin labeled G-4 or even AG-3 to be extremely valuable, but generally it will be a coin that is almost unavailable in higher grades. Books and publications monitor the coin market regularly, just like the stock market is monitored, and they describe a coin's type, date, and grade, assigning a price to every one unless that grade would have no value.

In general, coin collectors loathe cleaned coins, so artificial cleaning by adding any chemical will detract greatly from a coin's value. A true coin collector will say the dirt in the creases is a positive attribute and much preferable to a cleaned coin.

25. A good title for this passage would be

   A. The Financial Benefits of Coin Collecting
   B. How Popularity and Availability Affect Coin Value
   C. Coin Grading — One of the Most Important Skills in Coin Collecting
   D. How to Grade Coins — A Detailed Study

26. The word talent in the second sentence is closest in meaning to

   A. ability
   B. pay
   C. source
   D. money

27. The author describes a coin's popularity as involving all the following except

   A. grade
   B. how well the artist created the work
   C. the depiction on the coin
   D. the coin's material

28. The word scarce in the second paragraph is closest in meaning to

   A. popular
   B. old
   C. rare
   D. valuable

29. The author implies that availability is primarily related to

   A. the popularity of a coin
   B. the material used to create a coin
   C. the age of a coin
   D. the number of coins of a given type and date that they were minted

**30.** The author implies that the most important feature of a coin is its

    **A.** grade

    **B.** date

    **C.** artist

    **D.** depiction

**31.** Organize the following according to grade from the highest to the lowest.

    **A.** AU-58

    **B.** MS-60

    **C.** AG-3

    **D.** VF-20

**32.** The one grading category that has the most numbered grades within it is

    **A.** Good

    **B.** Mint State

    **C.** Fine

    **D.** About Uncirculated

**33.** According to the author, the phrase contact marks means

    **A.** marks on a coin caused by banging from other coins

    **B.** defects in the minting process

    **C.** connections among coin dealers

    **D.** defects caused by cleaning

**34.** The word luster in the third paragraph is closest in meaning to

    **A.** value

    **B.** sheen

    **C.** marked

    **D.** material

**35.** According to the passage, a Mint State coin with which of the following characteristics would be graded the highest?

    **A.** One small contact mark, full luster, good eye appeal, and no hairlines

    **B.** One large hairline, diminished luster, good eye appeal, and no contact marks

    **C.** A small contact mark, a small hairline, foggy luster, and fair eye appeal

    **D.** No contact marks, luster affected by cleaning, average eye appeal, and no hairlines

**36.** All of the following grades would be possible except

    **A.** MS-64

    **B.** AU-56

    **C.** VF-30

    **D.** AG-3

**37.** The author implies that

    **A.** a low-grade coin never has value

    **B.** the only difference between an MS-60 and an AU-58 may be that the AU-58 has been in circulation

    **C.** cleaning a coin can increase its value

    **D.** one must be a professional in order to obtain information on coin value

GO ON TO THE NEXT PAGE

## Passage 4

Hepatitis C is an illness, unknown until recently, that has been discovered in many individuals. It has been called an epidemic, yet unlike most illnesses with that designation, it is not easily transmitted. It is accurately referred to as epidemic in that so many people have been discovered with the illness, but it is different in that these people have actually carried the virus for many years. It is only transmitted by direct blood-to-blood contact; casual contact and even sexual contact are not believed to transmit the illness. Hepatitis means an inflammation or infection of the liver. Hepatitis C is generally chronic, as opposed to acute. This means that it continues to affect the patient and is not known to have a sudden onset or recovery.

The great majority of people infected with the illness either had a blood transfusion before the time that the disease was recognized in donated blood, or experimented with injecting illegal drugs when they were young. Many victims are educated, financially successful males between the ages of 40 and 50 who experimented with intravenous drugs as teenagers. There are frequently no symptoms, so the illness is discovered through routine blood tests. Most commonly, people learn they have the illness when they apply for life insurance or donate blood. The blood test reveals elevated liver enzymes, which could be caused by any form of hepatitis, by abuse of alcohol, or by other causes. Another test is then performed, and the result is learned.

Because the illness produces no symptoms, it of itself does not affect the victim's life, at least at first. But the constant infection in the liver can eventually lead to cirrhosis of the liver, which is scarring and death of portions of the liver. The cirrhosis in turn can lead to liver cancer and, ultimately, death. Severe cases can be reversed with a liver transplant. Yet, because the virus may exist in the body for more than 20 years before being discovered, after reviewing the condition of the liver, doctors often suggest waiting and periodically checking the condition rather than performing radical treatment procedures. The liver's condition is determined by a biopsy, in which a device is inserted into the liver and its condition is viewed. If there is little or no cirrhosis, it is more likely that treatment will be postponed.

Treatment frequently causes more discomfort than the illness itself. It consists of some form of chemotherapy. Currently, the most frequent treatment is a combination therapy, with one drug injected three times a week and another taken orally, costing hundreds of dollars a week. The therapy causes the patient to have symptoms similar to influenza, and some patients suffer more than others. Unfortunately, many patients do not respond, or do not respond completely to the therapy. There is no alternative therapy at this time for non-responders, although researchers are continually trying to find a cure.

**38.** The author implies that

    **A.** physicians have been treating patients for hepatitis C for more than 20 years

    **B.** other forms of hepatitis were known before the hepatitis C strain was discovered

    **C.** hepatitis C is generally seen as an acute illness

    **D.** hepatitis C is easily transmitted through any type of contact

**39.** The word onset at the end of paragraph one is closest in meaning to

    **A.** illness

    **B.** termination

    **C.** inception

    **D.** treatment

**40.** The best title for this passage would be

    **A.** Treatment Choices for Hepatitis C

    **B.** The History of Different Forms of Hepatitis

    **C.** Hepatitis C—Its Characteristics and Treatment

    **D.** The Causes and Symptoms of Hepatitis C

**41.** The word great at the beginning of paragraph two is closest in meaning to

    **A.** vast

    **B.** magnificent

    **C.** small

    **D.** important

**42.** The word routine in paragraph two is closest in meaning to

    **A.** standard

    **B.** elevated

    **C.** required

    **D.** complex

**43.** The word they in paragraph two refers to

    **A.** symptoms

    **B.** illness

    **C.** enzymes

    **D.** people

**44.** The author implies that

- A. patients usually learn of the illness because they have severe symptoms
- B. liver transplants are a very common form of treatment
- C. many people with hepatitis C were not addicts but simply experimented with illegal drugs
- D. people are still in danger of acquiring the illness from blood transfusions

**45.** The author indicates that a biopsy is performed in order to

- A. prepare for a liver transplant
- B. determine whether one has the virus
- C. learn the degree of damage to the liver
- D. decide which form of drug to prescribe

**46.** The author implies that hepatitis C

- A. attacks rapidly
- B. does not affect many people
- C. only rarely results in liver cancer
- D. attacks the central nervous system

**47.** The author states that people sometimes choose not to take treatment for hepatitis C for all of the following reasons except

- A. the medicine must be taken intravenously
- B. the treatment does not work for everybody
- C. often the level of illness is not severe
- D. the side effects of the medicine are sometimes worse than the symptoms of the illness

**48.** The word its in the third paragraph refers to

- A. device
- B. liver
- C. biopsy
- D. doctor

# Answers and Explanations

1. **D.** In North and South America. This is explained in the first paragraph.

2. **D.** in the eastern part of North America. This is explained in the first paragraph.

3. **A.** extremely tiny.

4. **B.** the giant hummingbird.

5. **D.** The speed at which a bee hummingbird's wings beat is not actually known. The author explains in paragraph five that they have not measured this species yet.

6. **A.** they attach to the body at one point only. This is explained in the third paragraph.

7. **A.** A helicopter. This is the only aircraft listed that can hover and move in different directions.

8. **A.** beak. The bill or beak is the mouth of the bird.

9. **A.** meager.

10. **B.** The structure of the feathers as well as pigmentation. This is explained in paragraph four.

11. **A.** wing and possibly tail movement. This is explained in paragraph four.

12. **D.** The association is beneficial to each organism, although it provides more benefit to the fungus. This is indicated in the third paragraph, in which the author states, It appears that the fungus actually gains more benefit from the relationship than does the alga.

13. **B.** formerly.

14. **C.** A lichen constituted a single plant. This is indicated in the first paragraph, in which the author states, Previously, lichens were classified as single organisms until scientists had the benefit of microscopes . . . .

15. **C.** close.

16. **C.** the joint benefit each organism receives from the relationship.

17. **D.** the fungus uses the carbohydrates manufactured by the alga. This is indicated in the third paragraph, where the author states, Algae form simple carbohydrates that, when excreted, are absorbed by fungi cells and transformed into a different carbohydrate.

18. **A.** singular/plural. The author explains in the first paragraph that fungus and alga are singular and fungi and algae are plural forms of the words.

19. **C.** new organisms are grown from pieces of existing organisms. This is explained in the fourth paragraph, where the author states, Most botanists agree that reproduction is vegetative because portions of an existing lichen break off and fall away to begin a new organism nearby.

20. **D.** algae are more sensitive to light than fungi. This is explained in the third paragraph, in which the author states, Yet, fungi also contribute to the symbiosis by absorbing water vapor from the air and providing shade for the algae, which are more sensitive to light.

21. **D.** close.

22. **D.** strong.

23. **C.** harsh.

24. **D.** reduce soil erosion.

25. **C.** Coin Grading — One of the Most Important Skills in Coin Collecting.

26. **A.** ability.

27. **A.** grade.

28. **C.** rare.

29. **D.** the number of coins of a given type and date that they were minted.

30. **A.** grade. The entire passage indicates this is the most important.

31. **B, A, D, C: MS-60; AU-58; VF-20; AG-3**

32. **B.** Mint State. It has 11 numbered grades, from 60 to 70.

33. **A.** marks on a coin caused by banging from other coins. This is specifically stated in the third paragraph.

34. **B.** sheen.

35. **A.** One small contact mark, full luster, good eye appeal, and no hairlines. B has a large hairline and reduced luster. C has two kinds of marks and defective luster. D has been artificially cleaned, which you are told is a negative.

36. **B.** AU-56.

37. **B.** the only difference between an MS-60 and an AU-58 may be that the AU-58 has been in circulation. The distinction is that MS means Mint State, which also means uncirculated. About Circulated means only slightly circulated.

38. **B.** other forms of hepatitis were known before the hepatitis C strain was discovered. The author refers to hepatitis in general, and hepatitis C specifically, implying that there are others.

39. **C.** inception.

40. **C.** Hepatitis C — Its Characteristics and Treatment.

41. **A.** vast. The word in this context is an intensifier, modifying majority.

42. **A.** standard.

43. **D.** people.

44. **C.** many people with hepatitis C were not addicts but simply experimented with illegal drugs.

45. **C.** learn the degree of damage to the liver.

46. **C.** only rarely results in liver cancer.

47. **A.** the medicine must be taken intravenously. It is injected, but not in the vein.

48. **B.** liver.

# Arithmetic Reasoning

**Directions:** For each of the following questions, select the choice that best answers the question or completes the statement.

1. One gallon of paint covers 400 square feet. How many gallons are needed to cover 2,225 square feet?

   A. 5 gallons
   B. 6 gallons
   C. 7 gallons
   D. 8 gallons

2. A restaurant bill without tax and tip comes to $38.40. If a 15% tip is included after a 6% tax is added to the amount, how much is the tip?

   A. $6.11
   B. $5.76
   C. $5.15
   D. $2.30

3. The sum of 2 feet $2\frac{1}{2}$ inches, 4 feet $3\frac{3}{8}$ inches, and 3 feet $9\frac{3}{4}$ inches is

   A. 9 feet $\frac{7}{8}$ inches
   B. 9 feet $9\frac{5}{8}$ inches
   C. 10 feet $\frac{5}{8}$ inches
   D. 10 feet $3\frac{5}{8}$ inches

4. Doug earns 15% commission on all sales over $5,000. Last month, his sales totaled $12,500. What were Doug's earnings?

   A. $750
   B. $1,125
   C. $1,875
   D. $2,625

5. Fencing costs $4.75 per foot. Posts cost $12.50 each. How much will it cost to fence a garden if 10 posts and 34 feet of fencing are needed?

   A. $472.50
   B. $336.50
   C. $315.50
   D. $286.50

6. How much change would you get back from a $20.00 bill if you purchased 8 CD covers costing $1.59 each?

   A. $7.28
   B. $10.41
   C. $12.00
   D. $18.41

7. The scale on a map shows 500 feet for every $\frac{1}{4}$ inch. If two cities are 6 inches apart on the map, what is the actual distance they are apart?

   A. 125 feet
   B. 750 feet
   C. 2,000 feet
   D. 12,000 feet

8. A 10-foot rope is to be cut into equal segments measuring 8 inches each. The total number of segments is

   A. 1
   B. 8
   C. 15
   D. 40

9. Rayanne can read one page in two minutes. If a book has 80 pages, how long will it take her to read?

   A. 160 minutes
   B. 120 minutes
   C. 80 minutes
   D. 40 minutes

10. Three boxes are needed to hold 18 reams of paper. How many boxes are needed for 90 reams?

   A. 5
   B. 6
   C. 9
   D. 15

**11.** The area of the figure is

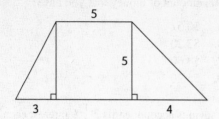

A. 42.5
B. 47
C. 52.5
D. 60

**12.** Cards normally sell for $3.00 each. How much was saved if 5 cards were purchased on sale for 2 for $5.00?

A. $2.50
B. $5.00
C. $12.50
D. $15.00

**13.** Mattie walked 45 yards north, 36 yards west, and 41 yards south. Jacob walked 16 yards north, 49 yards west, and 33 yards south. How much farther did Mattie walk than Jacob?

A. 20 yards
B. 22 yards
C. 24 yards
D. 28 yards

**14.** A cylinder whose height is 8 inches has a volume of $128\pi$ cm$^3$. If the radius is doubled and its height is cut in half, the volume of the resulting cylinder is

A. $64\pi$ cm$^3$
B. $128\pi$ cm$^3$
C. $256\pi$ cm$^3$
D. $512\pi$ cm$^3$

**15.** The figure contains 5 equal squares. If the area is 405, what is the perimeter?

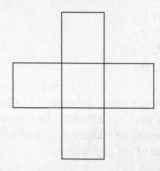

A. 81
B. 90
C. 108
D. 144

**16.** Find the length of $x$ in the figure.

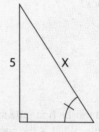

A. $6\frac{2}{3}$
B. $7\frac{1}{3}$
C. $8\frac{1}{4}$
D. $\frac{15}{4}$

**17.** Joann ate $\frac{1}{4}$ of a peach pie and divides the remainder of the pie among her four friends. What fraction of the pie does each of her friends receive?

A. $\frac{1}{3}$
B. $\frac{7}{12}$
C. $\frac{3}{16}$
D. $\frac{1}{8}$

GO ON TO THE NEXT PAGE

18. Max weighs 209 pounds. If he loses 2 pounds per week, how much will he weigh in 7 weeks?

    A. 191 lbs
    B. 195 lbs
    C. 202 lbs
    D. 207 lbs

19. An appliance originally costing $1,000 goes on sale one week for 25% off. The following week, it is discounted an additional 10%. What is the new sale price of the appliance?

    A. $650
    B. $675
    C. $750
    D. $900

20. Dennis ran a race in 2.2 minutes. Kayla ran the same race in 124 seconds. What is the difference between these two times?

    A. 2 seconds
    B. 8 seconds
    C. 14 seconds
    D. 22 seconds

21. A taxi ride costs $3.00 for the first mile and $1.00 each additional half mile. What is the cost of a 10 mile ride?

    A. $10
    B. $12
    C. $13
    D. $21

22. If 3 cans of soup cost $5.00, how much do 10 cans cost?

    A. $15.00
    B. $16.45
    C. $16.67
    D. $17.33

23. Kyle ran 3 miles in $17\frac{1}{2}$ minutes on Saturday, $4\frac{1}{2}$ miles in 22 minutes on Sunday, and 2 miles in 9 minutes on Monday. What is the average time per mile?

    A. 1.6 minutes per mile
    B. 5.1 minutes per mile
    C. 16.2 minutes per mile
    D. 17.8 minutes per mile

24. You have 40 nickels and 12 dimes. What is the total amount of money that you have?

    A. $0.52
    B. $3.20
    C. $4.60
    D. $5.20

25. A savings account earns $2\frac{1}{4}$% interest each year. How much simple interest is earned on a $1,000 deposit after a 5-year period?

    A. $22.50
    B. $100.00
    C. $112.50
    D. $150.00

26. Vanda put some water in the freezer. When she removed it, the water's temperature was 0° C. Leaving it out will raise the temperature 4° F each hour. At this rate, how many hours later will the water's temperature be 52° F?

    A. 4 hours
    B. 5 hours
    C. 13 hours
    D. 52 hours

27. Stanley can type 35 words per minute. If it takes him a half hour to type a document, about how many words are in the document?

    A. 900
    B. 1,050
    C. 1,500
    D. 2,100

**28.** Sandy bought $4\frac{1}{2}$ lbs of apples and 6 kiwi fruits. Brandon bought $3\frac{1}{4}$ lbs of apples and 9 kiwi fruits. If apples cost \$1.39 per lb and kiwis are 2 for \$1.00, how much more money did Sandy spend than Brandon?

    **A.** \$0.24

    **B.** \$0.94

    **C.** \$1.54

    **D.** \$2.32

**29.** Bryan borrows \$50,000 at an interest rate of 8% compounded annually. How much will Bryan owe after two years if he does not pay back any of the money during this time?

    **A.** \$8,000

    **B.** \$58,000

    **C.** \$58,160

    **D.** \$58,320

**30.** In a nut mixture, there are $1\frac{1}{8}$ pounds of almonds, $2\frac{3}{4}$ pounds of cashews, and $3\frac{1}{3}$ pounds of peanuts. The total weight of the mixture is

    **A.** $6\frac{1}{3}$ pounds

    **B.** $6\frac{23}{24}$ pounds

    **C.** $7\frac{5}{24}$ pounds

    **D.** $7\frac{7}{12}$ pounds

# Answers and Explanations

1. **B.** If one gallon covers 400 square feet, then $\frac{2,225}{400} = 5.5625$ or 6 whole gallons are need to cover 2,225 square feet.

2. **A.** The tax on the bill is $38.40 \times 6\% = \$2.30$. The amount, including tax, is $\$38.40 + \$2.30 = \$40.70$. The tip is $\$40.70 \times 15\% = \$6.11$.

3. **D.** First add the number of feet together and then add the number of inches.

$$2 \text{ ft} + 4 \text{ ft} + 3 \text{ ft} = 9 \text{ ft}.$$

$$2\frac{1}{2} \text{ in} + 3\frac{3}{8} \text{ in} + 9\frac{3}{4} \text{ in} = \frac{5}{2} + \frac{27}{8} + \frac{39}{4} = \frac{20}{8} + \frac{27}{8} + \frac{78}{8} = \frac{125}{8} = 15\frac{5}{8} \text{ in}.$$

$$15\frac{5}{8} \text{ in} = 1 \text{ ft } 3\frac{5}{8} \text{ in so all together } 9 \text{ ft} + 1 \text{ ft } 3\frac{5}{8} \text{ in} = 10 \text{ ft } 3\frac{5}{8} \text{ in}.$$

4. **B.** The amount of commissions over $5,000 is $\$12,500 - \$5,000 = \$7,500$. Earnings are $\$7,500 \times 15\% = \$1,125$.

5. **D.** The total cost for the posts and fencing is $(10 \times \$12.50) + (34 \times \$4.75) = \$125.00 + \$161.50 = \$286.50$.

6. **A.** The cost of the 8 CD covers is $8 \times \$1.59 = \$12.72$. The change received back is $\$20.00 - \$12.72 = \$7.28$.

7. **D.** The proportion $\frac{500 \text{ ft}}{\frac{1}{4} \text{ in}} = \frac{x \text{ ft}}{6 \text{ in}}$ can be used to find the number of actual distance. Cross multiply. $500 \times 6 = \frac{1}{4}x$ so $3,000 = \frac{1}{4}x$ and $x = 3,000 \times 4 = 12,000$ ft.

8. **C.** The total number of inches in a 10 foot rope is $10 \times 12 = 120$ inches. The number of 8 inch segments that can be cut is $\frac{120}{8} = 15$.

9. **A.** If 1 page can be read in 2 minutes, then 80 pages can be read in $80 \times 2$ or 160 minutes.

10. **D.** The proportion $\frac{3 \text{ boxes}}{18 \text{ reams}} = \frac{x \text{ boxes}}{90 \text{ reams}}$ can be used to find the number of boxes. Cross multiply. $3 \times 90 = 18x$ so $270 = 18x$ and $x = \frac{270}{18} = 15$ boxes.

11. **A.** Add the areas of the two triangles and the square to find the total area. The area of the square is $5^2 = 25$. Both triangles have a height of 5. The area of one triangle is $\frac{1}{2} bh = \frac{1}{2} \cdot 3 \cdot 5 = \frac{15}{2} = 7.5$. The area of the other triangle is $\frac{1}{2} bh = \frac{1}{2} \cdot 4 \cdot 5 = \frac{20}{2} = 10$. The total area is $25 + 7.5 + 10 = 42.5$.

12. **A.** Five cards at $3.00 each cost $5 \times \$3.00 = \$15.00$. If cards are 2 for $5.00, the cost per cards is $\frac{\$5.00}{2} = \$2.50$ so 5 cards would cost $\$2.50 \times 5 = \$12.50$. The amount saved is $\$15.00 - \$12.50 = \$2.50$.

13. **C.** Mattie walked $45 + 36 + 41 = 122$ yards. Jacob walked $16 + 49 + 33 = 98$ yards. The difference between these two distances is $122 - 98 = 24$ yards.

14. **C.** The volume of a cylinder is $\pi r^2 h$. In the original cylinder, $\pi r^2 8 = 128\pi$, so $r^2 = \frac{128\pi}{8\pi} = 16$ and the radius, $r$, equals $\sqrt{16} = 4$. In the new cylinder, the radius is doubled to 8 and the height is cut in half to 4. The resulting volume is $\pi \cdot 8^2 \cdot 4 = 256\pi$ cm$^3$.

15. **C.** The area of one square is $\frac{405}{5} = 81$. So the length of each side is $\sqrt{81} = 9$. The total number of sides in the figure is 12, so the perimeter is $9 \times 12 = 108$.

16. **A.** The proportion $\frac{5}{3} = \frac{x}{4}$ can be used to find $x$. Cross multiply. $5 \times 4 = 3x$ so $20 = 3x$ and $x = \frac{20}{3} = 6\frac{2}{3}$.

17. **C.** After eating $\frac{1}{4}$ of a pie, what remains is $1 - \frac{1}{4} = \frac{3}{4}$. If 4 friends share the remainder, then each received $\frac{3}{4} \div 4 = \frac{3}{4} \times \frac{1}{4} = \frac{3}{16}$.

18. **B.** If 2 pounds are lost each week, then after 7 weeks, $7 \times 2 = 14$ pounds are lost. The weight after 7 weeks is $209 - 14 = 195$ pounds.

19. **B.** The discounted amount after the first week is $\$1,000 \times 25\% = \$250$ so the sale price is $\$1,000 - \$250 = \$750$. The discounted amount after the second week is $\$750 \times 10\% = \$75$ so the sale price is $\$750 - \$75 = \$675$.

**20. B.** Convert 2.2 minutes to seconds. $2.2 \times 60 = 132$ seconds. The difference in the two times is $132 - 124 = 8$ seconds.

**21. D.** In a 10-mile trip, after the first mile, there are 9 additional miles. If each additional half mile is $1, then an additional mile is $2. The cost of the trip is $3 for the first mile + ($2 × 9) for the additional miles. $3 + $18 = $21.

**22. C.** The proportion $\frac{\$5.00}{3\,\text{cans}} = \frac{\$x}{10\,\text{cans}}$ can be used to find the cost of 10 cans. Cross multiply. $5 \times 10 = 3x$ so $50 = 3x$ and $x = \frac{50}{3} = \$16.67$.

**23. B.** Average is the total time divided by the total miles run. The total time is $17.5 + 22 + 9 = 48.5$ minutes. The total number of miles run is $3 + 4.5 + 2 = 9.5$. The average is $\frac{48.5}{9.5} = 5.1$ minutes per mile.

**24. B.** The total amount of money is $(40 \times \$0.05) + (12 \times \$0.10) = \$2.00 + \$1.20 = \$3.20$.

**25. C.** Interest = principle × rate × time. Interest $= \$1,000 \times 2\frac{1}{4}\% \times 5 = \$1,000 \times 0.0225 \times 5 = \$112.50$.

**26. B.** $0°$ C is equivalent to a Fahrenheit temperature of $0°\left(\frac{9}{5}\right) + 32 = 32°$ F. To become $52°$ F, it must rise $20°$ F. If it rises $4°$ F every hour, then $\frac{20}{4}$ or 5 hours later, it will be at $52°$ F.

**27. B.** There are 30 minutes in half hour. $30 \times 35 = 1,050$ words.

**28. A.** The cost of Sandy's purchase is $(4\frac{1}{2} \times \$1.39) + (6 \times \$0.50) = \$9.26$. The cost of Brandon's purchase is $(3\frac{1}{4} \times \$1.39) + (9 \times \$0.50) = \$9.02$. Sandy spent $\$9.26 - \$9.02 = \$0.24$ more.

**29. D.** The interest on the loan in the first year is $\$50,000 \times 8\% = \$4,000$. The amount that must be paid back after one year is $\$50,000 + \$4,000 = \$54,000$. In the second year, the interest would be $\$54,000 \times 8\% = \$4,320$. Thus, at the end of the second year, Bryan owes $\$58,320$.

**30. C.** $1\frac{1}{8} + 2\frac{3}{4} + 3\frac{1}{3} = \frac{9}{8} + \frac{11}{4} + \frac{10}{3} = \frac{27}{24} + \frac{66}{24} + \frac{80}{24} = \frac{173}{24} = 7\frac{5}{24}$ pounds.

# Mathematics Knowledge

1. Multiply $(2x + 1)(2x + 1)$.

   A. $2x^2 + 1$
   B. $4x^2 + 1$
   C. $4x^2 + 2x + 1$
   D. $4x^2 + 4x + 1$

2. $\frac{5}{16} + \frac{9}{24} =$

   A. $\frac{11}{16}$
   B. $\frac{14}{40}$
   C. $\frac{7}{20}$
   D. $\frac{14}{48}$

3. The sum of $\sqrt{50} + 3\sqrt{72}$ is

   A. $4 + \sqrt{122}$
   B. $4\sqrt{122}$
   C. $7\sqrt{2}$
   D. $23\sqrt{2}$

4. Simplify $5(a - 2) - (4a - 6)$.

   A. $a - 4$
   B. $a - 8$
   C. $a - 10$
   D. $a + 4$

5. What is the diameter of a circle whose circumference is equivalent to its area?

   A. 2
   B. 3
   C. 4
   D. 6

6. The cube of 8 is

   A. 2
   B. 24
   C. 512
   D. 8000

7. Find the area of a triangle whose base is 3 inches less than its height.

   A. $\frac{1}{2}h^2 - 3h$
   B. $\frac{1}{2}h^2 - \frac{3}{2}h$
   C. $\frac{1}{2}h - \frac{3}{2}$
   D. $\frac{1}{2}h^2 - 3$

8. Evaluate $3r^3 - 2s^2 + t$ if $r = -1$, $s = -2$, and $t = -3$.

   A. 2
   B. 4
   C. $-8$
   D. $-14$

9. The product of two numbers is 117. If one of the numbers is 9, what is the other?

   A. 11
   B. 13
   C. 15
   D. 17

10. Simplify $\left( \frac{a^{-3}b^2}{2ab^{-1}} \right)^{-3}$

    A. $\frac{2a^6}{b}$
    B. $\frac{8a^{12}}{b^9}$
    C. $\frac{a^8}{8b^3}$
    D. $\frac{a^{12}}{8b^9}$

11. There are five more boys in the kindergarten class than girls. If there are 27 children all together, how many are boys?

    A. 10
    B. 11
    C. 16
    D. 22

**12.** The area of the shaded region is

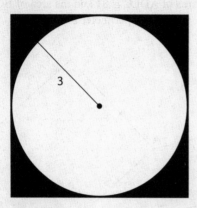

    **A.** $9 - 3\pi$
    **B.** $36 - 3\pi^2$
    **C.** $36 - 9\pi$
    **D.** $81 - 9\pi$

**13.** The product of the square of $x$ and three less than $x$ is

    **A.** $\sqrt{x}\,(x - 3)$
    **B.** $\sqrt{x}\,(3 - x)$
    **C.** $x^2(x - 3)$
    **D.** $x^2(3 - x)$

**14.** The cube root of 512 is

    **A.** 8
    **B.** 56
    **C.** $170\frac{2}{3}$
    **D.** 1536

**15.** What is the probability of rolling a sum of 9 using two dice?

    **A.** $\frac{1}{4}$
    **B.** $\frac{1}{9}$
    **C.** $\frac{5}{12}$
    **D.** $\frac{7}{36}$

**16.** If the diameter of a circle is increased by 100%, the area is increased by

    **A.** 50%
    **B.** 100%
    **C.** 200%
    **D.** 400%

**17.** Which mathematical statement best represents the following?

Six minus a number is four.

    **A.** $6 = n - 4$
    **B.** $6 < n + 4$
    **C.** $6 - n = 4$
    **D.** $n - 6 = 4$

**18.** Factor $2a^2 - 4ab + ab - 2b^2$

    **A.** $(a + 2b)(2a - b)$
    **B.** $(a - 2b)(2a + b)$
    **C.** $(2a - b)(a + 2b)$
    **D.** $(2a + b)(a - b)$

**19.** If $\frac{m}{n} = \frac{3}{5}$, what is the value of $5m - 3n$?

    **A.** 0
    **B.** $\frac{3}{5}$
    **C.** $\frac{6}{5}$
    **D.** 16

**20.** Floor tiling costs $13.50 per square yard. What would it cost to tile a room 15 feet long by 18 feet wide?

    **A.** $20
    **B.** $405
    **C.** $1350
    **D.** $3645

**21.** A rope is made by linking beads that are $\frac{1}{2}$" in diameter. How many feet long is a rope made from 60 beads?

    **A.** $2\frac{1}{2}$ ft
    **B.** 10 ft
    **C.** 30 ft
    **D.** 120 ft

**22.** If $2y + 6 = 3y - 2$, then $y =$

    **A.** $-2$
    **B.** 2
    **C.** 4
    **D.** 8

GO ON TO THE NEXT PAGE

**23.** $-3(-4-5) - 2(-6) =$

   **A.**  0

   **B.**  −5

   **C.**  15

   **D.**  39

**24.** Which of the following expressions represents the cost of 5 books and 3 magazines if books cost twice as much as magazines?

   **A.**  8$b$

   **B.**  8$m$

   **C.**  11$b$

   **D.**  13$m$

**25.** Squares ADEC, BCFG, and ABHI are shown. If the area of ADEC is 81 and the area of BCFG is 144, what is the perimeter of △ABC?

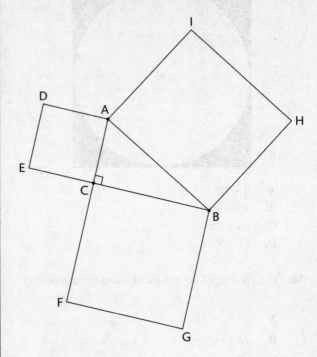

   **A.**  36

   **B.**  72

   **C.**  225

   **D.**  450

# Answers and Explanations

1. **D.** Using the distributive property, $(2x + 1)(2x + 1) = 4x^2 + 2x + 2x + 1 = 4x^2 + 4x + 1$.

2. **A.** The least common multiple of the divisors 16 and 24 is 48. $\frac{5}{16} + \frac{9}{24} = \frac{15}{48} + \frac{18}{48} = \frac{33}{48} = \frac{11}{16}$.

3. **D.** Simplifying $\sqrt{50} + 3\sqrt{72}$ yields $\sqrt{25 \cdot 2} + 3\sqrt{36 \cdot 2} = 5\sqrt{2} + 18\sqrt{2} = 23\sqrt{2}$.

4. **A.** $5(a - 2) - (4a - 6) = 5a - 10 - 4a + 6 = a - 4$.

5. **C.** The circumference of a circle is given by the formula $C = 2\pi r$, and the area of a circle is given by $A = \pi r^2$. If the circumference is equal to the area, then $2\pi r = \pi r^2$. Solving for $r$, $\frac{2\pi r}{\pi r} = \frac{\pi r^2}{\pi r}$ and $2 = r$. The diameter is $2r$, or 4.

6. **C.** The cube of 8 is $8^3 = 8 \times 8 \times 8 = 512$.

7. **B.** The area of a triangle is $A = \frac{1}{2} bh$. If the base is 3 inches less than the height, then $b = h - 3$. Substituting this value in for $b$ gives $A = \frac{1}{2}(h - 3)h = \frac{1}{2}h^2 - \frac{3}{2}h$.

8. **D.** Substituting the given values for $r$, $s$, and $t$ into $3r^3 - 2s^2 + t$ gives $3(-1)^3 - 2(-2)^2 + (-3) = 3(-1) - 2(4) - 3 = -3 - 8 - 3 = -14$.

9. **B.** Let $x$ be the unknown number. Then $9x = 117$ and $x = \frac{117}{9} = 13$.

10. **B.** $\left(\frac{a^{-3}b^2}{2ab^{-1}}\right)^{-3} = \frac{a^9 b^{-6}}{2^{-3}a^{-3}b^3} = 2^3 a^{9-(-3)}b^{-6-3} = 8a^{12}b^{-9} = \frac{8a^{12}}{b^9}$.

11. **C.** Let $b$ represent the number of boys in the class and $g$ represent the number of girls. Then $b + g = 27$. If $b = g + 5$; then $(g + 5) + g = 27$. $2g + 5 = 27$ and $2g = 22$ so $g = 11$. Therefore, the number of boys is $27 - 11$ or 16.

12. **C.**

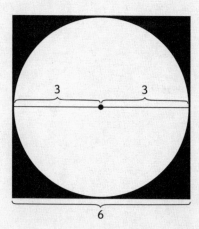

The area of the shaded region equals the area of the square minus the area of the circle. Since the radius of the circle is 3, the square has a side length of 6. The area of the square is $6^2$ or 36. The area of the circle is $\pi r^2 = \pi \cdot 3^2 = 9\pi$. The shaded region, therefore, is $36 - 9\pi$.

13. **C.** The square of $x$ is $x^2$. Three less than $x$ is $x - 3$. Their product is $x^2(x - 3)$.

14. **A.** The cube root of 512 is $\sqrt[3]{512} = \sqrt[3]{8 \times 8 \times 8} = 8$.

15. **B.** There are 4 possible ways to roll a 9 using 2 dice: 3 and 6, 4 and 5, 5 and 4, 6 and 3. The total number of possible outcomes when rolling 2 dice is $6^2$ or 36. Therefore, the probability of rolling a 9 is $\frac{4}{36} = \frac{1}{9}$.

16. **D.** The radius $r = \frac{d}{2}$. The area of the circle is $\pi r^2 = \pi\left(\frac{d}{2}\right)^2 = \frac{\pi d^2}{4}$. If the diameter is increased 100%, the diameter is $2d$ and $r = \frac{2d}{2} = d$. The area of the enlarged circle is $\pi r2 = \pi d2$. The enlarged circle is $\frac{\pi d^2}{\frac{\pi d^2}{4}} = \pi d^2 \div \frac{\pi d^2}{4} = \pi d^2 \cdot \frac{4}{\pi d^2} = 4$ or 400% bigger.

**17. D.** Six minus a number is shown by $n - 6$. So six minus a number is four is represented by $n - 6 = 4$.

**18. B.** Group the first two terms and the last two terms together. $(2a^2 - 4ab) + (ab - 2b^2)$ Factoring out common terms from each group gives $2a(a - 2b) + b(a - 2b)$. Common to both terms is $(a - 2b)$. Factoring this out results in $(a - 2b)(2a + b)$.

**19. B.** Cross-multiplying the proportion $\frac{m}{n} = \frac{3}{5}$ leads to the equation $5m - 3n$. Subtracting $3n$ from both sides results in the equation $5m - 3n = 0$.

**20. B.** The area of a room 15 feet wide by 18 feet long is $15 \times 18 = 270$ square feet. Since there are 3 feet in a yard, there are $3 \times 3$ or 9 feet in a square yard. Convert 270 square feet to square yards. $\frac{270}{9} = 30$ square yards. Since the cost is \$13.50 per square yard, the total cost is $\$13.50 \times 30$ or \$405.

**21. A.** 60 beads $\times \frac{1}{2}" = 30$ inches. Converting this to feet gives 30 inches $\times \frac{1\,\text{foot}}{12\,\text{inches}} = \frac{30}{12} = 2\frac{1}{2}$ feet.

**22. D.** Subtract $2y$ from both sides. $2y + 6 - 2y = 3y - 2 - 2y$ so $6 = y - 2$. Adding 2 to both sides gives $y = 8$.

**23. D.** Using the correct order of operations, $-3(-4 - 5) - 2(-6) = -3(-9) - 2(-6) = 27 - (-12) = 27 + 12 = 39$.

**24. D.** If books are twice as much as magazines, then $b = 2m$. 5 books + 3 magazines = $5b + 3m$. Substituting $2m$ for $b$ gives $5(2m) + 3m = 10m + 3m = 13m$.

**25. A.** Since the area of ADEC is 81, AC $= \sqrt{81} = 9$. Since the area of BCFG is 144, BC $= \sqrt{144} = 12$. Use the Pythagorean Theorem to find the length of the remaining side AB. $AB^2 = 9^2 + 12^2$ so $AB^2 = 81 + 144 = 225$ and $AB = \sqrt{225} = 15$. Therefore, the perimeter of the triangle $= 9 + 12 + 15 = 36$.

# Quantitative Comparisons

**Directions:** For each of the following questions, two quantities are given, one in each of Column A and Column B. You are to compare the two quantities and mark your answer sheet with the correct choice, based on the following:

Select A if the quantity in Column A is the greater;
Select B is the quantity in Column B is the greater;
Select C if the two quantities are equal;
Select D if the relationship cannot be determined from the information provided.

| Column A | Column B |
|---|---|
| **1.** $5^2$ | $2^5$ |

**2.** $$7 - 2a = 0$$

| | |
|---|---|
| $a^3$ | $\dfrac{1}{a^3}$ |

Note: Diagram not drawn to scale.

| **3.** $a + d$ | $c + b$ |
|---|---|

**4.** 5     The number of integers that satisfy both the inequality $6x - 18 < 0$ and the inequality $7 - 3x < 13$

**5.**     0.1% of $x$ is 2

| $x$ | 200 |
|---|---|

**6.**     $z > 0,\ y > 0,\ x < 0$

| $(3x)(3y)(3z)$ | $3(xyz)$ |
|---|---|

**7.**     $x$ and $y$ are negative integers

| $x^5$ | $y^2$ |
|---|---|

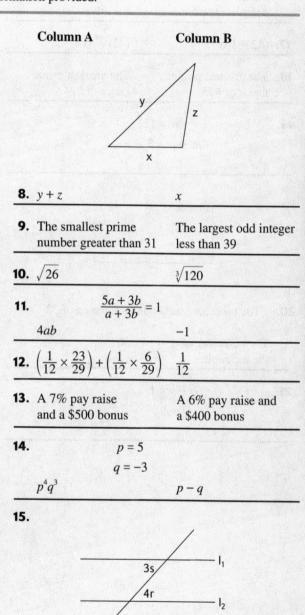

| Column A | Column B |
|---|---|
| **8.** $y + z$ | $x$ |
| **9.** The smallest prime number greater than 31 | The largest odd integer less than 39 |
| **10.** $\sqrt{26}$ | $\sqrt[3]{120}$ |

**11.** $$\dfrac{5a + 3b}{a + 3b} = 1$$

| $4ab$ | $-1$ |
|---|---|

| **12.** $\left(\dfrac{1}{12} \times \dfrac{23}{29}\right) + \left(\dfrac{1}{12} \times \dfrac{6}{29}\right)$ | $\dfrac{1}{12}$ |
|---|---|

| **13.** A 7% pay raise and a $500 bonus | A 6% pay raise and a $400 bonus |
|---|---|

**14.** $$p = 5$$
$$q = -3$$

| $p^4 q^3$ | $p - q$ |
|---|---|

**15.**

| $r$ | $s$ |
|---|---|

GO ON TO THE NEXT PAGE

| Column A | Column B |
|---|---|
| | |

**16.** Lauren drives from Buffalo to Rochester at an average speed of 50 miles per hour.

Gus drives from Rochester to Buffalo at an average speed of 40 miles per hour

| The amount of time it takes Lauren to complete the drive | The amount of time it takes Gus to complete the drive |
|---|---|

**17.** $(42 - 18)^2$ | $(42)^2 - (18)^2$

**18.** The greatest prime factor of 625 | The greatest prime factor of 224

**19.**
$$qa^2 - p^2 = 12$$
$$qa^2 + p^2 = 3$$

$q^2a^6 - p^4$ | 36

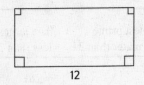

12

**20.** The preceding rectangle has an area of 72.

The perimeter of the rectangle | 36

**21.**
$$Qx - y = 1$$
$$Q - 1$$

$x$ | $y$

| Column A | Column B |
|---|---|

**22.** The average (arithmetic mean) of $a + 3$, $2a + 4$, and $2 - 3a$ | The average (arithmetic mean) of 0, 9, and 18

**23.** $\frac{x}{y} = \frac{5}{7}$

$x$ | $y$

**24.** $200\sqrt{5}$ | $(\sqrt{5} + \sqrt{5})^4$

**25.**

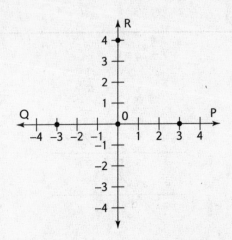

| The distance from point $Q$ to point $P$ | The distance from point $R$ to point $P$ |
|---|---|

**230**

# Answers and Explanations

**1. B.** Simply compute $5^2 = 5 \times 5 = 25$, while $2^5 = 2 \times 2 \times 2 \times 2 \times 2 = 32$.

**2. A.** Begin by solving the equation in the common information for $a$.

$$7 - 2a = 0$$

Subtract 7 from both sides

$$-2a = -7$$

Divide both sides by $-2$

$$a = \frac{7}{2}$$

Now, note that $\dfrac{1}{a^3} = \dfrac{1}{\left(\frac{7}{2}\right)^3} = \left(\dfrac{2}{7}\right)^3$. Therefore, we are comparing $\left(\dfrac{7}{2}\right)^3$ to $\left(\dfrac{2}{7}\right)^3$.

In general, when you cube a positive number greater than 1, it gets bigger, and when you cube a positive number less than 1, it gets smaller. Thus, $\left(\dfrac{7}{2}\right)^3 > \left(\dfrac{2}{7}\right)^3$.

**3. D.** Based on the properties of vertical angles, we know that $c = b$, and $a = d$. However, we have no way to compare the values of $a$ and $d$ to the values of $c$ and $b$.

**4. A.** Begin by solving the two given inequalities.

$$6x - 18 < 0$$

Add 18 to both sides

$$6x < 18$$

Divide both sides by 6

$$x < 3$$

$$7 - 3x < 13$$

Subtract 7 from both sides

$$-3x < 6$$

Divide both sides by $-3$

$$x > -2$$

The integers that solve both inequalities must be greater than $-2$ and less than 3. The only integers that satisfy these conditions are $-1$, 0, 1, and 2. Therefore, there are four such integers.

**5. A.** One way to determine the value of $x$ is to write 0.1% as its decimal equivalent, 0.001. Then, write the statement in the given information as an equation and solve for $x$.

$$0.001x = 2$$

Divide both sides by 0.001

$$x = 2 \div 0.001 = 2,000.$$

Therefore, $x > 200$.

**6. B.** To begin, note that $(3x)(3y)(3z) = 27xyz$, so we are comparing $27xyz$ to $3xyz$. Clearly, $27xyz$ has the larger absolute value of these two quantities. Note, however, that $x$ is negative, while $y$ and $z$ are positive. Therefore, $xyz$ is negative, which means that $27xyz$ and $3xyz$ are also negative. When comparing two negative numbers, the one with the larger absolute value is the smaller.

7. **B.** If $x$ and $y$ are negative, then $x^5$ is negative, while $y^2$ is positive. Any positive number is larger than any negative number.

8. **A.** In any triangle, the sum of the lengths of any two sides is bigger than the length of the third side.

9. **C.** The smallest prime number great than 31 is 37. The largest odd integer less than 39 is also 37.

10. **A.** No computations need to be performed to solve this problem; it can be solved by estimating the values of the quantities. To begin, note that since $\sqrt{25} = 5$, and $\sqrt{36} = 6$, then the value of $\sqrt{26}$ must be between 5 and 6. In addition, recall that $\sqrt[3]{125} = 5$, and so $\sqrt[3]{124}$ must be less than 5.

11. **A.** Begin by multiplying both sides of the equation given in the common information by $a + 3b$ to obtain the equation $5a + 3b = a + 3b$. If you subtract $3b$ from both sides, the result is $5a = a$. Subtract $a$ from both sides, and the result is $4a = 0$, which means that $a = 0$. If $a = 0$, then $4ab$ is also equal to 0.

12. **C.** Factor $\frac{1}{12}$ from each of the terms in the expression in Column A.

$$\left(\frac{1}{12} \times \frac{23}{29}\right) + \left(\frac{1}{12} \times \frac{6}{29}\right) = \frac{1}{12}\left(\frac{23}{29} + \frac{6}{29}\right) = \frac{1}{12}\left(\frac{29}{29}\right) = \frac{1}{12}$$

13. **D.** Without knowing the original salaries in each case, it is impossible to determine which entry is larger.

14. **B.** Simply note that $p^4q3 = (5)^4(-3)^3$ is negative, whereas $p - q = 5 - (-3) = 8$, which is positive. It is not necessary to evaluate $p^4q3$.

15. **B.** Since the two angles indicated in the diagram are alternate interior angles, we know that $3s = 4r$. For this to be true, $s$ must be bigger than $r$.

16. **D.** Without knowing if they took the same route, it is not possible to determine who took longer to complete the job.

17. **B.** Note, first of all, that $(42 - 18)^2 = 24^2$. Also, the quantity in Column B is the difference of two squares, and can therefore be factored:

$$(42)^2 - (18)^2 = (42 - 18)(42 + 18) = 24 \times 60.$$

Clearly, $24 \times 60 > 24 \times 24$.

18. **B.** Since $625 = 5 \times 5 \times 5 \times 5$, its greatest prime factor is 5. Since $224 = 2 \times 2 \times 2 \times 2 \times 2 \times 7$, its greatest prime factor is 7.

19. **C.** In order to quickly answer this question, multiply together the two equations given in the common information to obtain a new equation. On the left hand side we get $(qa^2 - p^2)(qa^2 + p^2) = q^2a^4 - p^4$, which is the same as the entry in Column A. On the right hand side we get $12 \times 3 = 36$, which is the same as the entry in Column B. Thus, the entry in Column A is the same as the entry in Column B.

20. **C.** The formula for the area of a rectangle is $A = lw$, so, in the given rectangle, we have $72 = 12 \times w$. Thus, $w = 72 \div 12 = 6$. The perimeter of this rectangle is $12 + 6 + 12 + 6 = 36$.

21. **C.** Since $Q^0 = 1$, it follows that $x - y = 0$. Therefore, $x = y$.

22. **B.** To find the average of each of these entries, add up numbers and divide by 3. To begin, $(a + 3) + (2a + 4) + (2 - 3a) = 9$. Since $9 \div 3 = 3$, the average of the entry in Column A is 3. In Column B, the three numbers add up to 27, and, since $27 \div 3 = 9$, the entry in Column B is larger.

23. **D.** This is a very tricky question. Initially, it might appear as if the answer is **B**, since it appears as if $y$ must be bigger than $x$. However, this is not necessarily true. If, for example, $x = -5$ and $y = -7$, then $\frac{x}{y} = \frac{5}{7}$, but $x$ is bigger than $y$.

24. **A.** In Column B, we have $(\sqrt{5} + \sqrt{5})^4 = (2\sqrt{5})^4 = 2^4 \times (\sqrt{5})^4 = 16 \times 25 = 400$. Since $\sqrt{5}$ is bigger than 2, however, $200\sqrt{5}$ is larger than 400.

25. **A.** To begin, the line segment between point $R$ and point $P$ is the hypotenuse of a $3 - 4 - 5$ triangle, and thus the distance from point $R$ to point $P$ is 5. On the other hand, the distance from point $Q$ to point $P$ is the distance from $(-3, 0)$ to $(3, 0)$, which is 6. Since $6 > 5$, the answer is **A**.

# Life Science

1. What is the probability that the first child of a couple will be a type B boy, if one parent has type AB blood and the other has type O?

   A. 25%
   B. 50%
   C. 75%
   D. 100%

2. The variations in the thickness of the annual rings produced by a tree would most likely be caused by which of the following factors?

   A. amount of sunlight
   B. amount of rain
   C. richness of the soil
   D. all of the above

3. The most highly developed portion of the mammalian brain that is used in the processing of thought is the

   A. cerebellum
   B. spinal cord
   C. cerebrum
   D. optic lobe

4. In the normal development of a human embryo, if the cells are separated at the two-cell stage, the result will be

   A. death for each cell
   B. identical twins
   C. fraternal twins
   D. one child male, the other female

*Use the following diagram of human lungs and respiratory system to answer question 5.*

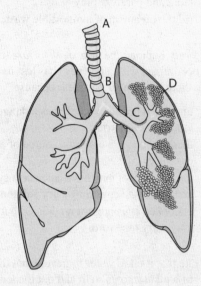

5. The actual gas exchange occurs in the structures marked

   A. A
   B. B
   C. C
   D. D

6. Most hospitals ban plants in a hospital room of a patient with respiratory problems because

   A. the moisture they release makes breathing more difficult
   B. the plants can cause $CO_2$ poisoning
   C. the plants will reduce the $O_2$ concentration at night
   D. the plants will produce too high an $O_2$ concentration level

7. If the pancreas of a dog is surgically removed, the dog will die shortly thereafter because

   A. it will be unable to properly regulate its sugar levels and it will be unable to adequately digest certain food materials
   B. it will contract diabetes
   C. it will starve
   D. it will go into shock from the surgery

GO ON TO THE NEXT PAGE

**8.** The function of specialized cells (called nematocysts) in coelenterates is to

   **A.** provide a rudimentary nervous system
   **B.** produce digestive juices
   **C.** sting and paralyze prey
   **D.** rid the organism of indigestible waste

**9.** Once very popular, the dish *steak tartare* (chopped raw beef mixed with a raw egg) has lost its appeal since there is a danger of illness because

   **A.** uncooked beef commonly has a dangerous amount of bacteria
   **B.** these foods are a common source of amoebic dysentery
   **C.** uncooked beef may have tapeworm cysts, and uncooked eggs may carry salmonella
   **D.** uncooked eggs present no danger, but beef may carry tapeworm

**10.** The rate that it takes water to travel from the roots of a plant into its stem and out the leaves is controlled by the

   **A.** mitochondria
   **B.** xylem
   **C.** phloem
   **D.** stomata

**11.** A critical process took place during the evolution of fish into amphibians. It was

   **A.** the loss of scales by the fish
   **B.** the loss of gills by the fish and the evolution of lungs in amphibians
   **C.** its new ability to use fins for locomotion on land
   **D.** its new ability to reproduce on land

**12.** Unicellular animals such as the paramecium were first described by

   **A.** Linnaeus
   **B.** Malpighi
   **C.** Hooke
   **D.** Leewenhoek

**13.** Freshwater fish must maintain certain levels of sodium in their systems in order to maintain a normal life. In order to do this, they actively transport sodium

   **A.** out through the kidneys and in through the gills
   **B.** out of the blood through the gills and into the blood through the kidneys
   **C.** into the blood both through the kidneys and gills
   **D.** into the digestive system without the use of gills or kidneys

**14.** The production of sex hormones is controlled by

   **A.** the testes and ovary
   **B.** the hypothalamus and FSH
   **C.** the pituitary and ovary
   **D.** a negative feedback system

**15.** In order for a mutation to have an evolutionary effect, it must occur in

   **A.** germplasm DNA
   **B.** a centriole
   **C.** the endoplasmic reticulum
   **D.** somatoplasm RNA

**16.** Picture a specific ecosystem in which rabbits are preyed upon by owls, hawks, and snakes. If wolves enter the system what is the most likely short-term outcome from the following choices of the addition of the wolves?

   **A.** The snake population would increase.
   **B.** There would be a greater depletion of the rabbits.
   **C.** The owls, the hawks, or the snakes, would become extinct.
   **D.** There might be a tendency for owls and hawks to prey on the wolves.

**17.** Which base is found in DNA but not in RNA?

   **A.** thymine
   **B.** cytosine
   **C.** guanine
   **D.** adenine

18. Photosynthesis utilizes light energy from the sun to manufacture an energy storage product that is one of the

    A. proteins
    B. sugars
    C. nucleic acids
    D. amino acids

19. In human males meiosis occurs in the

    A. Cowper's gland
    B. nephron tubules
    C. penis
    D. seminiferous tubules

20. Each of the following elements is present in all amino acids but not in sugars. Which one is NOT present in sugars?

    A. carbon
    B. hydrogen
    C. nitrogen
    D. oxygen

21. The dodo and the passenger pigeon became extinct a relatively short time ago. Which of the following would be the most likely cause of their extinction?

    A. snakes that ate their eggs
    B. a viral infection
    C. human predation
    D. malarial-type disease

22. As cells break down compounds, they yield energy, which is stored by the synthesis of another compound with a high-energy bond whose energy is readily available. This compound is

    A. ATP
    B. NAD
    C. glucose
    D. glycogen

23. Intelligent animal life on another planet is more likely to be aerobic rather than anaerobic because

    A. all planets have O2 atmospheres
    B. aerobes are about twenty times more efficient in extracting energy from foodstuffs than are anaerobes
    C. life has never existed in an O2-free environment
    D. breathing deeply enhances brain functions and intelligence

24. Solar energy is converted to chemical energy in plants through pigments such as chlorophyll. A red-orange pigment that functions similarly is

    A. biliverdin
    B. NADP
    C. cytochrome
    D. carotenoid

25. What is the function of the Golgi apparatus?

    A. to break up ingested food particles
    B. to prepare cell products for secretion
    C. to provide energy to the cell
    D. to enclose waste products

26. A compound that is split during photosynthesis is

    A. $H_2O$
    B. $CO_2$
    C. NADP
    D. ADP

27. Many people are familiar with the popular diet fad that is a high protein, high fat, low carbohydrate diet. Among the metabolic changes it causes are increased production of ketoacids, acetone breath, and acidic urine. These duplicate some of the symptoms of which metabolic disease?

    A. PKU
    B. diabetes mellitus
    C. Tay-Sachs disease
    D. lactose deficiency

GO ON TO THE NEXT PAGE

Practice Test 2

28. The technique of amniocentesis is used to detect which genetic abnormality?

    A. albinism
    B. muscular dystrophy
    C. manic depression
    D. Down's syndrome

29. Penguins who live in the Antarctic are much larger than penguins living in more temperate regions. Which of the following might explain this?

    A. In Antarctica, breeding seasons are short; as a result penguins there lay fewer and larger eggs than penguins in warmer climates.
    B. The fishes on which penguins feed are larger in cold water than in warmer water.
    C. Cold air contains a larger percentage of oxygen than warm air.
    D. Large bodies have smaller surface to volume ratio than small bodies.

30. Which of the following is the *best* reason for using mathematics in a study of populations? It allows us to

    A. define the limits of a population
    B. quantify and predict growth in population
    C. regulate population
    D. determine when we are working with a population

# Answers and Explanations

1. **A.** There is a 50 percent probability of the child having either A or B blood. This 50 percent is multiplied by the 50 percent probability of a boy to give 25 percent.

2. **D.** The thickness of the annual rings are influenced by any factor that affects the growth rate of the tree each year.

3. **C.** The spinal cord is not a part of the brain (B); and the optic lobe (D) is a specialized portion of the brain having to do with optics. Although the cerebellum (A) is part of the brain, it is NOT the part that is used in processing thought.

4. **B.** In normal development the resulting cells, particularly early in development, are identical.

5. **D.** The only structures thin enough to allow the passage of gas are the alveoli and the tiny ducts that lead to them.

6. **C.** At night, plants metabolize the sugar they make during the day; therefore they use $O_2$ and produce $CO_2$, possibly reducing the $O_2$ concentration in a closed room.

7. **A.** The pancreas is important both in the regulation of sugar in the body, and as a producer of digestive juices. Only choice (A) covers both of those functions.

8. **C.** The coelenterates use the nematocysts uncoil to sting and ensnare prey.

9. **C.** Raw beef can be infected with tapeworm or bacteria. In addition, the bacterium salmonella is often found in chicken eggs. Many restaurants today only serve meat well-done.

10. **D.** Only stomata are found on the leaf surface and have movable walls so as to be able to open or close and regulate the flow of water.

11. **C.** This change resulted in land-based creatures.

12. **D.** Leeuwenhoek is well known for inventing the microscope and seeing unicellular microscopic forms.

13. **C.** A fish gets sodium into the body via the blood through the two structures that allow penetration of water.

14. **D.** The manufacture of sex hormones requires a variety of interactions. Each of the other choices are components of some of the interactions, but choice **D** is all-encompassing.

15. **A.** Only germplasm DNA is passed from parent to offspring in a constant manner. Unless this process occurs, there is no means for a mutation to be carried into a lineage.

16. **B.** While all of these choices may apply, in the short-term, there will be a greater depletion of the rabbits.

17. **A.** Thymine is found only in DNA.

18. **B.** None of the other responses is an energy storage product, nor are directly involved in photosynthesis.

19. **D.** Semen includes sperm produced by meiosis.

20. **C.** All organic compounds have carbon, hydrogen, and oxygen. (C), nitrogen, forms the amino group of all amino acids.

21. **C.** It is most likely that human predation was the primary cause of their extinction. Although each of the other factors may have had an effect on their diminished population, only choice **C** would have had such a major effect on the populations of both groups of birds.

22. **A.** ATP is the energy currency of all living cells. Energy from breakdown of glycogen, glucose, fats, and proteins, etc., is used to form the high-energy phosphate bond converting low energy ADP to ATP. NAD functions in electron transfer reactions.

23. **B.** Intelligent animal life requires a great deal of energy. Since anaerobes are inefficient in extracting energy from molecules, the logical answer is **B**.

24. **D.** The clue to this answers lies in the word "carotenoid." The pigment is red-orange, like a carrot, and therefore (D), carotenoid, is the answer.

**25. B.** The Golgi apparatus prepares cell production for secretion.

**26. A.** The $H_2O$ is split into hydrogen and oxygen. None of the other molecules is split in photosynthesis.

**27. B.** Diabetes mellitus is a disease that involves a lack of active insulin, and thus sugar cannot enter the cells to be metabolized. The resulting symptoms are similar to the effects of this diet.

**28. D.** Down's syndrome (formerly called mongolism) is caused by the presence of an extra chromosome, and thus can be detected from a karyotype (photographic examination of stained chromosomes) made from any cultured fetal cells.

**29. D.** One of the most important factors is maintaining a constant body temperature. Body size (D) is critical in this respect.

**30. B.** is the only response involving quantification.

# Physical Science

1. Which of the following is the basic action of most cutting tools?

   A. principle of work
   B. fulcrum
   C. lever
   D. inclined plane

2. A golf ball and a Ping-Pong ball are dropped in a vacuum chamber. When they have fallen halfway down, they will have the same

   A. velocity
   B. potential energy
   C. kinetic energy
   D. rest energy

3. Most metals are solids and most common non-metals are gases. Which of the following pairs of metal and non-metal are exceptions (i.e., metal is a liquid and nonmetal is a solid)?

   A. gold and nitrogen
   B. mercury and sulfur
   C. sodium and sulfur
   D. mercury end nitrogen

4. Based on the principle of conservation of energy, energy can be

   A. created but not destroyed
   B. destroyed but not created
   C. both created and destroyed
   D. neither created nor destroyed

5. Which of the following is <u>not</u> a properly balanced chemical equation?

   A. $BaO + H_2O \rightarrow Ba(OH)2$
   B. $SO_3 + H_2O \rightarrow H_2SO_4$
   C. $H_2 + O_2 \rightarrow H_2O$
   D. $CH_4 + 2O_2 \rightarrow CO_2 + 2H_2O$

6. According to Einstein's theory of relativity,

   A. space and time are aspects of each other
   B. energy and mass are aspects of each other
   C. both of the above
   D. none of the above

7. The use of lubricants cannot reduce

   A. rolling friction
   B. sliding friction
   C. static friction
   D. inertia

8. Which of the following compounds illustrates ionic bonding (electron transfer)?

   A. $MgCl_2$
   B. $CH_4$
   C. $HCN$
   D. $H_2O$

9. The quantity of heat required to change the temperature of a unit amount of a substance by 1°C is called its

   A. specific heat capacity
   B. heat of fusion
   C. heat of vaporization
   D. mechanical equivalent of heat

10. Alpha, beta, and gamma radiation are the three major products of natural radioactive decay. Which of the following is (are) the most penetrating radiation?

    A. alpha rays
    B. beta rays
    C. gamma rays
    D. they are all equally penetrating

11. When a vapor condenses into a liquid

    A. it absorbs heat
    B. it generates heat
    C. its temperature rises
    D. its temperature drops

12. The acceleration of a rock thrown upward is

    A. greater than that of a rock thrown downward
    B. the same as that of a rock thrown downward
    C. smaller than that of a rock thrown downward
    D. zero until it reaches the highest point in its situation

GO ON TO THE NEXT PAGE

13. Two elements cannot be combined chemically to make

    A. a compound
    B. another element
    C. a gas
    D. a liquid

14. A pinch of salt is added to a glass of water. The result is

    A. an element
    B. a compound
    C. a solution
    D. a heterogeneous substance

15. An airplane travels 250 miles in half an hour at constant velocity. Its velocity is

    A. 125 miles per hour
    B. 250 miles per hour
    C. 500 miles per hour
    D. 1000 miles per hour

16. A refrigerator

    A. produces cold
    B. removes heat from a region and transports it elsewhere
    C. causes heat to vanish
    D. changes heat to cold

17. Given the following atoms, which one is the heaviest?

    A. hydrogen
    B. iron
    C. lead
    D. uranium

18. If you were designing a dam, you would design it to be thicker at the bottom than at the top. Why?

    A. Pressure is greater with increasing depth.
    B. Surface tension exists only at the surface of liquids.
    C. A dam would not look right with a thin bottom.
    D. Water is denser at deeper levels and therefore exerts greater pressure at the bottom of the dam.

19. A body with constant velocity has

    A. a positive acceleration
    B. a negative acceleration
    C. zero acceleration
    D. a constant acceleration

20. If an automobile tire explodes, the air that was contained in that tire

    A. increases in temperature
    B. decreases in temperature
    C. remains the same
    D. increases in pressure

21. Under which of the following conditions would the carbonation in an open bottle of a carbonated beverage be retained the longest?

    A. low temperature and low pressure
    B. low temperature and high pressure
    C. high temperature and low pressure
    D. high temperature and high pressure

22. Which of the following is an example of nuclear fusion?

    A. $_{92}^{235}U + _0^1n \rightarrow _{56}^{139}Ba + _{36}^{94}Kr + _0^1n$
    B. $_1^2H + _1^3H \rightarrow _2^4He + _0^1n$
    C. $_{92}^{234}U \rightarrow _2^4He + _{90}^{230}Th$
    D. all of them

23. The silver coating on the glass surfaces of a thermos cuts down on

    A. the conduction of heat energy
    B. the convection of heat energy
    C. the radiation of heat energy
    D. bacteria growth

24. The needle of a magnetic compass

    A. aligns itself perpendicular to a magnetic field
    B. aligns itself parallel to a magnetic field
    C. rotates continuously in the magnetic field of an electric current
    D. is affected only by permanent magnets

**25.** The following equation represents a reaction that takes place in water containing dissolved silver nitrate:

$$Cu + 2\,AgNO_3 \rightarrow 2\,Ag + Cu(NO_3)^2$$

Which of the following statements about this reaction is not true?

A. The symbol Cu may represent a piece of copper wire placed in the solution.
B. Silver metal is precipitated out in this reaction.
C. Silver is a more reactive metal than copper.
D. There is no change in the nitrate ion in this reaction.

**26.** The property of light waves that leads to the phenomenon of color is their

A. amplitude
B. velocity
C. wavelength
D. density

**27.** In a vacuum, the velocity of an electromagnetic wave

A. depends upon its frequency
B. depends upon its wavelength
C. depends upon its amplitude
D. is a universal constant

**28.** Copper (Cu) has an atomic number of 29 and a mass number of 64. One copper atom, therefore, has how many protons?

A. 27
B. 29
C. 31
D. 35

**29.** The bending of a beam of light when it passes from one medium to another is known as

A. refraction
B. reflection
C. diffraction
D. dispersion

**30.** According to the equation $E = mc^2$,

A. mass and energy when combined travel at twice the speed of light
B. mass and energy when combined travel at the speed of light squared
C. energy is actually mass traveling at the speed of light squared
D. energy and mass are related

# Answers and Explanations

1. **D.** The basic concept is the inclined plane. In order to cut material, it is necessary to wedge a tool between two parts of the material.

2. **A.** Both objects would have the same acceleration, and therefore must have the same velocity.

3. **B.** Experience should indicate that all metals are solids except mercury, which is a liquid. This eliminates choices A. and (C). Also, from common knowledge, we know that nitrogen is a common gaseous component of air.

4. **D.** The conservation of energy, the most fundamental principle of science, is that energy can neither be created nor destroyed.

5. **C.** In order for an equation to be balanced, the number of each type of atom on either side of the arrow must be the same. The only equation that is not balanced is (C)—there are two H atoms on each side, but two O atoms on the left and only one on the right.

6. **C.** In relativistic theory both space and time and mass and energy are aspects of each other.

7. **D.** Lubricants are used to reduce friction, but has nothing to do with inertia, which is related to mass.

8. **A.** $MgCl_2$ is the only compound composed of a metal and a non-metal. An ionic bond is formed when electrons are transferred from a metal atom (Mg, in this case) to a non-metal atom (Cl, in this case). This produces a salt with metallic positively charged ions and non-metallic negatively charged ions in a geometrical crystal structure. The other three compounds are composed of only non-metals. Non-metals bond by sharing electrons (covalent bonding).

9. **A.** The statement given is the definition of specific heat capacity. B and C refer to heat flows for a change of phase of a material.

10. **C.** Gamma rays are electromagnetic rays and are the most dangerous and penetrating—lead shielding of substantial thickness is required as protection from them. Alpha particles (helium nuclei) and beta particles (high-energy electrons) are stopped by paper or thin sheets of metal.

11. **B.** When a vapor condenses into a liquid, heat must flow out of the vapor. The temperature will remain constant during the transition.

12. **B.** The acceleration of any object in free flight on the surface of the earth is the acceleration due to gravity. Therefore **B** is the answer. All the other statements imply some other kind of acceleration.

13. **B.** An element cannot be subdivided into more basic elements.

14. **C.** Salt added to water will dissolve, the result being a solution.

15. **C.** The calculation of velocity is displacement per time. In this case we have 250 miles divided by 1/2 hour. The result is 500 miles.

16. **B.** A refrigerator transports heat from inside to the outside.

17. **D.** Uranium has the largest atomic weight, or a greater number of neutrons and protons, than any of the other elements listed.

18. **A.** A dam is thicker at the bottom than at the top because pressure increases with increasing depth of water.

19. **C.** Since acceleration demands a change in velocity, constant velocity can only occur with zero acceleration.

20. **B.** Air contained in an exploding automobile tire undergoes a rapid explosion and decrease in pressure; both contribute to a lowering in temperature.

21. **B.** More gas (carbonation) will stay in solution at low temperature; heating will generate more gas. Also, when the cap is opened, the gas is released since pressure is lessened.

22. **B.** Fusion is the combining of smaller nuclei to produce a larger one. Choices **A** and **C** are examples of fission, the breaking down of a large nucleus into smaller ones.

23. **C.** The silver coating in a thermos bottle reflects radiation, which reduces the amount of radiant heat energy transfer.

24. **B.** The needle of a magnetic compass aligns itself parallel to a magnetic field. It is affected not only by permanent magnets, but also by electromagnets.

25. **C.** You must first recognize that the symbol for copper is Cu, silver is Ag, and a nitrate ion is $NO_3$. Thus, choices **A**, **B**, and **D** are true. The correct answer is *a false* statement (C). What is occurring in the reaction is the displacement of silver (Ag) from a solution of silver salt by copper (Cu).

26. **C.** The wavelength of a light wave is related to the spectral color it exhibits.

27. **D.** In a vacuum, all electromagnetic waves have the same velocity, namely the velocity of light.

28. **B.** Twenty-nine protons.

29. **A.** When a beam of light passes from one medium to another, its velocity changes, leading to a change in direction of the beam. This phenomenon is known as refraction.

30. **D.** The equation $E = mc^2$ relates mass and energy. It says nothing about the speed of travel for either the mass or the energy.

# APPENDICES

The following is a list of Nursing Associations and their current Web addresses. If you have any questions about specialties, you should contact them. As you progress in your studies, you may find new areas of interest, and many of these associations have forums where you can pose specific questions about the career areas.

Academy of Medical-Surgical Nurses
http://amsn.inurse.com/

Air & Surface Transport Nurses Association
http://www.astna.org/

Alliance for Psychosocial Nursing
http://www.psychnurse.org/

Alpha Tau Delta
http://www.atdnursing.org/

American Academy of Ambulatory Care Nurses
http://www.aaacn.org/

American Academy of Nurse Practitioners
http://www.aanp.org/

American Academy of Nursing
http://www.nursingworld.org/aan/

American Academy of Wound Management
http://www.aawm.org/

American Assembly for Men in Nursing
http://people.delphiforums.com/brucewilson/

American Assisted Living Nurses Association
http://www.alnursing.org/

American Association of Colleges of Nursing
http://www.aacn.nche.edu/

American Association of Critical-Care Nurses
http://www.aacn.org/

American Association of Diabetes Educators
http://www.aadenet.org/

American Association for the History of Nursing
http://www.aahn.org/

American Association of Legal Nurse Consultants
http://www.aalnc.org/

American Association of Managed Care Nurses
http://www.aamcn.org/

American Association Neuroscience Nurses
http://www.aann.org/

American Association of Nurse Anesthetists
http://www.aana.com/

American Association of Nurse Assessment Coordinators
http://www.aanac.org/

American Association of Occupational Health Nurses
http://www.aaohn.org/

American Association of Office Nurses
http://www.aaon.org/

American Association of Spinal Cord Injury Nurses
http://www.aascin.org/

American Board of Nursing Specialties
http://www.nursingcertification.org/

American Case Management Association
http://www.acmaweb.org/

American College of Health Care Administrators
http://www.achca.org/

American College of Healthcare Executives
http://www.ache.org/

American College of Nurse-Midwives
http://www.acnm.org/

American College of Nurse Practitioners
http://www.nurse.org/acnp/

American Forensic Nurses
http://www.amrn.com/

American Health Care Association
http://www.ahca.org/

American Holistic Nurses Association
http://ahna.org/

American Nephrology Nurses Association
http://anna.inurse.com/

American Nurses Association
http://www.nursingworld.org/

American Nurses Foundation
http://www.nursingworld.org

American Nursing Informatics Association
http://www.ania.org/

American Organization of Nurse Executives
http://www.hospitalconnect.com/

American Pediatric Surgical Nurses Association
http://www.apsna.org/

American Psychiatric Nurses Association
http://www.apna.org/

American Radiological Nurses Association
http://www.arna.net/

American Society of Pain Management Nurses
http://www.aspmn.org/

American Society of PeriAnesthesia Nurses
http://www.aspan.org/

American Society of Plastic Surgical Nurses
http://www.aspsn.org/

Association of Camp Nurses
http://www.campnurse.org/

Association of Community Health Nursing Educators
http://www.uncc.edu/achne/

Association of Nurse Advocates for Childbirth Solutions
http://www.anacs.org/

Association of Nurses in AIDS Care
http://www.anacnet.org/

Association of Pediatric Oncology Nurses
http://www.apon.org/

Association of periOperative Registered Nurses
http://www.aorn.org/

Association of Rehabilitation Nurses
http://www.rehabnurse.org/

Association of Women's Health, Obstetrics, & Neonatal Nurses
http://www.awhonn.org/

Baromedical Nurses Association
http://www.hyperbaricnurses.org/

Case Management Society of America
http://www.cmsa.org/

Dermatology Nurses Association
http://www.dnanurse.org/

Developmental Disabilities Nurses Association
http://www.ddna.org/

Emergency Nurses Association
http://www.ena.org/

Endocrine Nurses Society
http://www.endo-nurses.org.

Hospice and Palliative Nurses Association
http://www.hpna.org/

Infusion Nurses Society
http://www.ins1.org/

International Society of Psychiatric-Mental Health Nurses
http://www.ispn-psych.org/

League of Intravenous Therapy Education
http://www.lite.org/

National Association of Clinical Nurse Specialists
http://www.nacns.org/

National Association of Hispanic Nurses
http://www.thehispanicnurses.org/

National Association for Home Care
http://www.nahc.org/

National Association of Independent Nurses
http://www.independentrn.com/

National Association of Neonatal Nurses
http://www.nann.org/

National Association of NP's in Women's Health
http://www.npwh.org

National Association of Orthopedic Nurses
http://www.orthonurse.org/

National Association of Pediatric Nurse Practitioners
http://www.napnap.org/

National Association of School Nurses
http://www.nasn.org/

National Association of School Nurses for the Deaf
http://www.nasnd.org/

National Association of State School Nurse Consultants, Inc.
http://lserver.aea14.k12.ia.us/swp/tadkins/nassnc/nassnc.html

National Black Nurses Association
http://www.nbna.org/

National Conference of Gerontological Nurse Practitioners
http://www.ncgnp.org/

National Federation of Licensed Practical Nurses Inc.
http://www.nflpn.org/

National League for Nursing
http://www.nln.org/

National Nursing Staff Development Organization
http://www.nnsdo.org/

National Organization for Associate Degree Nursing
http://www.noadn.org//

National Organization of Nurse Practitioner Faculties
http://www.nonpf.com/

Nurse Practitioner Associates for Continuing Education
http://www.npace.org/

Nurses Christian Fellowship
http://mason.gmu.edu/~jmerritt/nncf.html

Nursing Ethics Network
http://jmrileyrn.tripod.com/nen/nen.html

Nursing Organization of Veterans Affairs
http://www.vanurse.org/

Oncology Nursing Society
http://www.ons.org/

Sigma Theta Tau International Honor Society of Nursing
http://www.nursingsociety.org/#

Society of Gastroenterology Nurses and Associates
http://www.sgna.org/

Society of Pediatric Nurses
http://www.pedsnurses.org/

Society of Urologic Nurses and Associates
http://www.duj.com/suna.html

The American Association of Nurse Attorneys
http://www.taana.org/

Uniformed Nurse Practitioner Association
http://unpa.org/

Visiting Nurse Associations of America
www.vnaa.org

# State Boards of Nursing

The purpose of the State Boards of Nursing is not only to grant licensing and support for nurses, but they also serve to protect the consumer. If you have questions about your local board, you can contact them directly, either through their websites or by mail, telephone, or fax.

Alabama Board of Nursing
770 Washington Avenue
RSA Plaza, Ste 250
Montgomery, AL 36130-3900
Phone: (334) 242-4060
FAX: (334) 242-4360
http://www.abn.state.al.us/

Alaska Board of Nursing
Dept. of Comm. & Economic Development
Div. of Occupational Licensing
3601 C Street, Suite 722
Anchorage, AK 99503
Phone: (907) 269-8161
FAX: (907) 269-8196
http://www.dced.state.ak.us/occ/pnur.htm

Arizona State Board of Nursing
1651 E. Morten Avenue, Suite 210
Phoenix, AZ 85020
Phone: (602) 331-8111
FAX: (602) 906-9365
http://www.azboardofnursing.org/

Arkansas State Board of Nursing
University Tower Building
1123 S. University, Suite 800
Little Rock, AR 72204-1619
Phone: (501) 686-2700
FAX: (501) 686-2714
http://www.state.ar.us/nurse

California Board of Registered Nursing
400 R St., Ste. 4030
Sacramento, CA 95814-6239
Phone: (916) 322-3350
FAX: (916) 327-4402
http://www.rn.ca.gov/

Colorado Board of Nursing
1560 Broadway, Suite 880
Denver, CO 80202
Phone: (303) 894-2430
FAX: (303) 894-2821
http://www.dora.state.co.us/nursing/

Connecticut Board of Examiners for Nursing
Division of Health Systems Regulation
410 Capitol Hill Ave. MS# 12HSR #340308
Hartford, CT 06134
Phone: (860) 509-7624
FAX: (860) 509-7286
http://www.state.ct.us/dph/

Delaware Board of Nursing
861 Silver Lake Blvd
Cannon Building, Suite 203
Dover, DE 19904
Phone: (302) 739-4522
FAX: (302) 739-2711
http://professionallicensing.state.de.us/boards/nursing/index.shtml

District of Columbia Board of Nursing
Department of Health
825 N. Capitol Street, N.E., 2nd Floor
Room 2224
Washington, DC 20002
Phone: (202) 442-4778
FAX: (202) 442-9431

Florida Board of Nursing
4080 Woodcock Drive, Suite 202
Jacksonville, FL 32207
Phone: (904) 858-6940
FAX: (904) 858-6964
http://www.doh.state.fl.us/Mqa/nursing/nur_home.html

Georgia State Board of Licensed
Practical Nurses
237 Coliseum Drive
Macon, GA 31217-3858
Phone: (912) 207-1300
FAX: (912) 207-1633
http://www.sos.state.ga.us/plb/lpn/

Hawaii Board of Nursing
Professional & Vocational Licensing Division
P.O. Box 3469
Honolulu, HI 96801
Phone: (808) 586-3000
FAX: (808) 586-2689
http://www.state.hi.us/dcca/pvl/areas_nurse.html

Idaho Board of Nursing
280 N. 8th Street, Suite 210
P.O. Box 83720
Boise, ID 83720
Phone: (208) 334-3110
FAX: (208) 334-3262
http://www.state.id.us/ibn/ibnhome.htm

Illinois Department of Professional Regulation
James R. Thompson Center
100 West Randolph, Suite 9-300
Chicago, IL 60601
Phone: (312) 814-2715
FAX: (312) 814-3145
http://www.dpr.state.il.us/

Indiana State Board of Nursing
Health Professions Bureau
402 W. Washington Street, Room W041
Indianapolis, IN 46204
Phone: (317) 232-2960
FAX: (317) 233-4236
http://www.state.in.us/hpb/boards/isbn/

Iowa Board of Nursing
River Point Business Park
400 S.W. 8th Street
Suite B
Des Moines, IA 50309-4685
Phone: (515) 281-3255
FAX: (515) 281-4825
http://www.state.ia.us/government/nursing/

Kansas State Board of Nursing
Landon State Office Building
900 S.W. Jackson, Suite 551-S
Topeka, KS 66612
Phone: (785) 296-4929
FAX: (785) 296-3929
http://www.ksbn.org

Kentucky Board of Nursing
312 Whittington Parkway, Suite 300
Louisville, KY 40222
Phone: (502) 329-7000
FAX: (502) 329-7011
http://kbn.ky.gov/index-old.htm

Louisiana State Board of Nursing
3510 N. Causeway Boulevard, Suite 501
Metairie, LA 70003
Phone: (504) 838-5332
FAX: (504) 838-5349
http://www.lsbn.state.la.us/

Louisiana State Board of Practical
Nurse Examiners
3421 N. Causeway Boulevard, Suite 203
Metairie, LA 70002
Phone: (504) 838-5791
FAX: (504) 838-5279
http://www.lsbpne.com

Maine State Board of Nursing
158 State House Station
Augusta, ME 04333
Phone: (207) 287-1133
FAX: (207) 287-1149
http://www.state.me.us/nursingbd/

Maryland Board of Nursing
4140 Patterson Avenue
Baltimore, MD 21215
Phone: (410) 585-1900
FAX: (410) 358-3530
http://www.mbon.org/main.php

Massachusetts Board of Registration
Commonwealth of Massachusetts
239 Causeway Street
Boston, MA 02114
Phone: (617) 727-9961
FAX: (617) 727-1630
http://www.state.ma.us/reg/boards/rn/

Michigan CIS/Office of Health Services
Ottawa Towers North
611 W. Ottawa, 4th Floor
Lansing, MI 48933
Phone: (517) 373-9102
FAX: (517) 373-2179
http://www.michigan.gov/cis/0,1607,7-154-10568—-,00.html

Minnesota Board of Nursing
2829 University Avenue SE
Suite 500
Minneapolis, MN 55414
Phone: (612) 617-2270
FAX: (612) 617-2190
http://www.nursingboard.state.mn.us/

Mississippi Board of Nursing
1935 Lakeland Drive, Suite B
Jackson, MS 39216-5014
Phone: (601) 987-4188
FAX: (601) 364-2352
http://www.msbn.state.ms.us/

Missouri State Board of Nursing

3605 Missouri Blvd.

P.O. Box 656

Jefferson City, MO 65102-0656

Phone: (573) 751-0681

FAX: (573) 751-0075

http://www.ecodev.state.mo.us/pr/nursing/

Montana State Board of Nursing

301 South Park

Helena, MT 59620-0513

Phone: (406) 444-2071

FAX: (406) 841-2343

http://www.discoveringmontana.com/dli/bsd/license/bsd_boards/nur_board/board_page.asp

Nebraska Health and Human Services System

Dept. of Regulation & Licensure, Nursing Section

301 Centennial Mall South

Lincoln, NE 68509-4986

Phone: (402) 471-4376

FAX: (402) 471-3577

http://www.hhs.state.ne.us/

Nevada State Board of Nursing

1755 East Plumb Lane

Suite 260

Reno, NV 89502

Phone: (775) 688-2620

FAX: (775) 688-2628

http://www.nursingboard.state.nv.us

New Hampshire Board of Nursing

P.O. Box 3898

78 Regional Drive, Bldg B

Concord, NH 03302

Phone: (603) 271-2323

FAX: (603) 271-6605

http://www.state.nh.us/nursing/

New Jersey Board of Nursing
P.O. Box 45010
124 Halsey Street, 6th Floor
Newark, NJ 07101
Phone: (973) 504-6586
FAX: (973) 648-3481
http://www.state.nj.us/lps/ca/medical.htm

New Mexico Board of Nursing
4206 Louisiana Boulevard, NE
Suite A
Albuquerque, NM 87109
Phone: (505) 841-8340
FAX: (505) 841-8347
http://www.state.nm.us/clients/nursing

New York State Board of Nursing
Education Bldg.
89 Washington Avenue
2nd Floor West Wing
Albany, NY 12234
Phone: (518) 473-6999
FAX: (518) 474-3706
http://www.nysed.gov/prof/nurse.htm

North Carolina Board of Nursing
3724 National Drive, Suite 201
Raleigh, NC 27612
Phone: (919) 782-3211
FAX: (919) 781-9461
http://www.ncbon.com/

North Dakota Board of Nursing
919 South 7th Street, Suite 504
Bismark, ND 58504
Phone: (701) 328-9777
FAX: (701) 328-9785
http://www.ndbon.org/

Ohio Board of Nursing
17 South High Street, Suite 400
Columbus, OH 43215-3413
Phone: (614) 466-3947
FAX: (614) 466-0388
http://www.state.oh.us/nur/

Oklahoma Board of Nursing
2915 N. Classen Boulevard, Suite 524
Oklahoma City, OK 73106
Phone: (405) 962-1800
FAX: (405) 962-1821
http://www.youroklahoma.com/nursing/

Oregon State Board of Nursing
800 NE Oregon Street, Box 25
Suite 465
Portland, OR 97232
Phone: (503) 731-4745
FAX: (503) 731-4755
http://www.osbn.state.or.us/

Pennsylvania State Board of Nursing
124 Pine Street
Harrisburg, PA 17101
Phone: (717) 783-7142
FAX: (717) 783-0822
http://www.dos.state.pa.us/bpoa/nurbd/mainpage.htm

Rhode Island Board of Nurse
Registration and Nursing Education
105 Cannon Building
Three Capitol Hill
Providence, RI 02908
Phone: (401) 222-5700
FAX: (401) 222-3352
http://www.health.state.ri.us

South Carolina State Board of Nursing
110 Centerview Drive
Suite 202
Columbia, SC 29210
Phone: (803) 896-4550
FAX: (803) 896-4525
http://www.llr.state.sc.us/pol/nursing

South Dakota Board of Nursing
4300 South Louise Ave., Suite C-1
Sioux Falls, SD 57106-3124
Phone: (605) 362-2760
FAX: (605) 362-2768
http://www.state.sd.us/dcr/nursing/

Tennessee State Board of Nursing
426 Fifth Avenue North
1st Floor - Cordell Hull Building
Nashville, TN 37247
Phone: (615) 532-5166
FAX: (615) 741-7899
http://www2.state.tn.us/health/Boards/Nursing/

Texas Board of Nurse Examiners
333 Guadalupe, Suite 3-460
Austin, TX 78701
Phone: (512) 305-7400
FAX: (512) 305-7401
http://www.bne.state.tx.us/

Utah State Board of Nursing
Heber M. Wells Bldg., 4th Floor
160 East 300 South
Salt Lake City, UT 84111
Phone: (801) 530-6628
FAX: (801) 530-6511
http://www.commerce.state.ut.us/

Vermont State Board of Nursing
109 State Street
Montpelier, VT 05609-1106
Phone: (802) 828-2396
FAX: (802) 828-2484
http://vtprofessionals.org/opr1/nurses/

Virginia Board of Nursing
6606 W. Broad Street, 4th Floor
Richmond, VA 23230
Phone: (804) 662-9909
FAX: (804) 662-9512
http://www.dhp.state.va.us/

Washington State Nursing Care Quality
Assurance Commission
Department of Health
1300 Quince Street SE
Olympia, WA 98504-7864
Phone: (360) 236-4740
FAX: (360) 236-4738
https://fortress.wa.gov/doh/hpqa1/HPS6/Nursing/default.htm

West Virginia Board of Examiners
for Licensed Practical Nurses
101 Dee Drive
Charleston, WV 25311
Phone: (304) 558-3572
FAX: (304) 558-4367
http://www.lpnboard.state.wv.us/

Wisconsin Department of
Regulation and Licensing
1400 E. Washington Avenue
P.O. Box 8935
Madison, WI 53708
Phone: (608) 266-0145
FAX: (608) 261-7083
http://www.drl.state.wi.us/

Wyoming State Board of Nursing
2020 Carey Avenue, Suite 110
Cheyenne, WY 82002
Phone: (307) 777-7601
FAX: (307) 777-3519
http://nursing.state.wy.us/